MICHAE

44 DAYS

75 SQUADRON AND THE FIGHT FOR AUSTRALIA

hachette
AUSTRALIA

First published in Australia and New Zealand in 2016
by Hachette Australia
(an imprint of Hachette Australia Pty Limited)
Level 17, 207 Kent Street, Sydney NSW 2000
www.hachette.com.au

This edition published in 2017

10 9 8 7 6 5 4 3 2

National Library of Australia
Cataloguing-in-Publication data:

Veitch, Michael, author.
44 days: 75 squadron and the fight for Australia/Michael Veitch.

ISBN: 978 0 7336 3881 7 (paperback)

Australia. Royal Australian Air Force. Squadron, 75 – Biography.
Australia. Royal Australian Air Force. Squadron, 75 – History.
World War, 1939–1945 – Campaigns – Papua New Guinea.
World War, 1939–1945 – Aerial operations, Australian.
World War, 1939–1945 – Aerial operations, Japanese.

940.544994

Cover design by Luke Causby, Blue Cork Designs
Cover images courtesy of Australian War Memorial (AWM 017004)
and author's collection
Author photo courtesy of Gina Milicia
Text design by Bookhouse, Sydney
Maps by Kinart
Typeset in Garamond by Kirby Jones
Printed and bound in Australia by McPherson's Printing Group

The paper this book is printed on is certified against the Forest Stewardship Council® Standards. McPherson's Printing Group holds FSC chain of custody certification SGS-COC-004121. FSC promotes environmentally responsible, socially beneficial and economically viable management of the world's forests.

To my three wonderful Australians:
Zoe, William and Thomas

Contents

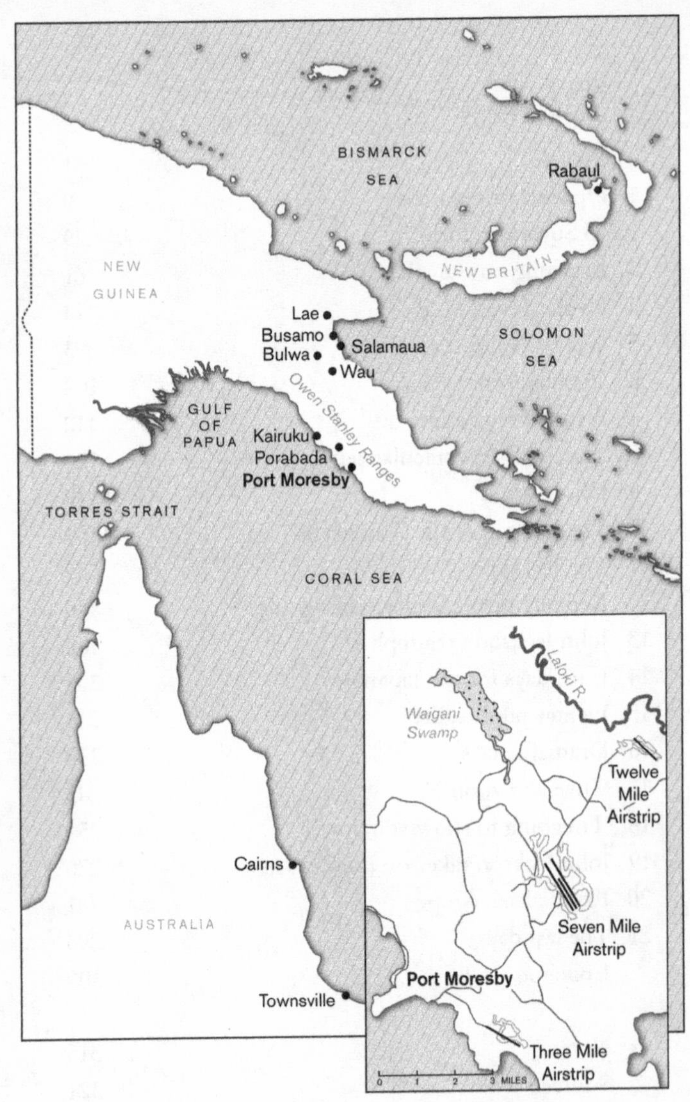
BISMARCK
SEA
Rabaul
NEW BRITAIN
NEW
GUINEA
Lae
Busamo
Salamaua
Bulwa
Wau
SOLOMON
SEA
Owen Stanley Ranges
GULF
OF
PAPUA
Kairuku
Porabada
Port Moresby
TORRES STRAIT
CORAL SEA
Cairns
AUSTRALIA
Townsville
Laloki R.
Waigani
Swamp
Twelve
Mile
Airstrip
Seven Mile
Airstrip
Port Moresby
Three Mile
Airstrip
0 1 2 3 MILES

Prelude

Early one evening in May 1942, nine dishevelled young men, barely recognisable as fighter pilots by the filthy remnants of uniform that hung off their jaundiced and emaciated frames, gathered under a fading canvas army tent to be addressed by their commanding officer.

Behind them stood the last of their P-40 Kittyhawk fighter aircraft – just three battered, patched-up machines held together with butchered parts and wire by exhausted maintenance crews who had been working around the clock for as long as anyone could remember.

Alongside the aircraft lay a narrow, dusty strip of well-worn dirt that served as a runway, the featureless expanse of bush that, for the last six weeks, had served as both home and front line in a fierce and unrelenting air battle stretching beyond it. This was Seven Mile Strip on the outskirts of Port Moresby. It was a hellish place: hot, fetid, disease ridden, an instant bog when it rained, choking dust-dry when it didn't. There were no buildings, no facilities and no relief. Not from the heat, not from the monotony, not from the stress, and especially not from the enemy. It was a place where even the cooling breezes from the nearby ocean never seemed to reach.

In early 1942, this dismal airfield scraped out of the New Guinea scrub represented the crucible in the most desperate crisis Australia had ever faced. Like its neighbour, Twelve Mile Strip, it was named for the distance it stood from the town it was now somehow supposed to protect, Port Moresby. And these men – these few poor bedraggled bastards – were somehow supposed to do the protecting.

As best they could, the men listened to the words of their leader, Squadron Leader Les Jackson. Just that day he had officially taken over as commanding officer from his brother, John Jackson, shot down and killed just a few days earlier. His Kittyhawk plunged into the side of nearby Mount Lawes with such force that its engine had embedded itself six feet into the ground. The only thing left to identify him was one of his flying boots, with a foot still inside, size 12. John Jackson was a big man.

Had one been there, one would have seen, behind the exhaustion, a bitterness in these men's eyes. Jackson's death, many of them believed, had been avoidable. Even pointless. His life had ended in the skies almost above where they now stood, after having been ordered to do something he'd countless times told them himself was impossible: taking on a Japanese Zero one-on-one in a dogfight. Couldn't be done, he'd said. Not with these machines, not these big heavy brutes. Everyone knew the nimble Zero could turn inside a Kittyhawk in an instant. 'On a sixpence,' one of their pilots, John Pettett, would say years later. Yet, that's what Jackson had been ordered to do by the shiny-arses with rings on their sleeves back at Moresby and Melbourne. Just get up there and do it, they'd told him, you'll see. And, loyal officer that he was, Jackson had obeyed. Proving them wrong cost him his life.

The young pilots had adored 'Old John' Jackson and his loss was devastating. The only thing that perhaps numbed their grief was the permanent haze of sickness and exhaustion that clung to them day and night. And now, John's younger brother, Les, was in charge. As they listened, many of them reflected silently on how two brothers could possibly be so unalike.

Word had just come through, Les told them, that the long-expected Japanese naval invasion force was on its way, headed for Port Moresby. It could be here any day. Pilots were needed to take off the following morning to try to stop it. Three exhausted pilots for three exhausted machines. Three, against an entire amphibious Japanese invasion fleet. Volunteers were needed. It was to be their last operation before being relieved by a squadron of American Airacobras, due at any time from Townsville. The men listened, expressionless. The whole thing sounded like a perfectly scripted suicide mission. And yet every one of them took a step forward.

This tiny, dishevelled gathering of worn-out young airmen was all that remained of the original twenty or so fresh young pilots of 75 Squadron, Royal Australian Air Force, formed barely two months earlier in Townsville – the first fighter squadron to be raised and flown in the direct defence of Australia. It had all been a panic-job, a handful of barely trained blokes just out of flying school, thrown together and rushed into combat. They were a mixed lot, among them a Queensland country teacher, a carpet salesman from Melbourne, an aspiring Sydney radio announcer and a quiet accountant from Launceston, who would blossom into one of the most fearless of them all.

Having hardly been given time to come to grips with handling their aircraft, let alone fighting in them, many of the men could count their hours in Kittyhawks on the fingers of one hand – some hadn't even survived the journey north from Australia. On their first day in action against the Japanese back in March, only four of their number could claim any combat experience at all, and that had been on the other side of the world in the African desert, fighting Germans and Italians. A very different kind of war from this.

But that was six weeks ago. There weren't many novices now.

For 44 days, in appalling conditions, flying aircraft that had been pushed to their limits and beyond, this group of men stood as the vanguard of their country's resistance to the juggernaut of Japanese aggression at the terrible dawn of the war in the

Pacific. For 44 days, in one of the most taxing climates on earth, they had stood by their aircraft – the metal often too hot to touch – waiting for the sound of three quick rifle shots, or the the yell, 'It's on!', before racing to their cockpits and taking off over the scrub and the jungle and the mountains to meet the finest, most hardened pilots flying the vastly superior aircraft that Japan's war machine had produced. For 44 days, they had fought a true David-and-Goliath struggle, had been shot at in high-level patrols, bombed and strafed daily on the ground – almost always outnumbered – and had watched their squadron's aircraft and its pilots gradually dwindle to almost nothing.

The 44-day air battle of Port Moresby was fought almost entirely over sea, jungle and a couple of airstrips, witnessed by no-one save a handful of Papuan locals who would glance up curiously at the white lines of vapour trails forming silently in the blue skies far above. Some historians have compared those 44 days to the Battle of Britain, with the stakes being arguably as high. But unlike Britain's epic aerial struggle, played out across hundreds of targets over southern England a year and a half earlier, this fight in the New Guinea skies revolved around just two: at one end, Port Moresby, its harbour and primitive airstrip coveted by the enemy, and at the other, the Japanese base at Lae on the north coast. In between were almost two hundred miles of almost uninhabited jungle, with the 14,000 foot razorbacks of the Owen Stanley Ranges rising perilously in the middle. The battle was a long-range duel, repeated day after gruelling day.

Also in contrast to their British counterparts, the men of 75 Squadron were completely alone. Incredibly, scandalously, despite years of warning, despite the advances and innovations achieved by Australian aviation during the First World War and its aftermath, this single squadron, this handful of green young men in borrowed aeroplanes, was all that could be mustered to meet the most formidable threat to their country in its history. And, unlike the First World War, this time there were no overbearing British generals to blame for the waste of Australian lives and resources. The mess Australia found itself in at the beginning of the Second World War was entirely of its own making.

Despite the odds, however, the men of 75 had given it back to the Japanese, and in spades. At the end of the battle, eighteen of Japan's previously invincible Zero fighters and Betty bombers lay in burnt-out pieces, scattered across jungle floors and sea beds, with 33 'probables' and another 30 destroyed or severely damaged on the ground.

It had been done by pilots and crews living in flimsy army tents, sleeping on camp stretchers, coping with mosquitoes, malaria and gastroenteritis, exacerbated by unspeakable food and the perils of tropical weather. But perhaps most wounding of all, the men of Australia's only front-line defensive fighter squadron were subject to the almost criminal interference – followed by the sullen neglect – of the higher echelons of the air force who, at one critical point in the battle, branded their hitherto successful hit-and-run tactics as cowardly, and slyly labelled them 'dingoes'. This, from experienced officers who should have had a clear understanding of the limitations of their aircraft as well as the tactics necessary to take on the superior Japanese machines. Barely did the officers even deign to visit the men at Seven Mile – just a short distance from their comfortable HQ – to see for themselves how it was being done.

•

But on this day in May, the men of 75 were beyond caring. What's one more trip anyway? they thought, consciously or otherwise, as they put themselves forward to take off for the next day's attack, in the face of overwhelming odds once again. Six weeks of combat had taken its toll: twelve of the squadron's pilots had been killed, and fifteen Kittyhawks lost from aerial combat, ground attack or accidents. In the end, it was down to just these three planes and a handful of pilots at the end of their rope. That was what was left of 75 Squadron by the end of the 44 days that Australia fought truly alone, in one of the most dramatic, yet least appreciated, chapters of our military history.

CHAPTER 1

Opportunity wasted

Almost every airman of the Second World War had, etched in his memory, the moment he realised he wanted to fly. For many, the flying bug bit early, and hard, and often it was an encounter with the brightest star in the dazzling firmament of Australian pre-war aviation, Sir Charles Kingsford-Smith. Admittedly, by 1932, Smithy's health was starting to fail and he was cash-strapped after another failed business venture, but at ten shillings a ride, this living legend gave thousands of young Australians their first taste of being aloft in his famous Fokker Tri-motor, *Southern Cross*, lifting off from airstrips and sporting ovals all over the country.

Smithy was far from alone in forging a vibrant Australian aviation identity. Names such as Charles Ulm, Bert Hinkler and two other Smiths had already entered into folklore. In 1919, Ross Smith and his older brother Keith had picked up knighthoods and £10,000 in prize money by taking off in a time-expired surplus Vickers Vimy bomber from a grass strip at Hounslow outside London and touching down in Darwin 28 days later, the first England-to-Australia flight. Nine years later, Bert Hinkler repeated the exploit – in half the time.

The 1920s and 1930s became a heroic age of Australian aviation. What just a few years previously had seemed flights of unimaginable duration were becoming an Australian speciality, with Smithy's epic 1928 crossing of the Pacific from California to Queensland in 83 hours, 33 minutes making him world famous. Nor were these feats confined to men. Australians could boast of Nancy-Bird Walton and her victory in a 1936 air race from Brisbane to Adelaide, and in 1927, one Millicent Bryant became our first female holder of a commercial pilot's licence. A decade later the now sadly all but forgotten Maude Lores Bonney became the first person to fly the 18,000 miles from Brisbane to her native South Africa in a tiny German-built Klemm monoplane.

In 1928, Australia established the world's first air ambulance, the Royal Flying Doctor Service, and boasted a plethora of airlines including, by the mid 1930s, Ansett, Australian National Airways (ANA), and what would evolve into one of the air industry's greatest and most enduring institutions, Qantas, which had already been operating for over a decade.

Virtually all of Australia's aviation pioneers had forged their careers in the country's nascent air force, the Australian Flying Corps (AFC), which did not even exist by the time most of them were young adults. Formed in 1912, the AFC grew alongside the global expansion of military aviation during the Great War, and by 1918 boasted eight squadrons, many of which had distinguished themselves fighting in the Middle East and over the Western Front. Bert Hinkler, for example, proved himself a brilliant mathematician and inventor, flying in Italy and developing instruments and flying gadgets that were used for decades, while Kingsford-Smith brought down four enemy aircraft over the Western Front before he was shot down in 1917, losing part of his foot and earning the Military Cross.

In August 1921, under the enthusiastic guidance of Wing Commander Richard 'Dickie' Williams – a non-smoking, teetotal son of a Cornish copper miner, now an Australian Flying Corps hero of the 1917 Palestine campaign against the Turks – the AFC emerged as the Royal Australian Air Force (RAAF). Initially, Williams had friends in high places, such as Prime Minister Billy Hughes, who described himself as a 'fanatic' for aviation, and approved of Williams forging for the RAAF a uniquely Australian identity. Under Williams as Chief of Air Staff – a role he would hold three times over seventeen years – the RAAF began to develop its own strategy based on its unique geographical situation, half a world away from events in Europe. In 1925, Williams drafted a major study of air warfare from an Australian perspective entitled 'Memorandum Regarding the Air Defence of Australia' in which – as a lone voice – he presciently framed the emerging threat from Japan.

As a boy in the late 1970s, I had a brief encounter with an ageing Dickie Williams in a Melbourne bookshop, specialising in military matters, I used to frequent. Several times a week after school I would catch the tram into the city, still in my uniform, to haunt this Aladdin's cave, usually remaining until being thrown out at closing time. Here I would pore over the myriad volumes of aeroplanes, hardly buying anything – much to the exasperation of the ever-patient bookshop owner – but laying the foundation of a lifetime's obsession. One afternoon, a small, immaculately dressed and very old man entered, ramrod straight and wielding a stick he seemed not to actually need. Marching – almost literally – up to the counter, he asked the proprietor in a firm voice, 'Do you hold a copy of *These Are Facts*?' The owner, who looked suddenly quite nervous, stammered out, 'Er, yes, I think we do, sir, I'll just find it for you.' As he went to retrieve the volume however, he was stopped. 'I don't want to buy it,' said Williams. 'I was just seeing if you had it. I wrote the bloody thing!' Upon that, he turned and marched out the front door. Dickie Williams would have been around 88 at the time, and as he left, the proprietor of the bookshop no doubt sighed with relief that he had thought to stock several thick hardback copies of the air marshal's autobiography.

Like Australia, Japan had benefitted from the sequestration of Imperial Germany's Pacific territories during and after the First World War. As one of the victorious Allied powers, part of Japan's spoils were the Caroline Islands, complete with the superb natural harbour of Truk, which could easily protect any navy of prodigious size. Australia, having forced the Germans out of its possessions of New Britain and New Guinea in 1914 by some remarkable naval exploits, was determined, under the ever bellicose Hughes, to hold onto them, creating for itself something of a mini-empire in the South Pacific. Japan too dreamt of an empire of its own, one considerably larger.

Having been hermetically sealed for over 300 years until the late nineteenth century, at the dawn of the twentieth, Japan began to develop audacious territorial ambitions, spurred on in no small part by its shock victory over Imperial Russia in the Russo-Japanese War of 1904–05. In the naval Battle of Tsushima, the almost virgin home-built Japanese fleet annihilated that of Russia, destroying eight of the Tsar's battleships and killing 5000 of his seamen for the loss of just over 100 Japanese. In terms of air power, too, Japan was quick to appreciate its importance. Even before the conclusion of the First World War, Japan had begun to plan for the next.

By 1918, Japan had founded its first aircraft manufacturing company, Nakajima, and a few years later a steamship company named Mitsubushi began to diversify into aircraft production, inviting technical assistance from Britain's famed Sopwith company to help them along. After their 1932 invasion of China, much of Japan's aircraft industry came under government control and, in strict secrecy, its output soared. For the moment, the militarists in Tokyo were more than happy not to challenge the wider world's prevailing, mostly racist, assumptions concerning the supposed inferiority of Japanese industry, particularly in the quality of its aircraft.

Dickie Williams, showing a flair for strategy lacking in many of the politicians of his day, believed firmly that Australia would one day be seen as an obstacle to Japan's dreams of a Pacific empire, and the flashpoint, he was certain, would be New Guinea. Shortly after submitting his report, he took to the skies in a small, open-cockpit seaplane to conduct a survey of the various New Guinea territories, including its eastern islands, and began to formulate a plan to defend them, with particular emphasis on the types of aircraft that would be required for the job.

However, fierce disputes over the limited Australian defence budget – as well as the insecurities of the navy and army around the very existence of this brazen new service that they saw solely as a threat to their own – led the Scullin Labor government, in 1929, to advise the end of the RAAF's status as an independent service. This advice, thankfully, was ignored, but the RAAF's budget, particularly after the onset of the Great Depression, never saw it expand much beyond the parameters of a large, private flying club.

Williams' determination, coinciding with Japan's invasion of Manchuria, saw something of a re-evaluation of the importance of air defence, and in the mid 1930s, modern aircraft were ordered to fill the RAAF's expanding ranks: Seagull floatplanes, Hawker Demon biplane fighters and Avro Anson multi-purpose aircraft from Australia's traditional source of weaponry, Great Britain. But what was really needed to meet any threat from the north were modern front-line fighter aircraft, and these were proving almost impossible to obtain. Britain had begun to manufacture Spitfires and Hurricanes, but London, desperate to re-arm itself, had made it abundantly clear that none of these would be heading in Australia's direction any time soon. America provided some modern Hudson bombers, which would be almost all that Australia would have to hit the Japanese when the time came in late 1941 and early 1942, but its capacity for production at that time was limited and fighters were again excluded from the equation.

In 1936, therefore, Williams, now an air vice-marshal, became instrumental in establishing the somewhat revolutionary notion of a local Australian aircraft manufacturing industry, in the form of the Commonwealth Aircraft Corporation (CAC). To head it up, he selected a brilliant pilot, engineer and industrialist, Wing Commander Lawrence Wackett. At a time when not so much as a motor car was being produced locally, the CAC would need a gargantuan effort to turn out modern military aircraft from scratch. Nevertheless, a delegation was sent around the world to find a suitable aircraft type that could be produced in Australia from the ground up, with the North American Aviation company's NA-16 type trainer eventually settled on to satisfy the RAAF's needs.

After an extremely short tooling-up period and the establishment of a factory at Fishermans Bend in Melbourne, the result, in March 1939, was the CAC Wirraway, Australia's first ever home-grown aircraft. Sadly, as a product of compromise, it would prove completely unremarkable in every way, particularly when hurled – idiotically – at the Japanese in Malaya, Singapore and Rabaul in the weeks after Pearl Harbor. On the eve of war, the RAAF still found itself with no modern fighter but a hotch-potch of just under 250 various other aircraft including Avro Ansons, Hawker Demon biplanes, an assortment of trainers, plus just seven all-Australian Wirraways. Added to this, only half of the twelve nominal squadrons on the RAAF's books were operational, a picture virtually unchanged from the conclusion of the First World War.

During this period of belated pre-war expansion, accident rates and training problems inevitably increased, prompting a public outcry, with much of the blame aimed at Williams. To appease popular and press opinion, and seizing a chance to rein in their increasingly quarrelsome chief of air staff, the Lyons government commissioned a report into the RAAF, which, when released in 1938, amounted to little more than a thinly veiled attack on Williams personally, which many believed had been the true purpose of the exercise in the first place. Hence, in early 1939, just before the outbreak of war, when Williams' insights and energies were most needed, the 'father of the RAAF' was unceremoniously packed off to England for 'training' with the Royal Air Force (RAF) in order to 'broaden his experience'. It is said he learned of his new appointment by reading about it in the newspapers.

Once out of the way, the government quickly began dismantling many of Williams' modest innovations. When the European war broke out in September 1939, they reluctantly agreed to bring him home early, but then further added to his misery by refusing to return him to his old job. Instead, Prime Minister Menzies appointed as the RAAF's new chief of air staff a completely unremarkable RAF air marshall, Sir Charles Stuart Burnett, who had to be dragged out of comfortable retirement and shipped to Australia to accept the RAAF's top job. To add insult to injury, it transpires that Burnett had also been Williams' junior commander when in Palestine twenty years earlier. It would prove to be one of the most catastrophic appointments in Australian political history.

Whatever small steps Williams had been able to make towards meeting the Japanese threat when it arrived were reversed upon the arrival of Air Marshal Burnett. In April 1940, despite the overwhelming evidence of the build-up of Japanese aggression, Burnett somehow gleaned 'a continuous lessening of the probability of an attack on Australian territory by Japan'. Williams' plans for an independent fighter force were scrapped, and the RAAF's resources were instead diverted into what amounted to a training department for Britain's RAF. From the end of April 1940, as part of its obligations to the Empire Air Training Scheme, the RAAF sent over a thousand aircrew per month to serve in the United Kingdom or the Western Desert Campaign, half a world away from their soon to be threatened homeland.

As the Pacific War approached, a panicked Menzies belatedly announced a major expansion of the RAAF's home defence capabilities, even agreeing – finally – to a vague notion of a defensive chain, stretching through New Guinea, the Admiralty Islands, the New Hebrides and New Caledonia with Port Moresby as the hub. Airstrips in outlying places such as Lae, Salamaua, Rabaul and Wewak were bolstered, and squadrons were equipped with modern aircraft such as the Lockheed Hudson bomber and Catalina flying boat, hurriedly delivered from America.

Unbelievably, even at this eleventh hour, precious resources such as the RAAF's No. 1 Squadron – the first unit to become operational with the Hudson – were offered to Britain for the defence of Singapore, in the belief that the survival of this supposedly impregnable fortress would be a bastion against Japan's further aggressions. This, despite all of Japan's Pacific bases being located thousands of miles from Singapore, as a quick reference to any school atlas would have confirmed. No. 1 Squadron was quickly followed by another Hudson unit, 8 Squadron, and, in September 1940, No. 21 Wirraway Squadron also headed north to Sembawang airfield in Malaya, where it flew the Brewster Buffalo, another virtually useless aeroplane, which had been rejected by the RAF for use in both the European and desert theatres of operation. When the Japanese struck in December 1941, the squadrons were all but wiped out.

In late January 1942, Rabaul, the former capital of the Australian mandated territory of New Guinea, was invaded. Its coastal defences, lacking overhead protection, were shattered by dive bombers without firing a shot. The speed of Japan's advance astounded not only the local defenders, many of whom were chased down and put to death in summary executions, but also the higher echelons of the RAAF, who could scarcely believe the reports coming back from reconnaissance flights over the island. One pilot, Bob Yeowart from Queensland, at first thought the fleet of ships he observed unloading at Rabaul to be American, until he noticed fighters with red circles on their wings being launched from an aircraft carrier.

Such was the level of unreality that, even after Rabaul's fall, Air Marshal Burnett was indulging notions of preparing a reconnaissance and defensive ring from New Caledonia to New Guinea, which, he declared, could be supported by 'forces from the mainland', a ludicrous notion now completely bypassed by reality.

On 19 February, it was Australia's turn when Darwin was bombed by exactly the sort of carrier-based force dismissed for years by Burnett as being incapable of threatening the Australian mainland. On this fateful morning, nearly 200 Japanese aircraft wheeled in over Darwin Harbour undetected and began to make havoc. No radar stations had warned of their arrival, and only after they began strafing and bombing ships in the harbour did the air raid sirens begin to wail into life. At least 242 people were killed, eight vessels were sunk and the myth of Australia's safety in isolation was exploded forever. Even the handful of long-range anti-aircraft guns that could be brought to bear against the second wave of high-altitude bombers that arrived over the city around midday were rendered useless due to faulty fuses. The Japanese leader of the raid that day, Mitsuo Fuchida, assessed Darwin's defences as 'contemptible'.

In a scene redolent with irony, Williams witnessed the attack personally. Recently returned to Australia and on his way further south after his enforced sojourn in Britain, he stood on the manicured lawn of the colonial-style Hotel Darwin, portable cine camera in hand, taking in the morning vista as the Japanese aircraft appeared overhead and proceeded to choose targets at will. The attack he had prophesised for 30 years – only to be ignored – was erupting around him. What went through his mind as he took shelter can easily be imagined.

Burnett, perhaps sensing his own glaring role in the catastrophe, made a quick visit to Darwin's battered aerodrome soon after the raid, mumbled platitudes about leadership and resilience, posed for the cameras then got back on his plane and headed back to Canberra.

Looking out across Darwin Harbour to the open waters of the Torres Strait in those days after Darwin's attack, one would have been forgiven for feeling the sense of a nation very much alone. Whether Japan had the intention or the means to actually invade Australia remains a debated topic among historians, but there is no doubt that it, at the very least, intended to isolate the island continent, control its waterways to the north, cut it off from help from its traditional allies, and establish a brutal hold over the islands and the hated European colonies of southern Asia.

The tragedy of Darwin laid bare the years of neglect, denial and wasted opportunities that saw Australia bereft of its own fighter defence force. Now, as Dickie Williams had predicted years earlier, New Guinea would become the crucible. Japan realised – as Williams well knew – that as long as Australian (and later, American) aircraft held Port Moresby as a base to launch attacks on the new conquests of its Pacific empire, it could never be secure.

In early 1942, Japan decided that New Guinea would be taken. It believed little effort would be required. The finest defences of the European and American powers had, after all, withered miserably before it. From already existing airfields on the New Guinea north coast at Lae and Salamaua, as well as recently conquered Rabaul, an aerial assault on Moresby would quickly reduce whatever resistance still remained in this colonial backwater, then in early May, an amphibious assault would see the town fall easily to Japanese hands. Singapore, Britain's Far East fortress, had toppled with just a shove, and the United States, still paralysed by the speed of Japan's Pacific blitz, was months away from deploying its power so far from home. Australia's own defences, decreed the Japanese, would be pitiful at best, if they existed at all.

In fact, the Japanese had already overplayed their hand. Had they not paused to consolidate their early gains after subduing Rabaul, and immediately launched against Port Moresby an assault of similar violence, there is little doubt that it would have similarly fallen.

At the end of January, the tiny Moresby garrison was ordered to hold out against an expected invasion from the sea. At that stage, Port Moresby's total air defence capacity consisted of one Hudson bomber and two Catalina flying boats, which had all been flown to their limits; as a result, the troops were not expected to last more than 36 hours. It was an opportunity the Japanese would never have again.

On 11 March, to little resistance, the Japanese began landing at Lae and Salamaua, soon establishing themselves at the landing strips there, bringing Port Moresby within an hour's flying time of its aircraft. It was understood that Moresby had an airstrip of its own, situated not far from the town. What the Japanese didn't know was that it was in a mess.

•

Seven Mile Strip, along with its smaller neighbour KilaKila, or Three Mile, began as a pre-war airstrip dating back to the early 1930s. American money had helped pay for its initial construction, with intentions that it be used as both a civil aerodrome as well as a refuelling spot for US aircraft travelling from Australia to their territories in the Philippines. It had, however, been poorly maintained.

Both Seven Mile and Three Mile had been slated for improvements to their capacities since 1939, but the larger Seven Mile, it was decided, would be given priority. The going was slow. In October 1941, Seven Mile began its military incarnation when American B-17 bombers touched down there briefly en route to their base at Clark in the Philippines (where, in a couple of months, they would be wiped out in Japanese attacks). By the time the first Japanese raids on Port Moresby and its airstrip began in early February, runway extensions had yet to be completed, and even permanent concrete barrack blocks with such luxuries as showers and flyscreens were still struggling to be built. Seven Mile's personnel were destined to remain under canvas for the time being.

In fact, Seven Mile's very viability as an operational air base was by no means certain. In February, panic gripped Port Moresby when, fearing imminent invasion, most of the civilian contractors, along with much of the population, left or were evacuated. In a shameful collapse of order and morale, shops and private houses were sacked, as recorded by Osmar White who recalled that: 'They had been abandoned in haste, and later looted. The doors stood open. One could see smashed furniture, crockery, papers scattered on the floor, draggled clothing, torn photographs.'

'An impression is rapidly growing,' stated a report by a senior air staff officer, 'that the policy of the Government is to let the garrisons at Port Moresby and Thursday Island go in the same way as that at Rabaul, and that no serious assistance will be given.'

Not that the defenders of Port Moresby had been idle in their belated preparations. Under the savage heat of a tropical summer, small bands of Australian army engineers had worked around the clock for weeks. Since Pearl Harbor, 200 miles of new roads had been bulldozed and blasted through jungles, across drained swamps and up mountain spurs, sometimes following the lines of old goat or mule tracks, performing in weeks feats of engineering which had been merely dreams of civil administrators for years. But work on Moresby's airstrips was incomplete, leaving them in a state, according to the RAAF's North East Area Command, 'designed for peacetime conditions in which aircraft cannot be dispersed except along runways'. The report went on to urgently require 'large labour gang and road-making units of the Army Department. Remaining contractors most cooperative but time factor against us unless very material and immediate assistance is forthcoming. Strongly recommend large work gangs work day and night to avoid continued repetition of this state of unpreparedness.'

This desperate outburst simply prompted a slanging match with the local army commander, General Morris, who, perhaps sensing the absurdity of expending his men's energies in preparing aerodromes that no aircraft would use, retorted that he was not prepared to 'use his limited labour to make dispersal bays, taxiways etc unless he can be assured that aircraft will be sent to occupy them, or that aircraft so occupying them will not be knocked out in the first few raids through lack of protection'.

The results of years of neglect and misguided priorities now seemed to be converging like a storm on this small airstrip just outside Port Moresby. Something would have to be done, and quickly. It was realised – finally – that modern fighter aircraft were essential to bolster the hub of New Guinea and its capital. Sporadic American units of the Army Air Corp had by this time begun to arrive in Australia, and the government optimistically put in an order for 700 P-40 Kittyhawk fighters, which began to arrive in dribs and drabs. At one stage, a batch of eighteen turned up and were earmarked to be forwarded to Seven Mile Strip, creating anticipation in Moresby that their arrival was imminent. However before they could be fully assembled from their crates at the RAAF base at Amberley, west of Brisbane, the order was countermanded by an American general who insisted they be deployed instead to join the losing battle currently underway in Java. Moresby would have to wait.

Renowned war correspondent Osmar White arrived at Port Moresby at this critical time to begin his long and brutally honest account of the entire New Guinea campaign. 'At two o'clock on the afternoon of 13 February 1942 a Lockheed Electra airliner landed at the Seven Mile airfield, Port Moresby, with 14 passengers. It was the last civil aeroplane to cross the Coral Seas from Australia.' He described the strip as 'A lonely sun-scorched clearing in the bush…a raw, metalled landing strip scooped out of a valley surrounded by low hills. The only aircraft on it were the Lockheed, an old Junkers transport pockmarked by bullets, and a single Hudson bomber.' His book *Green Armour* was considered an almost too frank assessment of Australia's unpreparedness when it was published in 1945, but it is now regarded as a classic of military writing.

As the early weeks of 1942 dragged on, Japanese aircraft began appearing above the undefended skies of Moresby with arrogant regularity. On the second night in February, the townsfolk of Moresby had been woken in their beds to the unfamiliar *krump* of bombs being dropped on the harbour by enormous four-engine 'Mavis' flying boats. The sound did not remain unfamiliar for long. By the end of March, Moresby had undergone no less than 22 Japanese air raids of various sizes. On 28 February, for example, 130 bombs were dropped, leaving houses and docks burning, while the Zero pilots flew low over the harbour, taking their time to line up and strafe ships and Catalina flying boats as they lay at their moorings.

Osmar White witnessed one such attack.

> I saw one crew die in a blazing hull that shot smoke and flames 400 feet above the placid harbour. The men had been asleep when seven Zeros came suddenly round the headland. They rolled and turned and looped with the skittish exuberance of Japanese fighter pilots who see no fighters to oppose them; then they blasted the bay shipping and the foreshores with cannon shells and incendiary bullets.

More and more brazenly, the Japanese bomber pilots, flying the fast new G4M 'Betty' medium bomber, would even make dummy runs on the target before leisurely turning around and dropping their bombs with confidence.

First World War veteran and now RAAF supply officer, Squadron Leader AE 'Ted' Church, who joined 75 Squadron as its highly capable equipment officer, experienced both the Port Moresby raids and the 44 days, leaving an account in a book published soon after the war, *They Flew Alone.* Of these early days in Moresby he writes: 'Every day Moresby or the 7 mile strip received two and often three raids. Flights of 18 and 24 big, twin-engined Mitsubishi bombers rode the clouds without let or hindrance. We on the ground could only gaze at them savagely, swear and dive for a slit trench as they sailed overhead.'

The town's sole anti-aircraft battery, situated on Tuagubu Hill, blasted away defiantly, but as its shells could reach no higher than 20,000 feet, Church speculated the Japanese pilots simply laughed at the bursts exploding harmlessly below them. 'Our inability to hit back or to prevent the continual raids developed an inferiority complex that gave the enemy superhuman powers.'

In a single week in March, the air raid sirens sounded over Moresby six times as the enemy once again appeared, targeting whatever it liked. On 7 March, ten aircraft appeared over the town at midnight, dropping 30 bombs in a seventeen-minute raid over barracks and army tents. Despite several times being driven off by the dogged and at times accurate anti-aircraft fire from gunners on the ground, without the protection of fighters, the Japanese could roam the skies at will.

Ted Church observed, however, that conditions at Seven Mile were set to improve, as the construction of a shower block, water system, fly-proof storerooms and proper kitchens with large stoves began to take shape. However: '…we should, of course, have known this was too good to be true. Exactly one week before we were to have moved in, the camp was the target for a large raid. Two hundred bombs fell in the hut area, and as the smoke and clouds of dust cleared away, our cherished dreams perished.'

Meanwhile, rumours of the Kittyhawks' arrival came and went, to be replaced by doubts that they would ever show up at all. In bitter soldiers' humour, the Kittyhawks became 'Tomorrowhawks', then as the weeks passed still with no sign of them, 'Mythhawks' and finally, 'Neverhawks'. But, far to the south, unknown to the people of the beleaguered town, things were finally beginning to move.

CHAPTER 2

75 Squadron forms

In late February, another consignment of around 75 P-40s, diverted from the deteriorating situation in Java, became available to the RAAF and arrived, still in their packing crates strapped to the decks of a cargo vessel, on Australia's shores. Whichever way they had come, the government was glad to receive them, and not a moment too soon. Plans were immediately drawn up to put them to use.

It was proposed that three new Kittyhawk squadrons, the first ever in the defence of the Australian mainland, be quickly raised. So, in Townsville on 4 March, 75 Fighter Squadron RAAF was founded, to comprise sixteen officers and 186 airmen, 28 of those being pilots. It would be allotted eighteen P-40 'E' Kittyhawk aircraft to be divided into two flights, as well as a headquarters flight. This was followed by No. 76 at Archerfield, Queensland, on 14 March, and, two days later, No. 77 at Pearce in Western Australia. Formed in haste in desperate times, 75 would go on to forge an illustrious history as one of the most famous units of the RAAF, still operating as a front-line fighter squadron 70 years later. At its conception, however, there was very little to work with.

In just over a week, from wherever they could be found, the diverse elements of a wartime fighter unit were thrown together from scratch. From the large Station HQ at Bankstown in Sydney came rookie pilots Arthur Tucker and Jim Norton; from SHQ Williamtown, Flying Officers Ron O'Connor, John Piper and Lloyd Holliday. Flying Officers Jeffrey Woods and Ken Lloyd came from 23 Squadron, then conducting maritime patrols off Brisbane, as did the future leader – and arguably 75 Squadron's most controversial personality – Flight Lieutenant Les Jackson. From Laverton came Pilot Officer Don Swann, a former signwriter and a 'practical man' who would soon prove himself as an effective squadron adjutant in the difficult weeks ahead.

Station Headquarters Canberra contributed several other young officers: Pilot Officer Oswald 'Ozzie' Channon, Flying Officer Barry Cox and sergeant pilots Vernon Sims, Stan Havard and Richard Granville. Recently returned to Townsville after the mauling of its Wirraways at Rabaul, 24 Squadron contributed Flight Lieutenant Bruce Anderson, Flying Officer Wilbur Wackett (the son of the well-known managing director of the Commonwealth Aircraft Corporation, Lawrence Wackett), Pilot Officer Geoff Atherton and Sergeant Ally 'Bink' Davies. Sergeant pilots Michael Butler and Bob Crawford, both of whom had witnessed the fury of the Japanese raid on Darwin, sheltering in slit trenches as the high-level bombers attacked their aerodrome, were relinquished by 12 Squadron. On that terrible day in Darwin, Butler had been sent aloft with two 112-kilogram bombs slung under his Wirraway, with orders to meet a suspected incoming Japanese invasion fleet. Lucky for him, there was no fleet to be found.

Some of 75's pilots were so raw they had yet to be assigned any posting whatsoever, with Pilot Officer John Le Gay Brereton – who would always be known by his nickname, 'Cocky' – arriving straight from No. 3 Service Flying Training School at Amberley, while Arthur Tucker had recently graduated at Deniliquin in New South Wales.

Only four men could be counted as having had operational experience in the Kittyhawk, all veterans of the Middle East campaign: Turnbull, Dave Ellerton, John Jackson, and the man who had been charged with the task of putting 75 together from scratch, Wing Commander Peter Jeffrey. Born in Tenterfield, Jeffrey had enjoyed a stellar career with the RAAF, joining up before the war then rising quickly to command 3 Squadron, and later still flying with 234 Wing operating Tomahawks and Kittyhawks in the North African desert. Jeffrey had been credited with at least five enemy aircraft shot down and many more damaged, although this tally was probably higher, as he was known to be a 'conservative' claimer. On one occasion, he landed behind the German lines beside a downed Kittyhawk to rescue its unlucky pilot, Flight

Lieutenant Cecil 'Tiny' Cameron, who at six foot four was the tallest man in the squadron. To make room in the rather small single-seat cockpit, Jeffrey discarded his parachute before somehow managing to fly back to safety with the not-so-tiny Cameron seated on his lap.

Jeffrey's skills both as a leader of men and an innovator were never better illustrated than in his instigation of the quietly revolutionary concept of the mixed rank pilots' mess. Traditionally, officers and NCOs occupied separate messes, even in postings as remote as the African desert, but Jeffrey, upon assuming command of 3 Squadron in February 1941, would have none of it. From now on, pilots, whether they wore stripes or rings, would sup together, sharing their skills and experiences of how to fight and how to survive in the hardship of the see-sawing desert campaign. Such threats to the traditional military class system were initially met with disapproval, but when the head of the entire Desert Air Force, Air Marshal Arthur Coningham, another 'colonial' from New Zealand, visited 3 Squadron to see this curious arrangement for himself, he approved, and it became standard for the Desert Air Force right across North Africa. By the end of his tour, Jeffrey wore the ribbons of both the Distinguished Flying Cross and Distinguished Service Order.

Returning exhausted to Australia in January 1942, but his tour complete, Jeffrey was put in charge of the major new RAAF facility at Bankstown. He did not remain there long. Summoned to Melbourne by the Air Board, he was solemnly and confidentially put in the picture as to the gravity of the situation to the north, and told that, in the board's opinion, he was the ideal man to pull together these three new squadrons, with his priority being to forge 75's raw assortment of men into a fighting unit and send them straight into battle.

His command, Jeffrey was told, would be in a supernumerary capacity, lasting until such time as the new squadron could be sent into action. Jeffrey baulked at this, insisting that as he was to be responsible for seeing the squadron become ready for battle, he should be given permanent command. With little choice, the Air Board agreed. When he expressed concern as to the level of experience of the pilots soon to be in his charge, Jeffrey was assured that all were experienced flying instructors, an outrageous lie given that only one man, Alan Whetters, would in any way fit that description.

And then there was the question of the time frame. In normal circumstances, Jeffrey could have expected to be able to give his men at least a hundred hours' flying time and a month to bond as a fighting team. These were far from normal circumstances, however, and he would have to do it all in less than a fortnight.

Anticipating the horrendous conditions that awaited his men and their aircraft in Port Moresby, Jeffrey was initially sceptical about what he regarded as the parsimonious allocation of just 75 Kittyhawks to furnish three whole new units. 'That's about enough to form one bloody squadron!'

was his initial response. Seventy-five aircraft were, however, all that was available, so 25 Kittyhawks was what he would be given – not very much to hold off the Japanese. But that task would ultimately fall to another man. Eager as he was to lead, Jeffrey had not counted on the strength of personality of a fellow veteran of 3 Squadron's Middle East campaign, Flight Lieutenant John Francis Jackson.

Jeffrey needed no convincing as to Jackson's skill and courage in battle – he'd seen it for himself in the desert – but nevertheless he believed Jackson had already done his time, and was still suffering from the nervous exhaustion that afflicted both men after their long desert campaign. 'John, look, when I sent you back from the Middle East, I thought you'd done your business and you're a bit operationally fatigued. You shouldn't be here at all,' Jeffrey had told him. Jackson disagreed. In view of his experience, and sensing the gravity of the situation he and 75 Squadron's green young pilots would soon be facing, Jackson believed he was the better man to lead them.

As Jeffrey recounted in an interview years later, 'he turned on me and said, "What in the bloody hell are you fighting for? King and Country or something? Well, I've got a wife and kids in Australia and no Jap bastard's going to get anywhere near them except over my dead body."' Despite his misgivings, Jeffrey felt the power in the man's convictions, and knew what he was capable of. So it was agreed that, having set up the squadron as best he could, Jeffrey would relinquish command to one of the greatest, and most unlikely fighter pilot commanders of the war, 'Old John' Jackson.

•

Photographs of John Jackson belie the classic young, lean and hungry fighter pilot image. Portraits of him are rare, but perhaps the best known is one taken in Libya some time in 1941 when he flew with 3 Squadron. Jackson, a big man, leans up against a Tomahawk fighter, towering above two fellow pilots, one with a hand in his pocket, the other holding a cigarette. Jackson's frame is half-turned towards the camera, the collar of his battle jacket pulled against the cutting North African wind. One can imagine the photographer having just made a joke, to which the men respond, and there is something about Jackson that makes you grin along with him.

Having just turned 34, Jackson was indeed considerably older than his fellow pilots, older, in fact, than fighter pilots just about anywhere. Born in 1908 to a family of well-off Queensland seed merchants, he attended Brisbane Grammar, and, rare for the time, travelled to Europe after the First World War with an odd, quasi-nationalist youth organisation called the Young Australia League, formed initially for the purpose of protecting the integrity of, of all things, Australian Rules Football.

By 1927, Jackson was running his own property 60 miles west of St George, and in 1933 he was in charge of Western

Queensland Motor and Engineering Works, as well as being a stock agent for the New Zealand Loan & Mercantile Agency Company. Inspired by the London to Melbourne Air Race of 1934, and mindful of how an aeroplane might assist his business, he travelled to Sydney, bought a tiny Klemm Swallow monoplane and learned to fly it. Soon he could afford to graduate to a considerably more impressive Beechcraft Staggerwing, and became a regular feature in the skies of western Queensland. When he joined the RAAF Reserve in 1936, known also as the Citizen Air Force, he discovered to his dismay that the machine he'd been piloting privately could outperform anything the air force could offer him at the time.

A few weeks after the outbreak of war in 1939, Jackson was called up, given the rank of pilot officer, experienced a brief stint on Wirraways with 23 Squadron at Archerfield, and in October 1940 was posted to 3 Squadron, which had just arrived in Egypt. Although a naturally gifted pilot, Jackson considered himself wholly underqualified to go into combat, citing his experience of air gunnery as 'practically nil'. His learning curve was steep and he quickly gained experience in fighting the Italians, Germans and the pro-German Vichy French. First, however, he would need to come to terms with flying obsolete cast-off RAF Gloster Gladiator biplanes, which he described as being in 'shocking condition and should be scrapped as unfit for further service'. This opinion was vindicated when his Gladiator ended up on its nose after suffering an engine failure on take-off. Jackson, fortunately, was unhurt.

The desert conditions were harsh with little in the way of comforts. Water was severely limited, and the constant dust storms coated everything – the men, their food, their bedding – with a fine covering of grit. Some of the pilots began to feel they were actually made of sand.

Eventually however, as a supply route to Britain opened up, the squadron began to receive Hawker Hurricanes, an aircraft Jackson adored. His victories quickly mounted. In a single action around Mersa Matruh in February 1941, Jackson shot down no less than three Stuka dive bombers. In April, he chalked up his fourth by an extraordinary piece of bluff. Firing his guns briefly at a marauding Stuka, he cursed as they jammed up and became useless. Rather than break off the attack, Jackson made dummy attacks at the German aircraft, forcing it to crash land in a dry riverbed. It was just the sort of determination and daring that he was to display many times over New Guinea.

After converting to the Kittyhawk's predecessor, the P-40 Tomahawk, Jackson took part in the campaign against the forces of Vichy France in Syria and Lebanon. In June, with the destruction of a Potez light bomber, he achieved his fifth victory to become an ace, and in July was promoted to flight lieutenant. One kill, a French Dewoitine fighter, scored late in the campaign, was set to be marked down as 'shared' with fellow ace, Bobby Gibbes. Instead, the two pilots tossed a coin. Jackson lost, and graciously gave the kill to his friend. By the end of his tour of operations in the Middle East, Jackson had been Mentioned in Dispatches and would soon be awarded the Distinguished Flying Cross (DFC).

Pilot Arthur Tucker described John Jackson as 'a true gentleman and friend to all', a big man, with a deep, friendly voice that hid a somewhat reserved personality. He clearly adored his wife, Betty, and wrote her many long and descriptive letters, many of which have survived. Viv Hill, a Queensland country dentist who went on to become a senior RAAF dental officer, remembered Jackson from his days around Gympie as 'a quiet, but genuine man who could talk to anyone with ease, and absolutely passionate about aviation'. At one stage, John tried to sell Viv his little Klemm monoplane, but the deal never quite came off.

Although he'd spent his life on the land, John seemed to enjoy the nightlife of Cairo when on leave, one of those people able to take anything in their stride. The function of a hotel bidet, however, perplexed him, and in a letter home he simply put it down to some kind of 'feminine-orientated device'. He was not averse to a drink, apparently, even having been placed 'on the dry' on his initial voyage to Egypt. He was fond of typical Australian larrikinism also. At one time, 3 Squadron was known by its simple but descriptive nickname, 'hydraulic', in that it could apparently 'lift anything', and Jackson played his part in upholding the unit's traditions. Once, he managed to obtain a car that had been spirited away from outside Cairo HQ, and was mortified when the rightful owner turned up to take it back, despite Jackson claiming to have painted it three different colours.

He was fair-skinned with thinning hair, and his eyesight, worn down under the glare of the Queensland and Middle Eastern skies, was notoriously unreliable. His hearing, according to Peter Jeffrey, was a little dodgy, and Arthur Tucker recalled that Jackson was 'so blind that he once led his flight halfway out into the Mediterranean chasing a spot on his windscreen'.

Arriving back in Australia in November 1941, and showing signs of nervous stress from the months of combat in the desert war, John was assigned, as was common with experienced pilots, to training. He hated every minute of it. Point Cook, near Melbourne, was something of a contrast to the deserts of Africa, but Jackson found no joy in his job at No. 1 Service Flying Training School, despite appreciating the value of the work being done there. 'I loathe this joint,' he wrote home. 'This training is a tough job and I take my hat off to the boys who have been doing it since war broke out...every one of these instructors is longing to be sent overseas, but I doubt if they have any chance of ever getting there – they are so valuable here.'

Jackson however, was soon to be back in action himself.

•

In 1939, Bill Deane-Butcher spent a year in surgery training at the Coast Hospital near the Sydney suburb of Randwick after gaining his medical degree at Sydney University. Overlooking the Pacific Ocean and beside the rolling greens of the New South Wales Golf Club, there were certainly worse places for a young surgeon to train, and coming from a respected medical family, Deane-Butcher no doubt contemplated a comfortable career ahead of him. He was an intelligent and thoughtful man, moved by the small human dramas of the medical profession. Decades later, he would recall a fourteen-year-old girl severely paralysed with polio, only her head visible at one end of an enormous respirator. For four months she was isolated, with even her parents forbidden to see her, Deane-Butcher virtually her sole companion. He never forgot the experience, nor the responsibility. 'I found the compassion of medicine a driving force,' he would later say.

Another young doctor taking surgery training that year was Rod Jeffrey, and the two men became friends. Also joining the medical staff was a Jewish refugee in his mid-thirties, not long escaped from Europe. Bill Deane-Butcher lived well into his nineties, but it took decades after the war for him to reveal to his son, Richard, the profound effect his Jewish friend had had on his life and career. 'That's the benefit of having a father who lives a long life,' Richard told me in an interview. 'They end up telling you things that they wouldn't have dreamed of when they were younger.' According to Richard, his father's friend was 'absolutely terrified of the Nazis and tried to convince people of the extent of their brutality, which he had witnessed first hand. He believed there was no way the Nazi machine could be stopped, and was convinced the war was a lost cause.'

In mid 1940, after the disasters of Dunkirk and the fall of France, Britain's demise seemed inevitable. Deane-Butcher noticed the demeanour of the doctor – whose name, to his lasting regret, he could never later recall – darken considerably. Convinced the Nazis would eventually arrive in Australia, where he would be tortured, the doctor began, openly and rationally, to talk to Deane-Butcher, as well as some of the other young doctors, about suicide. The talk went on for weeks.

One day, when on duty in emergency, Deane-Butcher received an ambulance. To his horror, the body of his young Jewish friend was inside, 'smelling strongly of cyanide'. The next day, both he and his fellow intern Rod Jeffrey decided to enlist. The director of the hospital, a forceful man by the name of Dr Walters, was aghast at losing two of his promising young interns and refused them permission to resign, so they simply snuck into the city that afternoon, walked into a recruitment office in Martin Place and signed up. 'Each of us signed up for both the army and the air force,' recalled Deane-Butcher. 'Six months later, Rod was called into the army, I went into the air force.'

Although given a uniform and an instant rank of Squadron Leader, Deane-Butcher's first job in the RAAF brought him little closer to the war. Installed in a pleasant flat in Brisbane where he was joined by his new wife, Elizabeth, Deane-Butcher spent a comfortable year assessing hopeful young airmen at the Brisbane recruiting centre and the nearby Elementary Flying Training School at Archerfield. Then there was the difficult but necessary job of travelling the countryside on recruitment trains, where the small party of RAAF officers wined, dined and danced to the point of exhaustion in every town they visited.

Deane-Butcher and Rod Jeffrey would go on to have very different wars, but in a conversation that in wartime probably should not have taken place, Jeffrey revealed that his brother, Peter Jeffrey, had just arrived back in the country from the Middle East and was now working up a brand-new unit of Kittyhawks that would soon be sent north to fight the Japanese. All this was of course, added Jeffrey, entirely secret. Bill Deane-Butcher listened with growing interest. He was now a man with a mission.

Deane-Butcher had met Peter Jeffrey via his brother before the war, but could in no way claim to be a friend. Despite this – and the wartime veil of secrecy that always surrounded the formation of new units – Bill somehow managed to discover that Squadron Leader Peter Jeffrey, the new CO of the yet-to-be-formed 75 Squadron, was currently in Adelaide. 'It was quite wrong of me, but I put in a trunk-line call from Brisbane and spoke to him,' he recalled years later. How he managed this piece of intelligence remains, even to his family, something of a mystery, but when Peter Jeffrey took the call from this forthright acquaintance he could barely remember meeting, he was both astounded and furious.

'I believe you're putting together a fighter squadron,' Deane-Butcher stated bluntly, to astonished silence at the other end of the line. 'Well, you'll need a medical officer, and I'm your medical officer.' It's not known whether Deane-Butcher revealed the source of his inside knowledge to have been Peter Jeffrey's very own brother, but, unperturbed by Jeffrey's indignation, he repeated his statement. Impressed by his determination, perhaps even sensing this was precisely the boldness he would be needing, Peter Jeffrey swallowed a little pride and told Deane-Butcher to report to the place the squadron would soon be heading, Townsville.

Dr Bill Deane-Butcher would go on to become one of the most important figures in 75 Squadron's 44-day campaign, remaining with it and its men for the duration of the battle. To some, he would evolve into a de facto squadron commander, particularly in the latter stages of the fight. Rod Jeffrey, meanwhile, would join the 2/26th Infantry Battalion, surrender with it at Singapore and experience the horrors of the Sandakan Death March, succumbing to beriberi in May 1945, just three months before the end of the war. Of the three doctors who began the war together, Deane-Butcher was the only one left alive.

'That's the way things happened in those days,' said his son, Richard. 'It was all very personal and it was a very small world.'

•

There is a portrait of Flying Officer John Piper, snapped just at the end of the 44 days, which – like that of his boss,

John Jackson – seems to run counter to the Second World War fighter pilot image, and yet, in a uniquely Australian way, perhaps exemplifies it. The first thing that strikes you is the beard, a sort of stump of a goatee, slightly manicured in a fashion that seems more akin to a beatnik of later decades, not the usual clean-shaven picture of 1940s airmen. His hair too, is just a little too long for the short-back-and-sides era. He wears an RAAF officer's cap, but almost jauntily and, with no sign of a shirt, one could imagine that it could easily be all that he is wearing. His eyes look heavenwards, and though weary, show a toughness, a determination, a 'bring it on' attitude, utterly devoid of fear. It's hard to imagine him ever having thrown a salute, but he was exactly the sort of man you would not want to come up against as an adversary.

Piper described himself as coming from 'the impoverished middle class', and was born in Melbourne in 1917, but grew up on a farm in Gippsland. As a result, he was a keen sailor and horseman. He joined the Light Horse at the beginning of the war, but had always liked the idea of flying though never thought he could afford the lessons. The RAAF thus seemed a logical path to follow. 'All I wanted to be was a fighter pilot. My ambitions were drink all night and fly all day. That was all I was really interested in.'

Piper had few illusions about either the war or his prospects, and said freely that 'none of us expected to come back. Well, I certainly didn't.' He looked forward to instruction in Canada and eventually being sent to Britain, but at the end of his training at Essendon and Point Cook, the Canadians were not quite ready, and so Piper stayed in Australia, accumulating the exceptionally high total of 150 flying hours.

A natural pilot who was 'never airsick, not even once', Piper flew Wirraways and Ansons on maritime escort patrols, then, as he said, 'for some extraordinary reason', was posted in July 1941 to an RAF squadron in Singapore flying the truly atrocious Brewster Buffalo. 'It was a very poor aeroplane,' Piper said. 'It was the only one I can remember that had a big red thing in the cockpit that said "Do not spin" because you wouldn't come out of it alive if you did.'

For a young air force officer, life in Singapore before Pearl Harbor was extremely pleasant, and Piper would always thank his lucky stars that he was brought back to Australia before the 'balloon went up'.

•

The manner in which the men who were to make up 75 Squadron discovered their destiny was often unconventional. Having completed his course on single engine Wirraways, Arthur Tucker, a former teacher from Queensland, was told he was to be seconded to the RAF, and contemplated a long route to the European war: weeks at sea in a convoy to the United States, then Canada for more training, and finally across the Atlantic to Britain. Awaiting embarkation at Bradfield Park in Sydney, Tucker watched the first contingent of his fellow pilots board the buses to take them down to Circular Quay. He would be on the next one. After a short time, the buses returned with the same load of somewhat bewildered airmen. No-one, it seemed, was going anywhere. Then the news of the Japanese attack on Pearl Harbor was announced. It was a shock to everyone. 'No discussion about Japan or their prospect of entering the war had been discussed whatsoever,' Tucker revealed in a series of interviews recorded in the 1980s. Pearl Harbor was, he said, 'a bolt out of the blue'.

As the air force digested the shock of this new Pacific War advancing towards their doorstep, Tucker and his fellow pilots cooled their heels for a few weeks at Bradfield Park – 'listening to wild rumours' – before about twenty of them were sent to an Operational Training Unit at Nhill in western Victoria, to basically repeat what they had already learned at their Service Flying Training School in Deniliquin. No-one seemed to know what it was they were supposed to be doing there, but for the moment, Tucker was happy to continue flying the cumbersome Wirraway – an aeroplane he rather liked – in much the same relaxed manner as he had done previously. 'There was nothing tactical we learned,' he recalled, 'and nothing much in the way of formation flying either. We weren't learning anything and we weren't being told anything. It was cloud-cuckoo land, looking back.'

In mid February, Tucker found himself being moved again, among a group of eighteen pilots, this time to RAAF Bankstown in Sydney where they were split between three new American squadrons being formed there. It was here, attached temporarily to the US 7th Pursuit Squadron, he would meet his new mount, the P-40 Kittyhawk. Instead of the familiar short, squat Wirraway, which Tucker likened somewhat to a bumblebee, he was now presented with a true thoroughbred. Initially, it was the Kittyhawk's shape that inspired him. 'Here we had an aeroplane with a great long nose,' he said. Even getting into the aircraft was a new experience. 'With a Wirraway,' he explained, 'you could step up onto it. But with the Kittyhawk, you had to really climb up into the thing.' Around him in the surprisingly roomy cockpit was the further shock of dozens and dozens of switches and dials, the function of many of them he could only guess at. 'I counted once that I had something like 77 different switches and levers in the Kittyhawk, all of which I had to know by feel.'

Then there was the smell. 'The smell of aeroplanes was always ominous,' said Tucker, and each type was different. As opposed to the air-cooled Wirraway, the Kittyhawk exuded the distinctive odour of the coolant glycol, an aroma indelibly etched in the minds of many airmen of the Second World War.

Bankstown was also where Tucker first encountered Flight Lieutenant Alan Whetters, from Melbourne. At 30, another older man, Whetters had initially been knocked back for pilot training upon applying to the permanent RAAF in 1934. So, having always had a love of 'mechanical things', he signed up as an engine fitter at Point Cook, a job at which he excelled. When, two years later, they finally allowed him to fly, he found he excelled at that too, even graduating to instructor in 1938.

Tucker would always speak of Whetters in glowing terms. 'A magnificent pilot,' he said, 'an instinctive one who liked to teach people.' After seeing him in combat over Moresby, Tucker would also add, 'He was a game bugger.'

Despite being initially looked down on by the other cadets, Whetters attributed his subsequent survival in combat to his experience and knowledge of aircraft engines. 'Never once did an aircraft fail me due to engine trouble,' he said in a series of interviews conducted many years later. He was also possibly helped by what he learned in his unlikely role as a weather pilot. Supposedly to avoid tedious parade ground duty, Whetters volunteered to conduct meteorological observation flights. In an open Hawker Demon biplane, he was required to read instruments fixed to the aircraft's wing-struts and record the information by writing it down on a pad attached to his knee. 'As a consequence,' he later reflected in magnificent understatement, 'your thoughts tended to be taken from the flying to obtain these readings.' Two Bulldog aircraft had crashed carrying out these operations prior to Whetters' stint in the job. The experience put him in good stead when later encountering the challenging weather over New Guinea.

Being the first two pilots to report to the American colonel in charge of the 7th Pursuit Squadron at Bankstown, Tucker and Whetters formed a lifelong bond. Tucker credited Whetters with giving him one of the most salient pieces of advice needed to survive in the air force, namely, 'Once you tell your story, stick to it and don't change a thing!' He would also be the first to allay Tucker's concerns about the powerful new aircraft they would soon be flying. 'The American colonel handed us the manuals,' said Tucker, 'and then told us that when we knew the "tits and bits" well enough to start the engine, we could fly it.'

Whetters took off first, completed a circuit without incident, landed and walked over to Tucker. 'Well, it's got a long nose,' he said breezily, 'but it's just like a Wirraway. You can't go wrong.'

Michael Butler recalled his introduction to the big aeroplane similarly: 'They said, "sit in that aeroplane and there's a sheet of paper. It says what's that for what's that for etc. After half an hour we'll test you out and away you go."'

'Awe-inspiring' is how Tucker recalled his own first impressions of the Kittyhawk. He still remembered taxiing down to the far corner of Bankstown on a bend of the Georges River, facing up the aerodrome's slight hill and 'pushing off' for his first flight. This, despite his view from the cockpit being restricted to the 'great lump of metal' of the expansive liquid-cooled V-12 Allison engine stretching up in front of him. 'When you were on the ground you couldn't see a thing without putting your head at forty degrees either side.' Nervously, Tucker opened the throttle for the first time, remembering what he had been told about landing the thing: 'Get lined up well back on the approach before lowering the flaps. If you turn with the flaps down, you'll spill the air out of them and go in.'

The Kittyhawk's power was such that Tucker found he was off the ground before he could even get his tail up. 'I had the feeling I had when a beautiful chestnut bolted with me, eleven years earlier, and all I could do was hang on for grim death.' Momentarily startled, he grabbed control of the stick, and executed the same tight circuit he had been practising in the Wirraway while at Nhill, landing on three points.

Michael Butler also recalled his first flight in the powerful new Kittyhawk:

> Well after the Wirraway it was quite extraordinary. You get in this thing and open the throttle of this huge engine and away you'd go. I can remember my first take-off. I was about 6000 feet up before I got the wheels up and the gills trimmed and all the other things you've got to do after take-off.

The Kittyhawk, the pilots realised, was a wonderful aircraft to fly, though care was needed to manage the immense power of the engine, particularly the torque swing, which Tucker described as 'intense, a lot more power than we'd ever had before. You had to remember to wind on three right rudder trim and three back to get her off the ground. If you forgot, or wound on the wrong trim, you'd very smartly put her into a ground loop and plough into something, and I certainly saw people do that.' One of his duties at Bankstown was as aerodrome controller, working with the American pilots who were just as inexperienced as he. 'I can tell you, there were an awful lot of aeroplanes bent there,' he said.

Michael Butler agreed that the American pilots also struggled:

> These poor fellas, they only had around 150 or 200 total hours of flying all types and they were absolutely scared stiff of the Kittyhawk. They were spinning them and ground-looping them, turning them over on their nose and getting lost and smashing up these lovely aeroplanes as fast as they were assembling them.

What Butler and his fellow pilots did not get much of a chance to do at Bankstown, however, was come to grips with the Kittyhawk in any meaningful capacity beyond taking off, flying around for a bit and landing. Barely 'three or four' familiarisation flights were all that he could recall of his time at Bankstown, with none of these including combat or formation practice, let alone firing the Kittyhawk's six half-inch guns.

One wet and miserable afternoon, Whetters was forced to improvise. 'The American major decided when we would fly,' he recalled. 'One afternoon he sent us up in heavy rain and a low mist. I decided the best way for me to fill in the time was just to circle the aerodrome.' In the poor conditions, Whetters lost track of home base and instead headed for the coast to regain his bearings. Unsure if he was even north or south of Sydney, he saw through a cloud break the smooth green track of a racecourse and decided to put down on it. Seeing a sign for Kembla Grange Racecourse, not far from Wollongong, he took off again and felt confident enough to head back to Bankstown by heading north and making a sharp left turn at Canterbury Road, which took him right to the front gate of the base.

Reporting to his American major that he had been required to make a forced landing – standard practice in the RAAF – the major looked at Whetters in shock. 'On a *racecourse*?' asked the American in a tone that made Whetters fear he was about to be put on report. But the man's surprise was genuine. 'Look, I'm not going to report you or call you a liar,' he said, 'but just tell me this, how the hell did you get around those turns?' The American had assumed, said Whetters, that he had landed on the actual track, instead of the open centre of the course, a detail which, at the time, he did not feel the need to correct. Arthur Tucker recalled the story as well, and reckoned that, in the eyes of the Americans at least, the Australian pilots' stocks rose sharply.

On Friday, 6 March 1942, Tucker celebrated his 22nd birthday with fellow pilot Jim Norton and some girls they had arranged to meet at Prince's Nightclub in Newtown. The two airmen were getting to know one another well, having been the very first two pilots to present themselves for duty – at exactly the same time – at the squadron's nascent beginnings with the US 7th Pursuit Squadron. At some stage in the evening, a misheard snippet of conversation led the fellows to believe the young ladies resided in nearby Ashfield, and at the end of the night they offered to escort them home. In fact, the girls lived in Bondi in Sydney's east – the opposite direction. A promise, however, was a promise – particularly to two educated young officers such as Tucker and Norton – and they dutifully saw the girls to their doors, missing the last tram back to town in the process.

Slogging their way on foot back to Wynyard Station in the small hours of the morning, the two young men contemplated the sleep-in they would be afforded on their day off, once they had waited long enough to catch the first train back to Bankstown. In the pre-dawn light, they crawled into bed, only to be rudely awakened almost immediately, it seemed, by an adjutant telling them to gather their things and prepare to get airborne. They were heading north.

Waiting on the tarmac, ten young pilots were addressed by their new leader, Wing Commander Peter Jeffrey, for the first time. He directed them to proceed to Garbutt airstrip in Townsville, refuelling at Archerfield in Brisbane, in preparation for heading to New Guinea. Years later, Jeffrey would confess to Graham Sivyer, a veteran himself and author of an unofficial biography of 75 Squadron, *The Magpie Fights Back*, that on the day, he could only find one map of the proposed route to Townsville, which he held close to him on the flight.

In the early morning gloom, slightly in shock, the young men peered around at the faces of their fellow pilots. Hardly anyone was familiar to anyone else. 'I knew Connor [sic] and Norton,' recalled Tucker, 'but the others had arrived from places like Williamtown and Canberra, and were complete strangers to me.' Even his CO was an unfamiliar face, despite Jeffrey having been stationed at squadron HQ Bankstown for some time.

'Never one to be lost for words,' as Tucker described himself, he proceeded to 'grumble' to the boss that they had only flown the aeroplane four times, never in formation, had done no instrument flying, lacked oxygen masks and did not even have use of their radios. This last point apparently arose after one over-zealous group captain had carefully collected the Kittyhawks' precious throat microphones and earpieces on their extraction from their packing crates and secreted them in a locker, the location of which could then not be found.

'Don't worry, I won't take you into cloud,' was the breezy assurance Tucker received from his leader when he aired his apprehensions. These remained less than assuaged, particularly as the group was about to take off without oxygen, limiting their ceiling to 16,000 feet at the most.

The men took off into a 'lousy, heavily polluted, fully overcast' Saturday morning sky, then proceeded to circle Bankstown in single file, waiting for one pilot who was struggling to start his engine. Eventually, ten aircraft in three flights pointed their noses to the north, Tucker in the starboard formation led by his friend from the previous night, Jim Norton, and Ron O'Connor, while on the far left, John Piper led another flight, all of them keeping an eye on their leader, Peter Jeffrey.

Not long into the journey, just as they passed the Hawkesbury River, the sky ahead loomed darker and lower. 'Suddenly, we were in cloud,' recalled Tucker, 'and quick as a wink, blind.' Remembering his instructions to simply trust his leader, Tucker kept his eyes glued to the wingtip to his right. But a glance into the 'office' of his cockpit told him immediately that they were all in deep trouble. 'I had been well trained by a good instructor in instrument flying,' he recalled, 'and so when I looked back I saw that our speed was up, and that we were in a tight, obviously descending spiral to the right.' Without radios, Tucker could not alert the rest of his formation, so decided all he could do was break away, ignoring his artificial horizon and flying instead by the more primitive but reliable 'bat and ball' on his instrument panel.

Straightening up out of the spiral, Tucker climbed on a northerly heading through a grey wall of glowering storm clouds. 'The cloud ahead of me started to brighten, but I was so anxious to get out of the clouds I fell for the old trick, pulled my nose up, and put her into a spin.' So down, once again, spiralled Tucker, in the first, and what could easily have been the last, spin he ever experienced in a Kittyhawk. But his cool head prevailed and applying the rules he had learned when in such a position in a Tiger Moth or Wirraway, he calmly extracted the aircraft from its potentially fatal dive, and climbed up through the cloud once again, this time with slightly more patience, emerging into the sun at 12,000 feet. Looking around, he found he was completely alone.

Keeping to a northerly heading, but having no any idea where exactly he should be flying, Tucker eventually spotted a Kittyhawk in the distance and 'thinking some company would be nice', made towards it. After a chase lasting half an hour or so, he caught up with it, only to watch it dive suddenly into an opening in the cloud bank. He followed at a steep angle and saw the sea several thousand feet beneath him. Emerging under the cloud bank and into heavy rain with the coast below, Arthur watched the leading Kittyhawk about a quarter of a mile ahead lower his wheels, put down his flaps and make a sharp left-hand turn. 'He looked like somebody who knew what he was doing,' he recalled, and figured he might as well do the same.

The rain was so heavy, Tucker could barely keep an eye on the tail of the aircraft in front, but suddenly realised he was over the edge of an aerodrome, with aircraft hangars flashing past on his left-hand side. In the midst of a fierce storm, and almost without realising it, Tucker had landed at the home of the RAAF's No. 1 Bombing and Gunnery School at Evans Head in northern New South Wales.

John Piper, the pilot Tucker found himself following, recorded his own recollections, confirming the chaos of the day.

> We got up towards Coffs Harbour and ran into a bit of light cumulus cloud. I started to climb through. Holliday and O'Connor didn't last ten seconds in the cloud and broke

> away. I went through and picked up 'Friar' Tucker on the other side...We broke down through a gap and flew under the cloud at a couple of hundred feet. We finally put in to Evans Head as I knew the strip was good, and with no maps I didn't feel like pushing on to Archerfield late in the evening in lousy weather.

The storm also caught Sergeant 'Bink' Davies.

> We ran into cloud near Kempsey and not being experienced did not keep formation. I knew the terrain so headed upwards to get above, finally seeing a thin patch with sea below, dived down under the soup, meeting a group circling at sea level. We stayed low to Archerfield, landing in rain.

Others in the formation had not been so lucky.

•

At the small timber community of Wauchope on the New South Wales central north coast, the local pub was filling, as it did most Saturday afternoons, with timber workers gathering to mark the end of another long week. At around four-thirty, not far from the town's outskirts, a young farming couple, Albert and Essie Freeman, suddenly heard the unfamiliar sound of an aeroplane engine followed by the sight of a lone single-engine plane skidding through the skies at a perilously low altitude before vanishing beyond the tree line. This was followed a few moments later by another aeroplane, this time heading west and equally as low. As they watched it clear a ridge, the aircraft clipped a tall dead tree standing alone in a paddock, flipped onto its back and skidded, tearing off its wings on a tree stump and bursting into flames. Albert raced to the scene but nothing could be done for the trapped pilot. It was all he could do to duck at the sound of exploding ammunition.

The first aircraft the young farmers had seen also crashed, as noticed by two workers on a small property nearby. As Stanley Meehan and Bob Teague toiled making repairs down a well, they felt the unmistakable concussions of an impact some way off, followed by the same distinctive crackle of ammunition. Mounting horses, they too headed towards a thin trace of smoke arising from bushland in the direction of Kempsey. When they finally found the scene, they were confronted by the sight of twisted metal and shattered trees. Close by, half suspended in trees, was the badly broken body of a pilot who, it seemed, had attempted to bail out of his aircraft.

The margin of luck or experience separating the fates of Jim Norton and Lloyd Holliday from their pal Arthur Tucker was no doubt a narrow one. Norton and Holliday were both raw graduates, having only completed their courses on Wirraways the previous January. Tucker had at least had some extra flying experience at an advanced training unit, but also credits his instructor, Jock Perrin, for versing him well in the technique of 'blind flying': when in difficult situations it was prudent to rely on the 'bat and ball' indicator rather than the more temperamental artificial horizon in his cockpit panel. It was a lesson that may well have saved his life that day, and not for the last time. Whatever the reason, breaking away from the formation when becoming aware of the spin which they were all in undoubtedly saved Tucker's life.

Holliday and Norton became 75 Squadron's first casualties. Aged 26, James William Norton had been a butcher by trade as well as a part-time lifesaver at Sydney's Bronte Beach. He had made an impact on local rugby, playing some 21 games for his Eastern Suburbs club. He left behind a wife and two children, and is buried in his hometown of Queanbeyan.

Lloyd Holliday was 23. He had attended Sydney Grammar School, and left a young widow, Lorraine. He is buried with his parents, Henry and Constance, in the Macquarie Park Cemetery on Sydney's upper north shore.

Ron O'Connor also came to grief in the perilous weather that afternoon, crash landing with his tanks on empty near Kyogle, but managed to walk away almost unharmed. His Kittyhawk, however, was written off. He too was enormously lacking in experience, having only flown a Kittyhawk for the first time three weeks before.

•

In just a couple of hours, 75 Squadron had lost two irreplaceable pilots and three aircraft without having fired a shot in the direction of the enemy. After regrouping and refuelling at Archerfield and Rockhampton from 44-gallon drums, the seven remaining aircraft proceeded to Garbutt airfield just outside Townsville, where they were joined by another flight of five Kittyhawks led up from Amberley by Flight Lieutenant Peter Turnbull to begin training.

There was an enquiry of sorts into the incident, for which all pilots were approached for comment. Arthur Tucker, characteristically, did not hold back, revealing, among other things, that despite being assured that his woefully inexperienced group of pilots would not be led into cloud, that is exactly what happened, with tragic results. His truthfulness, it seems, did his RAAF career no good whatsoever.

'It was seen that I had "tipped the bucket" on a highly regarded senior officer,' he recalled. His relationship with Peter Jeffrey – as well as some others of rank – did not improve, and Tucker believed he acquired a somewhat 'lippy' reputation. 'After that,' he said, 'I only had to blow my nose and I was in strife. It was very uncomfortable.'

CHAPTER 3

Learning on the job

Like most of Australia's military establishment, Townsville in March 1942 was ill-equipped for war or, from the way it looked to those who were there, anything else. By the time the men of 75 Squadron began to arrive, the schools were closed, the beaches were covered with barbed wire and civilians were streaming south to escape a predicted Japanese invasion. At Garbutt aerodrome, Bill Deane-Butcher, newly arrived from his previous station at Archerfield, expected something similar to a well-appointed aerodrome with 75 SQUADRON emblazoned over the guard gate. Instead he was presented with a motley collection of tents. 'Ten or fifteen recently erected tents stood in a paddock…boxes were being unpacked. A single table and chair in the open provided an office…there were a couple of water taps at the end of a long surface pipeline. Pots simmered on an open wood stove.'

Michael Butler, who had grown up on a large sheep and cattle station near Kapunda in South Australia, had joined the air force the day after war was declared, simply because he was 'keen on aeroplanes'. Beyond that, however, he hadn't given it much thought. Initially flying Wirraways with 12 Squadron in Darwin, his training, particularly in bombing, had been rudimentary.

> The bombs we were using in training were from the First World War and were that old they were all sort of oozing some sort of stuff which makes them highly dangerous. Why they couldn't have used some decent ones I don't know.

Upon arriving in Townsville to join 75 Squadron, he began looking for the adjutant, or somebody, anybody, of any authority.

> Honestly, you didn't know who was what because nobody wore any badges of rank…just hats and shirts and shorts but no badges of rank or decorations – nothing. It was quite hard for us to find who was in charge of the situation. I thought to myself, 'this is going to be a fairly informal crowd'.

Arthur Tucker was similarly underwhelmed, finding Garbutt practically deserted save for a Hudson bomber being held together with angle irons wired along its leading edge due to a cracked main spar, and an old and forlorn single-engine Junkers from the New Guinea goldfields as well as a couple of American B-17s in the hangar, which had come up from their base at Charters Towers for maintenance. 'Apart from that,' he said, 'the skies north of Brisbane appeared to be empty.'

Over the next week, the pilots and staff that would form 75 Squadron started to arrive from everywhere. Ground crew from as far away as Canberra and Darwin received their new postings and were on the move, and besides Peter Jeffrey's disastrous flight from Bankstown, a further batch of five Kittyhawks – still in their original American markings – were brought in from Amberley in Queensland, led by one of 75's most distinguished pilots, Flight Lieutenant Peter St George Bruce Turnbull. Already an ace with 3 Squadron, having nine kills and a DFC to his name, Turnbull would be mixing it with rookies. John Pettett, one of 75's most prominent pilots of the 44 days, described Turnbull as a quintessential Australian warrior:

> Pete Turnbull had been a jackeroo and had kicked around outback Australia most of his life, I think, and was a wonderful fellow. He had a great sense of humour and was completely coordinated; a very good-looking fellow too – very athletic kind of body and movements and everything and I think it all just came naturally to him.

In this new outfit, veterans of the Middle East such as Turnbull would be required to fly alongside green pilots barely out of their Elementary Flying Training School. It would not prove easy. 'I've seen reports of nine or even seventeen days of intensive training,' said Arthur Tucker, 'but there was actually none at all. I can only remember flying three times. There was no combat training, just flying around in V-formation.'

John Pettett, who had left school at fifteen to work at radio station 2UE in Sydney, and who had joined up the day after war was declared, recalled it similarly. 'In Townsville I had six days training. In fact, it wasn't really training at all, just getting used to the aeroplane and getting used to the other people and flying around as a squadron.' On 15 March, he flew for an hour of 'free flying and aerobatics', followed on 18 March by an hour and a quarter of 'squadron formation'.

There was some time devoted to 'shadow gunnery', where an aircraft would fly along one of Townsville's long deserted beaches at 200 or so feet, casting a shadow for a following aircraft to fire at in strafing manoeuvres, but ammunition was in such short supply the exercise was all but useless.

'I would think our conversion course onto Kittyhawks from Wirraways would be the shortest possible,' recalls Michael Butler.

> I don't think you could have made it any shorter. I think it averaged eight hours...we did a little bit of formation flying. No gunnery at all and certainly no tactics. When we were going up to Moresby, the leader of the flight, he said, 'when you take off from Horn Island I suggest you try your guns

> because you might need them when we get to Moresby'. I gave it a short burst and it was just like the heavens being let loose.

Slowly, Jeffrey began organising the squadron. In a practical decision, he insisted he be allotted a number of his former 3 Squadron aircraft tradesmen and ground staff, as each would be familiar with his standards, and his orders would need no follow-up. As more pilots arrived, two flights – B and C – were established with Flight Lieutenants John Jackson and Peter Turnbull as their respective commanders. A headquarters flight was also established under Pilot Officer Don Swann, as well as a servicing flight under the squadron's colourful engineering officer, Flying Officer Bill Matson, who had come up through the ranks as an airframe fitter.

At this point the true state of the Kittyhawks they would be taking into action in New Guinea was revealed. Having been transported across the Pacific in crates on the open decks of ships, many of the Kittyhawks' half-inch guns were rusted and had to be re-honed by the armourers, who complained that there was not nearly enough ammunition to do so properly. The Americans, pointed out one of Jeffrey's armourers, were allotted 200 rounds per gun to 'shoot them in', while the Australians were expected 'to merely hone the locks and trust to luck'. The armourers got their 200 rounds, but this meant there was virtually nothing left for the pilots to practise with. 'I know that I had never fired all the guns,' said John Pettett. 'I fired four guns at one time – only once on shadow firing – but the first time I used the whole six guns was against a Zero.' Pettett later estimated that before going into combat, he had flown the Kittyhawk for a total of twelve hours and 50 minutes, including the ferry flight from Townsville to Port Moresby.

Time was critical, however, and at a meeting with Wing Commander William 'Bull' Garing, the head of the RAAF's North East Area Command, Jeffrey was pressed on how soon his brand-new squadron would be ready for New Guinea. Jeffrey pointed out that the radios of his Kittyhawks still did not work, and some seemed to have not been fitted at all. Also the English-made microphones and oxygen masks they had been issued with on their arrival at Townsville did not fit their American aircraft. It would be, he said as calmly as his patience would allow, a couple of days yet.

John Pettett recalled the initial Kittyhawks as not even having functioning illuminated optical gunsights, the pilots having instead to rely on the 'ring and bead'. 'So you had like a ring out the front with a bead somewhere between it and your eye and you had to line up the bead with the centre of the ring – not very satisfactory.' The gunsight not being centrally aligned, the pilot was required to lean his head to the side of the cockpit to line up this elementary gunsight, actually placing himself outside the protective zone of the armour plate behind him. 'We got optical gunsights very shortly afterwards though and they were much more effective because the position of your head didn't make that much difference,' says Pettett. In New Guinea however, the bulbs that illuminated these sights would constantly blow, providing just one of the many operational headaches that would plague 75's pilots and crew throughout the 44 days. In one bright piece of news however, the original masks and throat microphones had been located at Amberley, and Peter Jeffrey sent an officer south to collect them.

Michael Butler recalls that not simply the radios but the aerials were not up to scratch. 'The receiving aerial,' he says,

> went from the wingtip to the tailplane and as soon as you got to a speed over around 250 miles an hour, bang, it would break and when you'd come down they'd fix it and put a new one on or something and away you'd go again. Next time, as soon as you get over that speed, bang. It seemed a simple thing to fix, and how helpful it would have been to have had radio to call up somebody if you were in trouble.

Arthur Tucker also earned himself an unexpected trip away from the squadron, ostensibly as one of three pilots sent on a ferry job to collect new aircraft, but he believed it was a form of punishment arising out of yet another run-in with squadron leadership over the matter of landings. In training, Tucker – and most of 75's newer pilots – had been taught to land their Wirraways on 'three points', when all of the wheels touched down at once, a technique they brought to Townsville when coming to grips with the Kittyhawk. The pilots found their new aircraft particularly favourable to a 'slipping approach' where the wingtip is pushed down and the nose held up with the top rudder, then kicked straight just before touch down. This way, he said, the P-40 'sat down on the runway like a well-trained puppy' with the extra drag of the tail wheel bringing the aircraft to a quicker stop.

It was a method that appalled the more cautious Americans, most of whom had no more experience of the Kittyhawk than did the Australians. 'The Yanks,' said Arthur, 'told us the way to land them was to get well back, straighten up and then come in. Then you set up and put the flaps down. If you turn with the flaps down, you'll spill the air out of them and you'll go in.' As a result, the Australian pilots watched on, bemused, as the Americans made what Tucker described as great long 'jumbo jet landings. When you think how afterwards we used to stand them on their tips and slide them in it appears ridiculous.'

The Squadron's rump of experienced Middle East pilots had their own ideas about how a Kittyhawk should be landed, and it was that group of men that would hold a great deal of power within 75. It was now decreed that the Kittyhawks be landed after the American-favoured faster approach on its main wheels, tail high until it dropped of its own accord. Tucker recalled that 'they had a terrible feeling that the aircraft would ground loop, so they would wheel them in [on the main undercarriage]. This took an awful lot of runway and caused a lot of accidents because the landing was too fast.'

The younger pilots were assured this made the aircraft more controllable on the ground but many of them saw it as bloody-mindedness on the part of the Middle East veterans and complained at having to relearn what had already been pressed into them. The rift caused bitterness along the squadron's already forming fault lines that took a long time to heal. Said Tucker:

> It was a disease of rushed squadrons generally throughout the war but it was particularly marked in 75 Squadron. You'd get people who came to be in authority who happened to go to school together, then other groups who had shared experiences who would be sent somewhere as a group. Only you didn't just import the friendships and loyalties, but the distrusts and dislikes as well.

Typically, the men from the various elements that made up 75 tended to stick together – from 23 or 24 Squadron, or the various Station Headquarters at Williamtown, Laverton or Canberra, and each, said Tucker, 'would be restive with the other groups. There was no chance of ever building up an esprit de corps, ever.'

But the small group of 3 Squadron Middle East veterans – John Jackson, Peter Jeffrey, Peter Turnbull and Dave Ellerton – as virtually the only men of 75 who could claim operational experience, were the most pronounced clique. Flight Lieutenant Bruce Anderson had tangled with a

Japanese 'Emily' flying boat with 24 Squadron in Rabaul, and Jeffrey 'Pop' Woods had some experience as a second pilot on Hudsons with 32 Squadron at Port Moresby, but theirs was the sum total of the squadron's combat experience in the Pacific. Hence the weight of responsibility fell heaviest on the Middle East men – looked up to as they were by the newer pilots. But as Tucker points out, the war they had seen thus far was vastly different from what they were about to experience in the tropics.

> There was a tremendous defeatism everywhere. No-one was confident the Japanese could be defeated at this stage of the war, and these men from the Middle East didn't have too much faith in what they'd be able to do either. You have to remember that the Japanese were undefeated, they'd swept all before them, and we were to be facing their very top men. The 3 Squadron blokes hadn't come up against anything like that.

The Western Desert had been a very different war: 'Africa was a mobile thing, rolling backwards and forwards over the desert like a gentlemanly game of tennis.' Moresby, by comparison, would be a pitched-in battle, 'a hard going thing', more akin to the Battle of Britain. 'Only in that case,' Tucker said, 'the enemy could choose from all the many English airfields. At Moresby, the Japanese only had one target, and we were sitting on it.'

And they were tired. Jeffrey made no secret of the fact to Graham Sivyer that, in his opinion, his Middle East veterans were 'time expired' or at the very least, had not sufficiently convalesced after the stress fatigue, injury or illness of their intense North African tour.

The staggered manner in which the new pilots arrived also added to Jeffrey's woes in moulding the men into a cohesive unit. The last of the initial batch of pilots, John 'Cocky' Brereton, arrived straight from training on 18 March, just two days before the squadron's departure for New Guinea.

At some stage during this week at Townsville, it was confirmed that John Jackson would lead the squadron. Whether Peter Jeffrey wanted to remain in command beyond 75's initial deployment to Port Moresby is unclear. He had, after all, just a few months previously completed a long tour of operations in the Middle East, and believed his 3 Squadron men were similarly wearing the fatigue of combat. But there was no doubting Jackson's energy and determination. After 'some very emotional verbal exchanges', which went against his better judgement, Jeffrey recommended Jackson be the man to take 75 into combat. Knowing his level of fearlessness, his eagerness for a fight, and perhaps considering his age, Jeffrey nevertheless believed Jackson was almost certainly going to his death.

This cursory period of training went on, when it could, still taking its toll. On 13 March, Sergeant Bink Davies made a tail-up landing according to the new doctrine of 'driving' the aircraft down on its two main wheels, but lost control of the aircraft on the runway. One wing stalled, dropped to the ground, and dragged his Kittyhawk violently to port. Davies vainly tried to correct by applying power, but his undercarriage collapsed, tearing through the underside of the wings. As the plane skidded finally to a halt, the watching ground crew knew immediately it was a write-off. Davies was lucky to be uninjured, but his recollections of the incident illustrated the young pilot's lack of experience.

> I was excused when Jeffrey found I had been trained on Ansons at Service Flying Training School, been sent to Fighter Operational Training Unit at Nhill where I got only about eight hours on Wirraways, then to Williamtown to the 9th Pursuit Squadron USAAC to convert to Kittyhawks, getting only three flights totalling less than three hours.

Five days later, another of the precious Kittyhawks was badly damaged, again in a landing mishap, when piloted by Sergeant Brown. Little wonder that, in a sober assessment of his pilots' skills on the eve of their departure to Port Moresby, Turnbull wrote to North East Area Command:

> On the whole, the standard of flying in 75 Squadron was high, but signs of under-confidence showed up in the pilots with less than 100 hours on the Wirraway type of aircraft.

> This would not have occurred had the pilots been allowed time for training...they were not up to operational standard.

He assessed that ten of his pilots had less than ten hours' flying time on the Kittyhawk before being expected to face combat.

Nevertheless, on 17 March, 33 ground crew and staff boarded a commandeered Qantas Empire flying boat that had seen better days and flew from Townsville to Port Moresby. The plane was said to be so overloaded that it 'wave-hopped most of the way'. This vanguard was met by the squadron's equipment officer, Squadron Leader Ted Church, who charged them with the tasks of establishing a field kitchen and erecting tents at Seven Mile Strip.

Two days later, John Jackson was appointed acting Squadron Leader and the Kittyhawks, with their drastically unprepared pilots, took off from Townsville to meet the battle-experienced and victorious Japanese air force.

CHAPTER 4

To the Seven Mile

Ready or not, John Jackson farewelled the first two Kittyhawks, flown by Barry Cox and Peter Jeffrey, as they took off from Townsville on 19 March on the first stage of the long haul up to Port Moresby via Cooktown, then Horn Island just off the tip of Cape York. Jeffrey made a quick trip on his own up to Port Moresby to inspect the strip at Seven Mile and, satisfied, flew back to Cooktown in North Queensland to guide his men. The next day, Jackson himself led another fourteen aircraft north to join them. A fuel problem forced Flying Officer Ken Lloyd to return briefly to Cooktown, resulting in a staggered series of starts and delays which eventuated in a group of four aircraft flown by Jeffrey, Channon, Wackett and Cox to arrive at Port Moresby some hours ahead of the rest. It was an arrival that nearly resulted in disaster.

The weary defenders of Port Moresby and its rugged airstrip had long heard talk of the imminent arrival of defenders from the south who would alleviate their virtually daily trial of being attacked by the dominant Japanese air power. For months they had expected the arrival of the much-vaunted Kittyhawks – and now they were on their way. The plan for their arrival was for the incoming Kittyhawks to circle an offshore shipwreck as a sign of recognition, before proceeding along a prescribed route inland to their new base at Seven Mile Strip.

At two o'clock on the afternoon of 21 March, the men of the 67th Anti-Aircraft Searchlight Battery were stationed at Seven Mile's temporary headquarters when an unfamiliar engine note was heard, and 'four fighter planes came low over our heads'. They recognised at once the RAAF roundel with its British-style red centre spot, not yet removed to avoid confusion with the Japanese 'rising sun', and cheered at the realisation that the 'Neverhawks' had finally appeared. Almost immediately, however, cheers turned to groans as the sound of machine guns, positioned around the airstrip, opened up.

Wartime communications, often unreliable, had failed completely on this day. Unaware of the Kittyhawks' arrival, the twitchy and rumour-weary machine gunners of the 39th Battalion watched as fighters approached from the southeast and circled the aerodrome low, well concealed against the surrounding hills in their freshly applied green camouflage, the same way many of the attacks of the ground-strafing Japanese Zeros had begun over the previous weeks. Another rumour that circulated soon after was that one of the gunners, seeing the letter code Z on the sides of one of the Kittyhawks, assumed it stood for 'Zero' and opened up. Whether or not this was the case, Alan Moore of the 39th Battalion – the young Lieutenant in charge of the Lewis gunners that day – recalled later in life that he, along with the rest of his group, did in fact interpret the red dot of the roundel as the Japanese 'rising sun'. It was promptly thereafter removed.

One machine gun fired and, despite the Kittyhawks approaching with flaps down and wheels extended – an obvious intention to land – others soon followed. At close range, the bullets tore into the brand-new machines as they completed their landing, the word only going up to cease firing when it became obvious to the gunners that these were the vanguard of their long-anticipated saviours. The four pilots were stunned by the reception and lucky to escape uninjured. One bullet actually passed through the horsehair-filled headrest of Peter Jeffrey's leading aircraft, barely more than an inch from the back of his skull. Leaping out of his aircraft, he was seen 'running around with his .38 service revolver, looking for someone to shoot'. All four Kittyhawks were damaged, and one of them would never fly again.

It was hardly the reception that anyone had anticipated, but there was little time to dwell, as the Japanese were due to make one of their regular visits. With tedious regularity, the Japanese had made a habit of sending over a daily reconnaissance flight in the form of a twin-engine Mitsubishi Ki-21 Sally bomber that would lumber its way across the Port Moresby skies, confident of meeting no serious challenge. It was a routine that had come to be regarded by the Port Moresby garrison as 'a necessary event, just like the heat and the mosquitoes'. The Sally would make a photo run over the harbour and Seven Mile Strip, then look around casually to decide where to drop the bomb it carried in its belly. Thus had it been for weeks. This day however, the script would run a little differently: less than two hours after their arrival, just before four pm, 75 Squadron was ordered to its first operational scramble.

Two of the four damaged Kittyhawks were quickly patched up, and Flying Officer Wilbur Wackett and his wingman, Barry Cox, took off on 75's first combat sortie. The short but fiery spectacle that followed, played out over the natural arena of Moresby Harbour, electrified the weary garrison, whose defenders had come to believe they would never see the day.

Confident the skies were still undefended, the Japanese pilot commenced his photo run at the low altitude of 10,000 feet, unaware that he had been spotted below by Cox and Wackett, who were now desperately climbing through the 4000 foot gap that separated them. Giving their Kittyhawks everything to make up the distance before the Japanese bomber turned and headed for home, the two attackers caught it, levelled out and commenced a classic 'stern and quarter' attack. One can only imagine the ghastly surprise of the Japanese crew, realising they were suddenly under fighter attack in these hitherto undefended skies.

The Sally skidded evasively as Cox and Wackett each gave the aircraft ten separate bursts from their combined twelve half-inch guns, a single bullet from which could easily punch a fist-sized hole through the Japanese aircraft's thin aluminium skin. The bomb doors were hurled open, and the load jettisoned. The doors themselves, noted the pilots, remained open. In vain, the Sally sought the cover of clouds. Cox fired into the port engine while Wackett concentrated on the starboard. Soon after lining up his aircraft behind the motors and pressing the firing button on his control stick, Cox noticed parts fly off the Japanese bomber, and smoke and oil reach back to him in a long dirty trail as the aircraft began to fly more erratically. The Sally rapidly lost height. Neither Cox nor Wackett had any idea of the spectacle they were creating for the hundreds of delighted men observing below.

Gunner Raymond Neil, as quoted in Mark Johnston's excellent and comprehensive study of Australia's entire Pacific air war, *Whispering Death*, remembered watching the skies above his head on this:

> typical tropical afternoon with about 60 to 70 per cent cloud cover. We observers were watching for the appearance of the Jap bomber between cloud breaks and trying to track his location by the sound of his engines. Imagine our delight to hear our fighters come on to the scene. Troops came out from cover on every hill and ridge and were screaming directions

> to our fighter pilots whenever the enemy aircraft appeared in a clear patch of sky. Unheard, of course, but a reflection of the long months of not being able to deal with an enemy aircraft outside the range of [the anti-aircraft guns]...

Above, Wackett and Cox were closing in on the Japanese bomber, now entering a death dive, and a fire was observed spreading through its fuselage. With another shot, Wackett delivered the coup de grace. At about 500 feet above the water, a couple of miles west of Moresby's Basilisk Beacon, just beyond the reef outside the main harbour, the Japanese aircraft was seen to explode before diving into the sea. Famed war correspondent (warco) Osmar White, on an adjacent hill, wrote that 'we onlookers fell on one another's necks, howling hysterically with joy', while Church remembered that 'on every hill and ridge around the shores of Moresby assembled spectator troops cheered this first victory over one of those who had been harassing us for months'.

Another famous warco who was there also – no less a figure than writer George Johnston – recalled that:

> two Kittys took off, intercepted [a Japanese bomber] over the mountains, drove her back, and after a brilliant attack shot her down in flames into the harbour. Too easy! Just before dusk a Lockheed escorted 13 more fighters in while truckload after truckload of troops cheered from the side of the road. First real evidence of aggression in this war. Whacco!

That victory above Port Moresby was a moment of extraordinary significance. Finally, it was seen that the Japanese, hitherto a juggernaut, riding their victories across Asia like an incoming tide, were not invincible. The men on the ground, impotent for so long under the Japanese command of the skies, saw with their own eyes that victory, if even on the small scale of the destruction of a single enemy bomber, was at least possible. If these young men, just arrived on the scene from the south in their Kittyhawks, could shoot down one Japanese aircraft, they could shoot down another, then another, and still more after that. Perhaps, after all, they were not destined to be starved, blasted or bayoneted out – or worse, taken prisoner – from their miserable holes surrounding Port Moresby. Things just might start going their way for a change.

The significance of the day was perhaps lost on Wackett and Cox, who may not have realised that they had just taken part in one of the most important moments in the RAAF's, indeed their country's, history: the launching of the first wholly independent defensive campaign in wartime, in the face of a direct threat to their homeland.

An hour after Cox and Wackett had achieved their very public victory, John Jackson's delayed formation was spotted, thirteen Kittyhawks in all, under escort from a Lockheed Hudson bomber. Their trip up from Horn Island had passed almost without incident, save for a lucky escape for Sergeant Ron Bailey, whose engine gave trouble in transit, forcing him to within 60 feet of the water, before it picked up again and saw him on to Port Moresby.

John Pettett was among them and remembered the day well. Flying number two to Les Jackson, they were just about to make their approach to Seven Mile when Les made a sudden tight turning dive down towards the harbour with, said Pettett, 'me belting along behind'. Les pulled out of the dive and began to circle something in the water. 'I was eventually able to gather sufficient wits to recognise the object as an aircraft I could not identify. It turned out to be the Japanese bomber shot down only an hour earlier by Barry Cox and Wilbur Wackett.'

This time there were no trigger-happy machine gunners lining up the approaching Kittyhawks. By now, word had gone around that finally, after months of rumours and hopes, speculations and disappointments, the planes to defend Moresby and take the fight to the Japanese had arrived. Osmar White recorded that:

> For miles around, men found they had business at the airfield. They came roaring up the road on lorries, cheering and laughing. They stopped, poured out of the vehicles, and stood staring with a mixture of awe and disbelief at the fighters on the ground...now there would be some kind of a fight, instead of a hopeless bloody walkover.

As Pettett put it in a television interview years later:

> These people were dead. They had no hope, no protection and felt the Japanese could just sail around anytime and take Port Moresby, which they of course tried to do eventually in the Coral Sea battle. But the arrival of the Kittyhawks just lifted the place. Wherever you went they'd just yell and scream and salute and wave at you.

•

For the moment, it was considered critical that the arrival of the Kittyhawks be concealed from the Japanese for as long as possible. After landing, John Jackson was briefed on the day's dramatic events and learned the critical piece of information that the Sally reconnaissance bomber had attempted to alert its base at Rabaul to the presence of these new fighters, but its radio transmissions had been jammed by the quick-thinking signals officer at the Port Moresby Wireless Station, Flight Lieutenant Max Haughton, who ordered a LAC (leading aircraftman) to hold down his Morse key. The tactic had appeared to work, as the Japanese base had been heard attempting to make contact with the lost bomber for some considerable time after its demise.

Late on 21 March, John Jackson was confirming Peter Jeffrey's opinion of him as never being one to shy from a fight, by devising a daring plan for the very next morning.

Church recorded that in his opinion, 'Morale rose a thousand per cent' in the aftermath of the victory over the harbour, and Jackson was determined it should stay that way.

A few hours before Wackett and Cox had been chasing the intruder, Hudsons of 32 Squadron – the only bomber unit to be stationed in Port Moresby and 75 Squadron's neighbours – were indulging in their own bout of spying over the Japanese base at Lae. Zeros had attacked the unescorted formation, and two crewmen had been wounded, but they returned with some excellent images of just what the Japanese were up to over the mountainous hump of the Owen Stanley Ranges barely an hour's flying time away.

Late in the afternoon of that first eventful day, the aerodrome control officer, Squadron Leader McIvor, arrived with the still-wet proof sheets of 32 Squadron's efforts and presented them to John Jackson. Wide eyed, the men pored over the images, not quite able to believe what they saw. There were the Japanese aircraft, neatly lined up wingtip to wingtip in rows along the Lae runway, fighters down one side, bombers down the other, and with still no idea of the arrival of 75 Squadron and its six-gunned Kittyhawks. Not one to let fortune slip through his fingers, Jackson thought dawn the next morning would be the perfect time to formally announce their arrival. He would divide his ten Kittyhawks into two flights, one under Peter Turnbull to provide top cover, the other led by himself to strafe the Japanese aerodrome.

75 spent a restless night with the men settling into their new, somewhat primitive, surroundings. Late on the evening of 21 March, Medical Officer Bill Deane-Butcher arrived at Moresby Harbour via Catalina flying boat along with a young

Tasmanian pilot, Geoff Atherton. Arriving at Seven Mile after dark, the men stumbled over rocks and pushed through head-high stretches of the ubiquitous kunai grass to arrive at the entrance of a large tent, sparsely furnished with a few wooden benches and bare tables. 'Flickering lamps provided our first glimpse of home,' remembered the doctor, along with 'a cup of tea and an enormous smile from a sweating bare-chested cook'.

That night, the men learned the failures of their mosquito nets – 'stifling, and inadequate at keeping out mosquitoes', according to one – and experienced for the first time the tropical night closing in around them like an oppressive dark blanket. 'The bush dark is really dark,' observed Deane-Butcher. John Pettett recalled little more of that first night besides attempting to dig a shallow trench around his tent to keep out the torrential midnight downpour.

At six o'clock the following morning, 22 March, the pilots were called to a pre-dawn briefing by John Jackson. He explained that he would lead the ground strafing along with Woods, Piper, Anderson and Cox, while Turnbull, Pettett, Brereton, Les Jackson and Wackett would stay above to tackle the inevitable counter-punch from the Zeros. They would use the element of surprise, and get in and out fast, with one pass in the early morning light, before the inevitable tropical build-up of the clouds made visibility untenable.

Half an hour later on this Sunday morning, wrote Bill Deane-Butcher, 'the dawn was shattered by the sound of engines' as 75's ten Kittyhawks lined up to take off for their audacious debut. Immediately, the inexperience of the pilots showed. One, who forever remained nameless, taxied the wrong way and, to Deane-Butcher's horror, prepared to take off from the west, straight into the path of the others, before his mistake was realised and he swung to the right.

The doctor's attention was soon drawn by the sight of another aircraft, which he recalled as 'a mound of blue metal crashing through the low scrub'. Whether through inexperience, nerves or the murk of the early tropical light, 'Cocky' Brereton opened his throttle to take off, then halfway down the runway swerved to avoid a parked Hudson bomber he had failed to notice past the long powerful nose of the Kittyhawk. John Piper saw the incident unfold in his rear-view mirror: Brereton's aircraft suddenly swinging out of the take-off line, skidding, then his wingtip ploughing into a mound of construction gravel on the side of the runway. With a terrible metallic screech, Brereton felt the Kittyhawk's undercarriage being ripped away as the aircraft swung in a whiplashing 180-degree ground loop, smashing his head against the reflector gunsight in front of him and knocking him out before the Kittyhawk came to rest just off the runway.

Rescue teams rushed to Brereton's badly broken aeroplane. Deane-Butcher and equipment officer Ted Church, travelling in a utility, were almost the first on the scene. Deane-Butcher was fond of 'Cocky' Brereton, describing him as 'small, wiry, intelligent and provocative... he had an unfailing capacity for getting into and out of trouble and for laughing in bad taste, hence his nickname'. With another doctor from 32 Squadron, Flight Lieutenant Adrian McGlynn, the three struggled to free Brereton's safety harness. On the unconscious young pilot's forehead, they could see 'a very nasty gash'. Now the crackle of flames could be heard as the aircraft's broken fuel system began to catch. Still Brereton's release remained jammed, until a mighty yank by Ted Church forced it to give way. Pulling the dead weight of Brereton from the aircraft as it caught fire, they certainly saved the man's life, and he escaped the incident with only minor injuries. Brereton survived the war, going on to study at Oxford and he eventually became a professor of ecology at the University of Armidale. Church's bravery was poorly rewarded; in the effort to free Brereton's harness, the strap of an expensive wristwatch, presented to him by the staff of his former employer, Buckingham's Department Store in Oxford Street, Sydney, broke and the watch fell into the cockpit to be consumed by the inferno.

The incident was the beginning of a close bond between two of the squadron's most important non-combatants, Church and Deane-Butcher. In his insightful memoir, *Fighter Squadron Doctor*, Deane-Butcher described Church as:

> a fascinating person. He was a tall, middle-aged Englishman, with ribbons from the First World War, a wide experience of life and great authority. He came to the Pacific Islands to collect butterflies for the Kensington Museum. He could

> command the natives in Pidgin English, fix a truck, tie knots and conjure up paw-paws. When I needed help, I'd ask Ted Church.

The remaining nine aircraft of 75 gained height over Moresby Harbour and headed over the mountains towards the Japanese aerodrome at Lae. John Piper recalled the scene vividly:

> Moresby looked glorious in the early morning – hills all softly green, and the harbour beautifully still, and the huge mountain range rising behind us with the humped-up cumulus cloud just squatting on the tops. Nine of us started out, and we bored up and up, to go over the mountains at about 14,000 feet. We went over, threading our way through these glorious silver mountains, and the sun started to rise. The whole took a glorious silver hue with the vivid green base. Terrifying beauty, really, as we were all on our way to make our first kill if possible. The sight was almost too much for me, and I almost forgot that I had about 25,000 pounds worth of machinery around me just for the purpose of killing people.

It had been many months since John Jackson had led a combat mission, and that had been above a vast desert on the other side of the world. But now, over the expanse of the Owen Stanley Ranges, his experience showed. Instead of heading straight for Lae, Jackson kept his raw squadron tightly together and swung them east out over the waters of the Huon Gulf. Anticipating both fighter defence and anti-aircraft fire, he would approach the target from the unexpected direction of the sea with the morning sun at his back. He hoped the glare would put off the Japanese ack-ack gunners for at least the first few crucial seconds of the attack.

At 12,000 feet, the formation split, Jackson's low flight peeling off towards the sea, skimming in over the water under broken cloud at just 1000 feet. Glancing below, Jackson saw with relief that the situation had not changed from the recce photos taken by the Hudsons 24 hours earlier. Down the centre of the runway was arranged the same neat line of around twenty Zero fighters, with a mixture of fighters and bombers similarly placed down either side of the airstrip. The four other Kittyhawks in Jackson's flight followed their leader down onto their conveniently presented targets. Jackson and Piper headed for the fighters, leaving the bombers to Cox, Anderson and Woods.

Jackson tore along the line of the Japanese fighters, arranged thus to make fuelling and maintenance simpler, but presenting like target practice to attacking aircraft. Smoke and flame erupted as bullets tore through fuselages and wing tanks, and the vague shapes of people could be seen scattering. It was all over in seconds. Some flak had come up at them, but to Jackson's surprise, neither he nor his aircraft had been struck so, ever the opportunist, he decided to break the cardinal rule of ground strafing: never go in for a second attack. Swinging sharply to the left above the far end of the

Japanese runway, he came around again, his escape route dead ahead, straight back out over the sea.

As expected, the Japanese had put up a dawn standing patrol of Zeros, which now swooped onto Jackson's formation. On the first run, Bruce Anderson's Kittyhawk had managed to avoid the light flak that came up from the seaward end of the runway but on the second he was caught as he turned into the attacking Zeros, the scene witnessed by Peter Turnbull who noticed 'one of our aircraft to be out of control and turn over on its side and dive downward with smoke streaming from it, toward a hill near Lae...the aircraft appeared to be definitely out of control and was lagging behind the other four aircraft that had done the ground strafing'. Anderson's aircraft was trailing white smoke – which may have been petrol or glycol – which meant his campaign was over almost before it had begun. As 75's first battle casualty, he was, ironically, the only pilot who had previously faced the Japanese, having flown a Wirraway during the doomed defence of Rabaul on the island of New Britain just eight weeks before. Sadly, this morning his experience counted for nothing. Anderson crashed to the jungle floor about six miles southwest of Lae.

Behind him, the remainder of Jackson's formation tore back along the burning line of Japanese aircraft, firing again, their vision obscured by smoke. Jackson again went for the fighters while Barry Cox led another attack on the dispersed bombers. John Piper flew so low that his wing clipped the propeller tip of a parked Japanese bomber. 'On that second run I got too low. When you're strafing you're supposed to come in and keep down as you're shooting, and you tend to get lower and lower and more and more horizontal and finally I hit a prop and it tore the gun out and severed my wing spar. It made a good bit of a clang.'

The collision also tore one of Piper's heavy Browning machine guns from its mount, but the Kittyhawk stayed in the air. 'Well, that was where a P-40 was excellent because it just didn't show any trouble at all, it just kept on going,' he said.

By this time, the attackers were being 'chased out' by the cannon-firing Zeros, and Piper recalled 'a very unpleasant ten minutes. My one vivid impression of the war is when you have a cannon attack from opposing aircraft, it's like cricket balls dipped in petrol, coming up slowly from behind and suddenly zipping past you.' Managing to shake off his pursuers, he flew the aircraft home as delicately as he could. Even after landing back at Seven Mile Strip, his dramatic day continued when, braking a little too hard while taxiing, he tipped his Kittyhawk onto its nose.

Meanwhile, Turnbull's top cover now came into action. Leading the second escorting formation, Wilbur Wackett noticed Turnbull waggle his wings and let fall his drop tank, then swoop down from 12,000 feet onto the Japanese, who were attacking Jackson's ground-strafing formation. John Pettett reflected on his single hour's shooting practice on the Kittyhawk, and that 'the only thing I had ever attacked in the air was a drogue that is not going to take any evasive action'. Flying

(AWM 034112)

A desolate place to fight. Seven Mile Airstrip, Port Moresby, in 1942, looking south-east.

(AWM OG2765)

Less agile than the Zero, but tougher. A line-up of RAAF Curtiss P-40 Kittyhawks being readied for action.

(AWM P1242.001)

The leader returns. Shot down by Japanese Zeros, Squadron Leader John Jackson arrives back at Moresby, showing little sign of his arduous fortnight trek through the jungle.

(AWM 15049)

A rough and ready lot. Pilots of 75 Squadron during a break in operations against the Japanese. *Left to right*: Flight Lieutenant Lex Winten, Squadron Leader Les Jackson, Flight Lieutenant John Piper and Flying Officer Peter Masters.

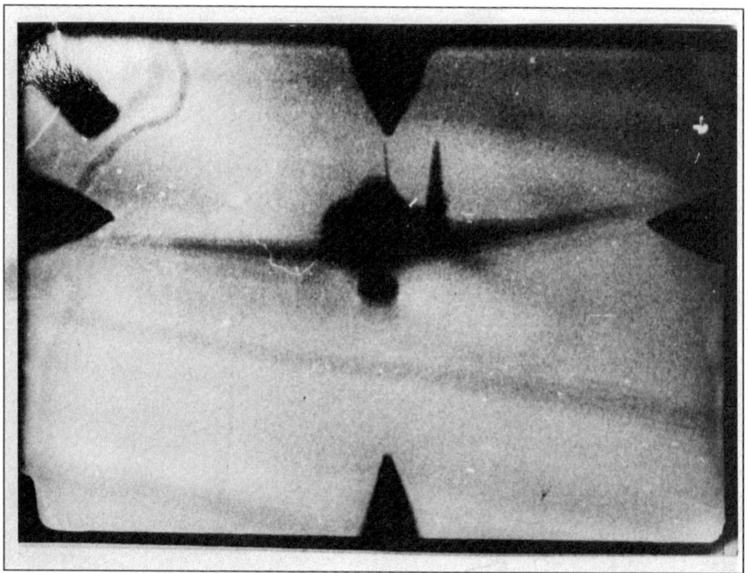

(Courtesy Peter Tucker)

The enemy in his sights. Bill Stuart's gun camera frames a Japanese Zero. Having yet to discard his 'drop tank', this Japanese pilot was most likely unaware of his attacker's presence.

(Courtesy Peter Tucker)

The informality of fighting in the tropics. *Right to left*: pilots Les Jackson, Peter Masters, Geoff Atherton and Alan Boyd.

(Courtesy Peter Tucker)

Flight Lieutenant Stuart Collie. A barrister in a former life, now 75 Squadron's intelligence officer.

(Courtesy Peter Tucker)

Corporal Alan Dyer cradles a 3.7-inch anti-aircraft shell while a fellow ground crew member looks on.

(Courtesy Peter Tucker)

Arthur Tucker: 'You wonder why I got malaria?'

Luxury, New Guinea jungle style. Bill Cowe at Bomana Camp, April 1942.

(Courtesy Peter Tucker)

(Courtesy Peter Tucker)

Just weeks out of training, 75 Squadron had to learn air combat the hard way. Alan Whetters (front, centre), with Arthur Tucker to his right, and Peter Masters to his left.

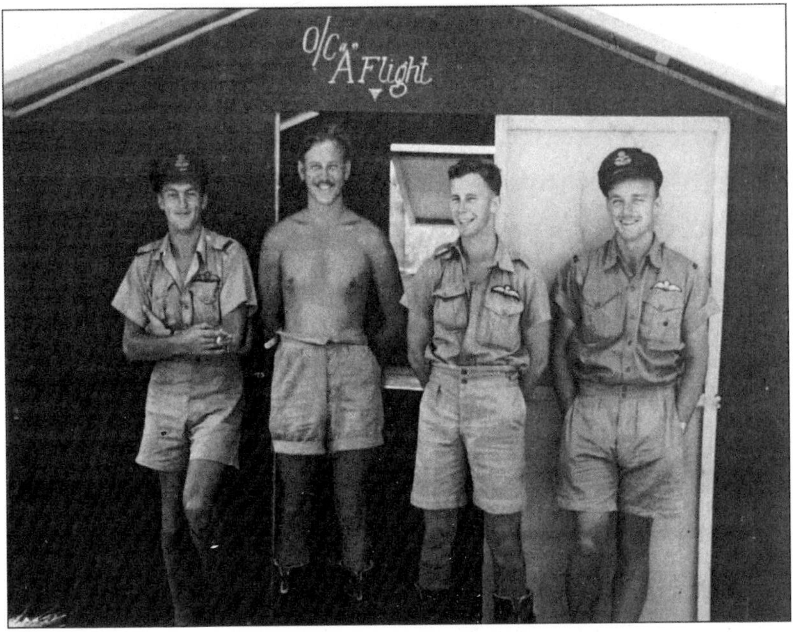

(Courtesy Peter Tucker)

Some of 75's young warriors. Cairns, December 1942. *Left to right*: Geoff Atherton, Sergeant Keith Wilson, Noel Todd and Arthur Tucker.

(Courtesy Peter Tucker)

A moment's relaxation before heading north again to face the Japanese. *Left to right*: Stan Hunt, Bill Cowe and Arthur Tucker. Carminya (near Mackay), 1942.

Petty Officer First Class Saburo Sakai. The only man to record the 44 days from the Japanese side.

(Author's collection)

(Author's collection)

The scourge of the Pacific skies in the early part of the war – the remarkable Mitsubishi A6M 'Zero' fighter.

wingman to Turnbull, Pettett watched him descend and make a beam and quarter attack on a Zero, which then executed the 'quite amazing manoeuvre' of a 'split S' stall turn, a speciality of the nimble Mitsubishi Zero whereby it could climb sharply in a vertical twisting corkscrew, turn, stall, then flick itself suddenly behind an attacking aircraft, turning the tables in an instant. As with the P-40's dive & zoom, this manoeuvre was the Japanese pilots' own means of both attack and escape: suddenly spiralling upwards to evade an imminent stream of bullets.

Michael Butler recalled his admiration of the skilled Japanese pilots:

> Their judgement was absolutely superb because as soon as you were getting almost in range they'd commence a stall turn and go up vertically and they'd leave it so late that you couldn't pull back to fire at them otherwise you'd go into a high-speed stall and the next thing they're on your tail.

Pettett seized his chance and fired at the Zero as it twisted to gain the advantage on Turnbull, but failed to notice him.

> This aeroplane had apparently been attacking the ground strafers and had pulled up into a climbing turn that the Zero did very well – a very steep climb and a sort of a flick turn to turn in the opposite direction...suddenly this character pulled up right in front of me and all I instinctively did was pull back on the stick and pull the trigger and allowing what

> I thought was enough deflection and that aircraft went down and I got one confirmed.

He did not later recall it being a particularly spectacular moment. The Zero, said Pettett, 'did not explode in a great burst of *Star Wars* in front of me or anything like that'. He simply noticed his bullets 'going pretty close' to his target with little immediate results, the whole thing lasting no more than four or five seconds. Nevertheless, he had achieved his first – and, as it transpired, only – kill, confirmed later by Wilbur Wackett, who was about to begin an extraordinary drama of his own. Turnbull also claimed a Zero in the engagement, bringing 75's tally to two.

Later, upon reflection, Pettett came to strongly believe that his victim had been the aircraft that, moments before, had shot down Bruce Anderson, and gained some satisfaction in the revenge of his fellow pilot. 'I had no reaction at all. I certainly didn't have any feelings at all for the Japanese pilot – no, none at all. I mean, he was there and trying to kill me and I was very lucky to get him.'

CHAPTER 5

Wilbur Wackett's ordeal

This first attack by Jackson and 75 Squadron, executed with daring and with the element of surprise, was considered a great success. In a report Jackson submitted to RAAF Headquarters on 30 March, he estimated that, of the twenty aircraft lined up along the runway at Lae, nine were destroyed and several others damaged. 'It is also believed from the pilots' reports that three bombers were also burnt.' The squadron had announced to the enemy that their one-way, virtually uncontested conquest of the skies over the vital hub of Port Moresby had now ceased, and that if they intended to take the port, they were in for a fight.

The day had come at a cost, however. Bruce Anderson, reportedly the first pilot to fire at the Japanese in New Britain, had been killed, and it was realised on the squadron's return that Wilbur Wackett was also missing. Airfield mishaps later that day took another two Kittyhawks out of action. As if John

Piper's day had not been eventful enough, he was scrambled later that afternoon to investigate a suspected patrolling enemy aircraft. On take-off, his undercarriage clipped a fuel drum, and a 'lonely two hours' was spent searching in vain for the Japanese aircraft. On landing, one of his wheels would not lock down, and the damage he caused to his aircraft's wingtip as it scraped along the runway took his aircraft out of action for some time.

Sergeant Stan Havard came to grief that day too when his aircraft caught the slipstream of another and crashed on take-off. He was, luckily, unhurt, but with Brereton's accident that morning, the tally of lost aircraft for this single day of action mounted to an alarming five.

It is, however, the story of Wilbur Wackett, one of the heroes of the previous day's downing of the Betty bomber over the harbour, that provides the attack on Lae's most remarkable saga.

•

At fifteen, the young Wilbur Wackett relocated from Sydney to Melbourne, when his already famous father, Lawrence, was given the job of running the Commonwealth Aircraft Corporation. Hence Wilbur had the unusual distinction of attending both Sydney and Melbourne Grammar schools, where he shone as a champion athlete. By 1939, he was a student at Melbourne University, but all he really wanted to do was fly aeroplanes. In March of that year, he applied for an air force cadetship.

Just a few weeks after the war began in September, Wilbur was given one of the RAAF's less glamorous jobs, flying convoy escort duties in quaint but antiquated twin-engine Avro Ansons up and down Bass Strait with 21 Squadron based at Laverton. His war would continue in this uneventful manner until January 1942, when he found himself posted to his birthplace, Townsville. Here, he joined the seriously depleted ranks of 24 Squadron rebuilding after their ill-fated defence of Rabaul where they lost ten aircrew, five Wirraways and four Hudson bombers. It was a brief posting, and on 12 March, Wackett joined the nascent 75 Squadron.

On the day he arrived at Moresby, his log book states that despite his many flying hours, only ten of those had been racked up on the Kittyhawk. By the time he was shot down over Lae on 22 March, it would be eleven.

As part of the top cover on the morning of John Jackson's first daring attack on Lae, Wackett, flying number two to Peter Turnbull, noticed his flight commander waggle his wings and release his detachable 'drop tank', a first sign that the Kittyhawk's radio/telephone sets had failed. Two Zeros from the Japanese dawn patrol had dived past Turnbull from 10,000 feet to pounce on the strafers below, but he had seen them late, and now plummeted after them.

Pushing his stick hard over, Wackett followed. As the two Zeros manoeuvred on Turnbull, they crossed Wackett's nose in line astern. In a split-second decision, he executed a sharp left turn and decided to attack the leading Japanese aircraft. As the grey outline of the Zero took shape in front of him, Wackett no doubt reflected on his excellent, beam-attacking position from height, but cursed his illuminated gunsight, the bulb of which had blown, leaving him with only a blank windshield. Lining up on the Zero as best he could, he aimed in its general direction, allowed for a little deflection, and moved his thumb over the firing button.

But instead of the shuddering recoil of his six guns coursing back through his aircraft, only one seemed to be working – the remaining five had apparently jammed. Nevertheless, it was good shooting and he observed his tracer hitting the port wing of the Japanese aircraft as it turned sharply.

It was a costly victory. In Wackett's cockpit, all hell broke loose. His enthusiasm far outrunning his experience, he had failed to take into account the second Zero, which had lined up behind him, spraying him with 7.9-millimetre bullets. One ricocheted off his wristwatch, another exploded on the dash in front of him. Holes began to appear along his wings, accompanied by the sound of tearing metal. He was suddenly covered in horsehair as one shell tore through the padding in his headrest, spilling its contents. Then he heard a series of pings as projectiles struck the Kittyhawk's sole piece of armour plating just behind his head. Thick black smoke began pouring from the engine as ruptured oil lines came into contact with hot metal and the Allison motor began to run rough.

Instinctively, Wackett steered towards the protection of a bank of grey cloud and headed out to sea. Later he reported seeing two fighters in the distance, both on fire, plunging to the surface somewhere near the mouth of the Bowong River. Reasoning that his chances of survival were slightly better in water than crashing into the jungle uncomfortably close to an enraged Japanese base, Wackett contemplated the previously unthinkable notion of ditching. Then his engine failed.

Estimating he was somewhere between Lae and Salamaua, he emerged beneath the cloud about 1000 feet above the water. How far from land he was he could not tell, though he noted he was now heading back to the coast. Controlling the aircraft as best he could, Wackett braced his legs on the firewall and brought up his left arm to protect his face from the gunsight on his dash. He hit the water at 90 knots.

With its prominent air scoop under the nose – which inspired 112 Squadron RAF pilots to apply the famous painted 'shark mouth' in the western desert – the Kittyhawk was not an easy aeroplane to ditch in water. Wackett, however, survived the sickening jolt and doubtless uttered a prayer in thanks that the aircraft did not cartwheel. In seconds, however, he was up to his waist in water as the plane began to sink. Fighting his way out of belt and harness, he threw away his helmet and flying boots (an act he was soon to regret), twisted the small bottle of carbon dioxide on his Mae West life jacket and leapt into the water as his aircraft vanished underneath him.

Almost immediately, a large shark broke the surface of the water just feet away. Wackett later wrote a detailed narrative of the incident:

> my heart skipped a beat as I saw it, and I looked at the land which seemed 10 miles off. I started swimming. After a few strokes, I stopped to unroll my sleeves and pull my socks up over my knees as I thought this would make me less noticeable to the sharks...and wondered whether I should discard my revolver and water bottle as they weighed me down. I decided to leave them on as I was swimming into Japanese-held territory and might need them.

Having survived the strain of an air battle, then a dogfight and being shot into the sea, Wackett now had to summon the strength to find his way back to shore through miles of shark-infested sea. More sharks appeared, one of which swam alarmingly close to Wackett's extremely vulnerable form, but he played dead in the water for some time and they eventually disappeared.

The tropical sun beat down, and Wackett baked. Incredibly, he managed to keep up a slow swim for the next nine hours, gradually pulling his exhausted body towards the shore. He would grant himself the occasional luxury of a brief rest, rolling onto his back, but the stinging from the salt in his mouth and eyes was unbearable. And each time he stopped the current took him away from land, and he would have to paddle frantically to regain his momentum. Eventually he found himself a couple of hundred yards from a shoreline where 'two natives [were] standing beside a canoe and pointing toward me. They did not seem disposed to help.'

Eight feet from the shore, Wackett's feet struck bottom and he hauled himself over rocks to lay down, exhausted, on the sand behind the tide line. For some reason, he felt a desire to test his pistol and let off a shot, which startled the villagers and did nothing to make them warm to his presence. 'Several women screamed when they saw me and rushed into their houses,' he recounted.

Few of the inhabitants of Busamo, the village where he had come ashore, seemed willing to come to his aid, but fortune provided two boys, mission educated at Rabaul, who immediately expressed a willingness to help. A fierce argument erupted among the villagers, many of whom, fearing reprisals from the Japanese, insisted on handing Wackett over to them. Wackett listened, following the villagers' proceedings as best he could, no doubt experiencing a strong sense of vulnerability. Eventually, despite the wishes of many of the people, the boys decided to deliver Wackett to safety.

The trio trekked for four torturous days through the heat of a sweltering jungle. Setting out at dawn, not resting till dark, and with nothing to protect his feet save a pair of disintegrating government-issue socks, Wackett trudged, one agonising step at a time, in the company of his two life-saving guides. The first day they passed over rough country and the wear on Wackett's feet was terrible. Producing roots and other edibles, the boys offered them to the weary Australian airman, and he accepted. The first night, the villagers of Lega gave them shelter. But a night's rest did nothing to alleviate the terrible state of Wackett's feet; sores and cuts had begun to open and he doubted whether he could muster the strength to carry on the next morning.

At first light, they set off again, this time striking out over the range. Wet ground made some of the going slightly more bearable, but the progress over thick roots and vines was slow. Then, after a short midday rest, they entered leech country. 'They fastened onto one's toes and sucked the blood, and it wasn't long before we all had to stop and scrape them off with sticks. My feet were sore enough without leeches biting my toes!'

By six that evening, Wackett was 'practically done in'. with no sign of a village before them. Hoping perhaps his guides would decide to simply camp out on the jungle floor, they instead indicated this to be out of the question and so on they pressed, through the dark. Soon enough, they entered the outskirts of a village and were confronted by 'six powerfully built warriors with drawn bows and arrows aimed straight at my chest'. The guides again did the talking, and they were escorted to a hut where they spent the night. Without realising it at the time, Wackett had managed to climb 10,000 feet to the village of Marpos, which accounted for the sudden drop in temperature.

The following day the trio struck out towards another village, Bulwa, traversing steep gorges and crossing, then recrossing, fast-flowing streams. In between, and as if their odyssey had not been hideous enough, they had swamps to contend with which:

> held up our progress and often we were wading up to our waists in foul-smelling mud. That night we spent in such a swamp, the evil smelling slush and the millions of mosquitoes made sleep impossible. We stretched out on some banana leaves, and the guide, seeing I was troubled with my legs, sat up all night and massaged them.

At four o'clock the next day, the exhausted party finally arrived at Bulwa, where they met up with a detachment of the remarkable quasi-guerrilla New Guinea Volunteer Rifles (NGVR), who knew the terrain as well as any local. From here, and to his unspeakable relief, Wackett and his guides were taken by lorry to an NGVR outpost where his feet were at last treated by a medical officer. After a few days, they were transported to the unit's base camp where the guides were each awarded the not inconsiderable sum of twenty shillings for their astonishing and, unquestionably for Wackett, life-saving determination to see him to safety. It is noted that one of the men returned to his village, Busamo, with gifts for the elders, while the other requested to continue on to Port Moresby. The payment was a deliberate gesture, designed to warm the New Guinea populace to the idea of aiding more downed Allied airmen.

Still, Wackett's journey was not over. Travelling by lorry to Wau, he joined a party under the command of a lieutenant who planned to walk more than 150 miles to Port Moresby. After five days, fresh supplies needed to be sent for, and the party settled in to wait at a spot along the track. Wackett however, had had enough, and instead joined another group heading south under the command of a Lieutenant Strand.

After another four days' walking, the southern coast of the Huon Peninsula was at last reached, where the party boarded canoes bound for a mission station, then Kairuku on tiny Yule Island. Here, the luck that had somehow managed to ward off malaria gave out, and Wackett came down with it severely. Recuperating on the island as long as he dared, he joined another group heading to Moresby by any means they could. A seven-hour walk ensued, then a lift up in a plantation lorry, followed by another four-hour trek that took them within striking distance of the capital. A further trip by canoe took him as far as Porabada, where he was picked up by an army truck and finally arrived in Port Moresby.

It would take a month to the day since being shot down over 180 miles away above Lae on his first mission for Wilbur Wackett to report back to 75 Squadron, having completed an odyssey of endurance and survival that defies belief. Wackett himself did not fly again from Port Moresby on account of his malaria, but reported the two aircraft he observed hitting the water as he himself was in trouble, confirming the claims of Peter Turnbull and John Pettett, who were each credited with a kill.

The loss of those two Zeros, as well as the daring raid on their base at Lae, had stunned the Japanese, and they would not be long in extracting revenge.

•

When the excitement of their initial attack of 22 March had passed, John Jackson counted the cost of the Lae action. Two of his aircraft lost over the target along with their pilots (one killed) and three more aircraft out of action due to airfield mishaps in a single day was, he knew, wholly unsustainable, whatever the result. The Japanese had lost too, but were now very much aware of 75's presence at Seven Mile, and would, he knew, be gearing up for a different type of air war. Nor would there be another opportunity to play the card of surprise. From now on, not only would the enemy be waiting for them at their bases, but Seven Mile Strip would become a target like never before. The following round in the battle for the skies above Port Moresby would set the pattern for the next 44 days. And it would begin the next morning.

CHAPTER 6

75 Squadron stays on

In his book, *Fighter Squadron Doctor*, Bill Deane-Butcher recalled that first Japanese attack on 75 Squadron vividly. That afternoon, he happened to be down near the pilots' tent adjacent to the airstrip when the single telephone attached to a pole connected to the fighter control room – a tunnel dug into the side of a nearby hill – rang loudly. 'It sounded harsh,' he said. 'Urgent directions came through the wire. It would be "on" in twenty minutes.' Around him, the squadron erupted into life. Flying gear was rechecked, trucks and aero engines roared into life. In a cloud of dust, Kittyhawks took to the air.

Fifteen minutes later there were more clouds of dust, accompanied by 'an almighty boom'. High up in the 'intensely blue sky' above him were arranged a neat pattern of Japanese bombers, just out of reach of 75's Kittyhawks.

Earlier that morning of 23 March, John Jackson, perhaps with a sense of foreboding, led the first dawn patrol over his new base. Nothing was sighted, but just before half past one that afternoon, every available Kittyhawk was scrambled to intercept two incoming flights of aircraft, which, as Deane-Butcher correctly observed, they were unable to reach. In this, their seventeenth air raid to date on Port Moresby, nineteen Japanese bombers escorted by just four Zeros – a testament to the effectiveness of the previous day's attack – arrived over Seven Mile, determined to put a quick end to this audacious challenge to their timetable for the conquest of New Guinea and beyond. In his own recollections, *They Flew Alone*, Ted Church recalled the sight of the Japanese formation: 'Cumulus clouds banked high above the mountains, ideal cover for a raiding party. Suddenly three shots rang out [the signal for attack] and from behind a cloud the 19 bombers sailed like tiny silver specks across the blue.'

Barely had the Kittyhawks climbed through 7000 feet when, above them, at 20,000, the Japanese bombers unloaded. As it happened, they were inaccurate, and their bombs missed the runway and caused little damage. The gunners behind the defensive 3.7-inch anti-aircraft guns aimed well, damaging three Japanese bombers, who turned for home after unloading their cargo.

It seemed the Japanese attack had fizzled out and perhaps the defenders could relax a little. Then, nearly an hour later, in a mirror image of the previous day's drama at Lae, it was the turn of the Zeros.

In the scramble to take off, two Kittyhawks became bogged in the mud near the runway as their pilots struggled to get them airborne. Ted Church was frantically attempting to shove the aircraft into the less-than-adequate dispersal pens adjacent to the runway even as the drone of engines loomed closer. Then four Zeros emerged from behind a hill, and, banking steeply, headed towards the airstrip.

Having done what he could to protect the marooned Kittyhawks, Church remembered with alarm another precious resource, the squadron's sole utility vehicle, which was currently sitting out in the open on the runway behind him, highly visible to any swooping aircraft, and for which there would be no foreseeable replacement. Racing back to his truck accompanied by a visiting Port Moresby barracks officer, Jock Russell, Church flew into the driver's seat and took off as fast as he could down the runway, trying to desperately think of somewhere, anywhere, on this scrubby, swampy airstrip that might pass for cover. In his search he momentarily 'quite forgot the Zeros and as the car raced along, we suddenly heard the spit-spit-spit of machine guns and the louder report of cannon immediately behind us'. It became obvious that Church and his small vehicle were a target for the Zeros, now screaming low over the airfield. 'Step on it! Can't you drive any faster?' was the less-than-helpful suggestion – 'with appropriate Australian adjectives' – from Jock Russell, who probably hadn't planned on seeing quite this much action on his visit to Seven Mile.

Throwing back a profanity in reply, Church 'pushed the accelerator to the floorboards', trying as best he could to dodge the bullets that were now spitting up the dust around him. Veering suddenly off the runway and coming to an abrupt stop, the two men leapt out and made their way on foot up nearby Morris Hill to observe the proceedings from what they assumed to be a safer vantage point. They were terribly mistaken.

The Zeros, possibly unable to capture a wildly careening vehicle in their gunsights, now concentrated on the considerably easier target of the grounded Australian fighters, two of which were quickly set ablaze, and a third damaged. The bold action of one of the ground crew, Alan Ramsay, prevented the tally from being far greater. Caught refuelling aircraft from the squadron's sole mobile petrol tanker as the strafing attack commenced, Ramsay refused to panic. He coolly disconnected the hose from the aircraft wing tank, even as the plane he was topping up was hit and flames began to take hold, before removing the precious tanker to safety. For his efforts, Ramsay was Mentioned in Dispatches.

It was also Bill Deane-Butcher's first exposure to the chaos of war. Pilots Les Jackson, Peter Turnbull and Barry Cox had been unable to get their aircraft started in time to intercept the Zeros. Deane-Butcher was walking towards them when he heard a shout and saw several quickly moving bodies take up what little space was afforded by the nearest slit trench. 'The four of us were caught in the open,' he recalled, 'and had nowhere to go.' Lying face down in a very thin looking patch of grass as the bullets of the Zeros 'sizzled all round us', Deane-Butcher could only 'speculate on how best to cover all my vital parts under one tin hat. Two shared priority – my head and my genitals. It came to me in a flash that in future, if I had any, I would need to carry two tin hats instead of one.'

The airfield defences now opened up, particularly the machine gunners, who had recently been bolstered by additional firepower from Port Moresby's three militia infantry battalions to a total of 27 Lewis and thirteen antiquated but functioning Vickers machine guns. Despite being armament from the World War One era, the defenders blasted away, catching the Japanese attackers in an unexpected cauldron of firepower. In a touch of irony, the gunners were joined by Peter Jeffrey, the man they had almost succeeded in killing on his arrival 48 hours earlier.

Having been prevented from becoming airborne due to an unserviceable motor, Jeffrey had to content himself with crouching beside the gunners in their pits and emptying his .38 revolver in the direction of the enemy as they zoomed past. In a repeat of John Jackson's daring double-dip strafe the day before, one of the Zero pilots peeled around and began to again line up the runway in his sights. Turnbull dived into a slit trench for cover as the aircraft passed by a second time but, his blood up, quickly re-emerged and emptied more rounds in its general vicinity. It is even possible – though it's more likely it was the machine gunners – that his aim was true, as the

Japanese aircraft pulled immediately into a steep climb, stalled, then dived nose-down towards Morris Hill – the spot where Ted Church and Jock Russell were currently taking cover.

As Church later wryly observed, an out-of-control aircraft hurtling towards the earth at several hundred miles an hour 'covers a lot of ground in a few moments', and he, like Deane-Butcher, felt somewhat exposed, with little more than his steel helmet for protection. 'A lot of body [was] showing outside the [helmet's] protective dome.'

Realising escape was impossible, the two beleaguered men attempted instead to push themselves into the protective bosom of the unyielding earth as the Zero slammed into the slope above them, ricocheted into the air and exploded 130 feet off the ground, its engine tearing off and careering 100 feet ahead, unleashing a torrent of shattered bits of aircraft all over the two officers. 'Burning oil and petrol spattered our shirts and shorts, pieces of aircraft flew in all directions,' said Church. The two men desperately attempted to slap out the flaming hot oil on each other's clothing. Exhausted, and with little that could be said, Church made the observation, 'That was a bit too close for general comfort, Jock.'

Despite the severity of the crash, the body of the Japanese pilot, Petty Officer Kyoichi Yoshii, was found largely unmarked some distance from the wreckage, though his cause of death was plain to see: a bullet wound to the right temple. Whether the fatal round emanated from the machine gunners or Peter Turnbull's .38 revolver would never be known.

On points, at least, the Australians had come off better in the attack on Seven Mile. Besides the Zero destroyed on Morris Hill, another was observed limping away to the north trailing a long white plume of smoke or petrol vapour. In the unlikely event it made it back to its base, it was certainly damaged, indicating the possible loss of two enemy pilots and aircraft for the same number of Kittyhawks destroyed on the ground, but no personnel injured. Nevertheless, over 1800 miles away, the very future of the squadron was being questioned.

After only three days of operations, seven of 75 Squadron's original seventeen Kittyhawks had been destroyed, in a place where, devoid of proper facilities of every description, the notion of repairing and maintaining the unit as an effective fighting force seemed remote indeed. Besides the Japanese counterattack on Seven Mile, 23 March was noted for two other incidences of significance. Firstly, the departure of Peter Jeffrey who, after setting up the squadron as best he could, handed it over finally to Jackson, then returned to the mainland to assist with the establishment of 75's sister Kittyhawk squadrons, 76 and 77. Secondly, after a sober assessment of 75's losses to date, a signal was sent from the Central War Office in Melbourne to the RAAF's North East Area Command, giving authority for 75 Squadron to withdraw to the relative safety of Horn Island, just off the tip of Cape York. Interestingly, the decision as to whether to act on this recommendation was left to the discretion of 75's already impressive new commanding officer, John Jackson.

The decision to withdraw would, he knew, be a serious one. Losses of men and aircraft at this rate could not be sustained, and the facilities at Seven Mile would continue to be dire. But what would be the message sent should the squadron retreat now? What of the hard-pressed militia who, nerves shot, had endured months of Japanese bombardment, and who had descended on Seven Mile in trucks to cheer the arrival of these Kittyhawks they thought would never arrive? What signal would it send to the country as a whole, should Australia's first independent defensive action in its history be seen to wither at its first encounter with the enemy? After discussing the matter with a senior RAAF officer at Port Moresby, Group Captain Charles Pearce, who expressed the opinion that, should the RAAF leave, 'the army would have to swim home' Jackson cabled Melbourne with his decision: 75 Squadron was going nowhere. For the next six weeks, come what may, this wretched airstrip in the bush seven miles from Port Moresby would remain their home and their battle line.

CHAPTER 7

A macabre routine

Despite being present at the squadron's inception and surviving – just – the terrible flight from Bankstown to Townsville, Arthur Tucker missed the first ten days of 75 Squadron's deployment to Port Moresby due to what he later described as his 'intransigence'. In his own words, he was always 'a bit of a rebel' and never a man to be intimidated into adhering to rules he believed foolish, or social norms he found irksome. He vehemently disagreed, for example, with the desert veterans' insistence on landing the Kittyhawks on two wheels rather than three, and let them know it. It was an altercation which, he believed, 'may have saved my life'.

Hailing from a long line of independent-thinking Celts, Tucker knew exactly why he was there risking his life, and it had little to do with 'king and country'. Then, as later in life, he nursed a healthy disdain for the monarchy. 'In our family, there was a lot of resentment towards the British way of doing things,' he recalled. 'Even now, I can tolerate the monarchy, but that's about all.'

When it came to politics, Tucker was self-taught, influenced by various instances during his formative years, such as the uncle, who, having survived the carnage of Gallipoli and the Western Front, absconded to Ireland near war's end and became witness to British cruelty during the struggles for Irish independence. Tucker also remembered coming across a newspaper story as a boy at Grammar school when preparing for a debate concerning the rising power of Japan. The story reported a recent visitor to Japan sighting a school map of Australia with the words 'your future home' printed across it. 'This was way back in 1934,' he said, and he never forgot it. 'By the time I was twenty, I was a big fella and wouldn't take any lip from anyone.'

So, after yet again arguing with his superiors on a matter he felt strongly about, Tucker 'drew a short straw', and instead of being sent north to Moresby, headed south to Bankstown to collect a spare aeroplane that, as it turns out, couldn't be found. 'Then they suddenly decided aeroplanes weren't as important as men,' and with four other pilots, he was put on a train back to Townsville, then loaded onto an American Flying Fortress, and arrived at Port Moresby in the first week of April.

Tucker's first impressions of his new home were not encouraging. 'The living was hard,' he said. 'Seven Mile was a dreadful little 'drome. It was still being extended at one end and had bumps, up and down like a country road, and not much wider.' It had, he said, been so hurriedly bitumened the previous November that 'heavy aircraft sank and bogged. At the southern end, a major water main ran under the strip and had leaky joints so the army dug a drain along the side to relieve the build-up of subsoil water – a trap for the unwary when swinging off to clear the strip.'

At the other end were the standby and operations tents but no buildings of any description. John Pettett too recorded his first dismal impressions:

> Living conditions were poor. Now, I had lived at home with my parents and for a short time with my wife in a little flat and then in messes where we had comfortable beds with clean sheets and pillows and all the conveniences. Plenty of showers; toilets and everything. But at Moresby we were living in tents. I had never been in a tent in my life until now. When we got into these tents, well the cots were set up – no pillows, just straw palliasses on wire cots. We had blankets but no sheets of course.

Everyone appeared to be sick, and very soon, he would be too. A few days later, when recording his first combat in his log book, he would write 'shits' beside the proscribed description of the action. 'That wasn't fear,' he explained, 'that was the fact that it was trickling down my legs. I had gastroenteritis, everyone did.'

Despite this ordeal, Tucker remembered his first encounter vividly. 'I was flying number 2 to Alan Boyd, a Middle East veteran with whom I had a good relationship.' Boyd had told Tucker to stick close to his wing so the more experienced pilot could keep an eye on him. 'The bombers were high and, as usual, we climbed up underneath as they headed home lickety-split over the Owen Stanleys,' he explained. 'Then came a radio warning: Zeros above!' For the rest of his life, Tucker thought long about the next few, somewhat surreal, moments of his first combat, and how they could so easily have been his last. 'Under heavy stress,' he later rationalised, 'the mind seizes on trivialities.' Flying along perfectly straight and level, Tucker said he became mesmerised by the sight of 'five or six large cigar-shaped belly tanks, tumbling down end over end just ahead of us'. Above him, the Japanese were jettisoning their fuel tanks to ready themselves for combat, and perhaps glanced over to see Tucker flying along apparently in a world of his own. 'Then I woke up, searched urgently around and could see no aeroplane at all, enemy or friendly. What a target I had been presenting!' From that moment on, he was never to forget the universal fighter pilot adage: never, ever, fly straight and level in a combat zone.

Arriving back at Seven Mile, Tucker expected one or more strips to be torn from him for losing contact with his flight commander, but the remonstration never came and the moment was forgotten in the ensuing weeks of battle. It was more than 50 years later, at a reunion, when he recalled the incident to Alan Boyd and asked what had taken place that day, that he discovered the truth. It transpired that Boyd had in fact seen the

Zeros above and pulled up his Kittyhawk's nose to fire, but the recoil of his guns had sent his aircraft into a violent spin from which he was only just able to recover below 10,000 feet. Boyd too, it seems, hadn't been able to say anything that day, but was relieved nonetheless that his charge was unharmed. The two men let their respective indiscretions pass without comment.

Tucker and his fellow pilots now fell into the peculiar, grim and often macabre routine that made up the 44-day battle for the skies above Port Moresby. When not in action, there was little for the pilots to do on the strip. There were no recreational facilities except tents that provided the most basic of messes and standby facilities. There was not a laundry nor even a proper toilet. For their bodily functions, the men simply took a shovel and a scrap of newspaper – if they could find some – and wandered into the kunai grass. This, in itself, proved a nightmare for Bill Deane-Butcher, who faced unwinnable battles against gastro, dengue fever and other diseases of the tropics.

The day would begin early at Seven Mile, at around five in the morning, when the pilots were roused from their tents to wash and shave as best they could from a trough or bucket. Their gear was assembled: helmet, oxygen mask, goggles, throat microphone and parachute. Also essential was their British Mae West life jacket, although the less-cumbersome American-issued examples were more popular.

Those scheduled to fly on the daily security patrol were picked up and driven to their aircraft, while others made their way to the standby tent to await the order to scramble, should word come through of a Japanese raid. The men ate, slept and flew in the same clothes, usually shirt and shorts, which gradually faded from khaki to a washed-out pale green. There was no saluting, and a casual attitude towards rank in general. Out here, according to Whetters, what was the point?

At the breakfast tent, the men lined up to be treated to monotonous and unappetising fare that contributed little to either health or morale. Arthur Tucker remembered it only too well. 'They were feeding us on tinned bacon which was dreadful, tropical spread which was worse, baked beans, and somewhere or other they'd captured a Liberty Ship's supply of herrings in tomato sauce, which we called "goldfish".' Tinned butter became rancid in the heat, and food that did not arrive tinned was dried. Powdered milk was perhaps tolerable, but particular revulsion was reserved for the powdered eggs, which not undeservedly were dubbed 'yellow death'. Dehydrated mutton needed to be soaked overnight, but the vile-smelling result, 'a form of meatloaf' was barely worth the wait. 'It was all vile stuff,' remembered Tucker. The more diplomatic Alan Whetters was philosophical. 'Well, I guess that it was all they had at the time, but it certainly was deficient in what you would call normal food.'

John Jackson, who was a keen amateur photographer, captured the only moving images of 75's deployment at Port Moresby during the 44 days. The brief minute or so that remains, taken from his wind-up hand-held movie camera, show a series of skinny and self-conscious young men, informally dressed beside a few very temporary looking tents in front of the monotonous grass and bush landscape. One fellow has found a slouch hat, which sits too large on his head as he eyes the camera, unsure what to do. The sequence would have been taken during one of the many periods of waiting, which was a feature of life for the pilots of the squadron. At one stage the squadron's intelligence officer, Stu Collie, identified by his distinctive bald pate, can be seen standing outside a tent topless and also looking self-conscious.

Here at the standby tent the men would relax as best they could, talking, writing letters, lounging on incongruous pieces of furniture that Bill Deane-Butcher had purloined from abandoned Port Moresby houses to give the pilots something to sit on. A wind-up gramophone played the few worn-out old records time and time again. To tent poles were nailed a few pictures of pin-up girls or a calendar. For some reason, John Piper remembered, gambling – even for matchsticks – was not yet a feature of the pilots' life as it would be when the squadron took part in the great Milne Bay battle later that year.

There were times, however, when even such a rudimentary facility as the standby tent was not used by the pilots. Alan Whetters recalled a particularly intense period of air activity in late April, when he was required to remain beside his aircraft in the dispersal area for ten days straight from dawn till dusk.

Beer was available, but without refrigeration it could barely be kept below lukewarm. In terms of quantity, memories seem to vary. Whetters remembered that of an evening 'we would go to a main tent, and share half a bottle of beer, and then I, and I assume the others, would retire to the sleep tents'. Arthur Tucker recalled a less generous ration. 'You did your job, you went home at night. We used to get one bottle of beer between two people about three days a week I think, and you'd have that and go to bed and get up in the morning, put on your clothes, and go down to the strip again before dawn.'

John Pettett remembered struggling to even drink the beer.

> I don't know whether the whole squadron was given beer, but we rather spoilt pilots did, but we couldn't drink it. A mate of mine, Bink Davies, tried to share one bottle but we could never finish it – it was warm, anyway. So we didn't use our ration of beer. Otherwise there was no drink at all. The hotel at Port Moresby had been brand new just before the war, I believe, but that had been practically destroyed after the civilians had left.

As he had instituted when in command of 3 Squadron, Peter Jeffrey formed an all-ranks pilots' mess at Seven Mile, where the men could meet, talk, share their limited ration of beer, and discuss tactics and ways to fight and survive. It had been revolutionary in the North African desert, but here it seemed a logical, and particularly Australian, way of doing things, although it was by no means to become a universal pattern in all RAAF establishments across the Pacific.

John Pettett recalled that 'there was no recreation; there was nothing to do. We could only sit around and write letters and the gambling came later at Milne Bay. We were on duty either down at the strip or we were off duty. That's the way we worked it: we had two days on and one day off.'

Curiously enough, one of the few recreations available to the pilots was fishing. Port Moresby operated Halvorsen cruisers on the harbour as a rudimentary form of air/sea rescue, but would take pilots out for a jaunt on the water on their non-flying days. Hand grenades rather than rods were the angling methods of choice and, on a good day, the fish caught could supplement the uninspiring creations of the squadron mess tent. 'There is an island off Port Moresby Harbour called Fisherman's Island and we caught 560 tailor one day with hand grenades,' John Pettett explained. 'That was our only recreation. Otherwise, if we went on duty, we stayed back in the camp and wrote letters.'

Always, however, when waiting around for something to happen, a sour sense of tension would lurk behind the relaxed figures of the fighter pilots and their outward appearance of sangfroid.

Suddenly, three shots from a pistol, or simply the shout from Stu Collie of, 'It's on!' would, almost with a sense of relief, awaken the men from their stupor of inactivity. 'That's when your heart jumped up into your mouth,' recalled Pettett.

> If your aircraft was fairly close you would race to it otherwise you would jump on the back of a utility truck and were driven to your aeroplane. You would hop off and jump into the cockpit and the crew would jump up beside you, throw

> the straps around your shoulders and grab them from down below and start to get those connected while you got your helmet on and strapped that on and plugged it into the intercom thing and your oxygen mask too. That's when it was really scary, the moment of truth.

Once airborne, the men would attempt to climb as high and as fast as possible to get above any incoming enemy aircraft. Almost always, with as little as twenty minutes' warning, they were too late. 'It was very important that we were in a position to dive on them if they were making a raid,' remembered Alan Whetters, 'but unfortunately I cannot recall this ever happening.'

John Pettett concurred. 'Our strafing job over Lae the day after we arrived is the only time I ever saw an enemy aeroplane below me, the rest were above – bombers and fighters. So we didn't have enough time. Our rate of climb was not that great.'

From a modern perspective, one of the most confounding aspects of the story of 75 Squadron's 44 days was the apparent lack of cohesion in its tactics against the Japanese. Alan Whetters had arrived at Seven Mile on 2 April, and spoke briefly with John Jackson, who he had known at Point Cook. In terms of what the job ahead of Whetters entailed, 'little was said'. Jackson, however, did press the importance of climbing hard to meet the Japanese, but beyond that simple maxim, the tactics as understood by the pilots were, to say the least, loose. 'This was one of the unusual conditions of the squadron. I cannot recall any information whatsoever on the tactics to be employed. All that we did was take off together, meet the enemy, and then operated as individuals. As a consequence we were operating far and wide.'

Arthur Tucker has similar recollections. 'With regard to flying organisation, there was none. The leader would take off and you scrambled to follow him. We didn't have any tactics at all, except that we tried to stay together and tried to stay alive.'

From the moment they were airborne, however, the pilots would scan the skies around them, and push from their minds the terrible danger they were soon to face. They would form up loosely, then climb as fast and as steep as their heavy aircraft would let them in the thick, tropical air. It had been stressed that the Zero was the far superior aircraft in terms of speed, climb and manoeuvrability, and John Jackson told his pilots 'on no account' were they to try to dogfight with them. The ideal position for the Kittyhawk pilots to attack was from above, with the sun behind, and then tear down through the Japanese formation and use their aircraft's far superior firepower against the more lightly armed and armoured Zeros and Japanese bombers. Then, using the Kittyhawk's heavier weight and its powerful Allison engine, they would let gravity take care of the rest, putting the plane into a steep dive that the Zeros simply could not match. It was called 'dive and zoom'.

Tucker remembered that:

> you climbed up, you tried to stay together, you had a squirt at something, and if it looked as though they got on your tail

> you bunted – that was, put everything in one corner – dived away to get up speed, and then come back and have another go, but on no account were you to try to dogfight the Zero because that was not on, and that you just kept on doing that while you could and that was it.

It was effective but ad hoc. None of the pilots could ever recall attending a briefing or having a larger sense of what was to be done, or any official instructions regarding the do's and don'ts of flying and fighting. Some of them undoubtedly chatted among themselves in the mess, lying around in chairs waiting for the call to get airborne, but the lack of any fighting policy was one of the stranger aspects of 75 Squadron's life at Port Moresby. 'We would get into the air immediately,' said Alan Whetters, 'but then we were still as individuals, and we just chased one another until we formed a formation.'

One way or another, new pilots learned that the most effective way of avoiding a direct attack from the rear was the tactic of 'everything in the corner', the so-called 'bunting' as described by Tucker. This involved throwing the rudder hard over and pushing the stick to the pilot's far left or right corner. For the Japanese pilot attacking from the rear, the Kittyhawk would effectively disappear in front of him as it plummeted earthwards. Here, the Kittyhawk's Stromberg Carlson direct-injection carburettor put it at a distinct advantage, and against an aeroplane as formidable as Japan's amazing Mitsubishi Zero, the Kittyhawk pilots needed every advantage they could find.

CHAPTER 8

The Zero's spectacular reign

The Zero's reign over the skies of the southwest Pacific was short but spectacular. This revolutionary aircraft, demanded by the Japanese military to prevent the mauling their unescorted bombers had experienced over China, was to be unlike anything the world had ever seen. Developed in 1937, the Zero was the brainchild of the Mitsubishi company's 33-year-old designer, Jiro Horikoshi, who is said to have thrown the original brief across his desk in despair when reading the list of specifications demanded. It was decreed that the Zero should have enormous range, a speed of well over 500 miles an hour, be at least as manoeuvrable as some of its slower predecessors, and have a wingspan of not more than 39 feet to enable it to be launched from the deck of an aircraft carrier. It was also required to be armed not only with machine guns but also the destructive power of cannon to perform as an interceptor against enemy bombers as well as a defensive fighter. These contradictory elements – particularly the demand of carrier operation, which usually required a large wing area for low-speed control, linked with a demand for speed, which required higher power and a smaller wing – made the Zero an exceptionally difficult aeroplane to construct. The Nakajima Aircraft Company, which was also given a chance to compete for the project, withdrew early, claiming the demands were impossible.

Horikoshi persisted, however, believing the key to meeting this new aircraft's challenging requirements was radical weight reduction. He elected for a relatively small, 950-horsepower Nakajima Sakae engine to reduce the fuel load, and excluded every single ounce of unnecessary weight. This included eliminating self-sealing fuel tanks, and – especially bad news for the pilot – armoured windshields as well as the traditional heavy piece of armour plate that, in most fighter aircraft of the time, protected the pilot from attacks from the rear.

The Zero – named for the last digit of the Japanese Imperial year in which it entered service, 2600 – was constructed of a new light but sturdy Extra Super Duralumin, a kind of aluminium that allowed for spars and ribs to be shaved to the thinnest of margins without loss of strength or integrity. This radical aircraft also incorporated features such as flexible control cables, which could prevent pilot over-correction at high speed by absorbing some of the movement to the control surfaces.

When it was unleashed in 1940, the Zero sent shockwaves through the aviation world. In its debut engagement in Japan's long-running war with China, it shot down 27 Soviet-built fighters of the Chinese Nationalist air force without loss. After Pearl Harbor, Zeros tore through an array of British and American aircraft types in Malaya and Singapore and quickly established a reputation that filled its adversaries with dread. The plane was indeed fast and, with drop tanks, boasted a range of over 1800 miles. It could perform seemingly impossibly tight turns and was superbly constructed. Later in the war when an intact example was captured and examined, it amazed its American assessors with its flush rivet construction and one-piece wing and fuselage assembly. 'Built like a fine Swiss watch,' one of them noted, a far cry from the earlier rumours men like Arthur Tucker heard, that the Zero was simply an inferior hotch-potch copy of a number of Western designs, put together 'with bamboo and spittle' and flown by pilots short of stature and with poor eyesight.

But the Zero had its faults. Indeed, like a fine Swiss watch, it could also be fragile, and with neither armour to protect the pilot nor self-sealing tanks to prevent it becoming a fireball in combat, Allied pilots soon found that, providing you could actually hit the thing, a relatively small number of rounds was enough to deliver the Zero a mortal wound. It was also a complex and difficult aircraft to manufacture, unlike the less agile but more solid American types, and the downside of the flexible control cables was that almost superhuman strength was required by the pilot to control the plane, particularly at high speed.

It was also poorly armed, with the compromise in weight reduction resulting in it simply not being able to carry effective firepower. Its two 7.7-millimetre machine guns were faster firing, but did not carry anything like the punch of the Kittyhawk's six half-inch Brownings, and its cannon, though powerful, could only fire 60 rounds before its modest magazine was exhausted.

The Zero's adversary during the 44 days, the Kittyhawk, or something very like it, had been around since the mid 1930s. It was born out of the Hawk, an all-metal monoplane fighter built by the Curtiss Aeroplane and Motor Company of Buffalo, New York, designed to lift American aviation to somewhere near the standards currently being reached in pre-war Europe. Over the next decade, it would undergo four significant incarnations, all of which the Americans referred to simply as 'Warhawk', but which the British and Commonwealth air forces, who used the aircraft far more than the Americans did, dubbed 'Tomahawk'. Then the much better armed 'D' variant, the Kittyhawk, was developed. The Australian ace Clive Caldwell, the highest-scoring Kittyhawk ace anywhere, described it as an aeroplane with 'almost no vices'. That was probably an exaggeration, but a testament nonetheless to the P-40D's rugged durability and power to deliver a punch. It was not, however, a ballerina, and could not be compared to its contemporaries such as the Spitfire or Messerschmitt 109.

When put up against the Zero, the Kittyhawk was double its weight, possessed less than half its rate of climb, and was not even in the picture when it came to manoeuvrability at equivalent speeds. Its V-1710 Allison engine also lacked a two-stage supercharger that would have enabled it to perform at higher altitudes. As a result, its optimal operating ceiling hung around 15,000 feet. Higher than this it became sluggish, and in the thin atmosphere above 20,000 feet the craft would, in aviation parlance, just 'fall out of the sky'.

John Piper was even-handed about the Kittyhawk's pros and cons, saying:

> its strength was it was very strong; very robust and well armour-plated, and it was quite fast. But other than that it didn't have anything much. It had a poor ceiling. From twenty-two to twenty-five thousand feet we were just sort of wallowing round the place. If you found yourself at high altitude making a head-on attack on Japanese bombers, well by the time you'd got around and caught up again, you know, the day was nearly over.

The Kittyhawk was rugged, which the Zero simply was not. According to Arthur Tucker, the Kittyhawk 'was just *the* aeroplane for the conditions we were going into'. Michael Butler talked of the Kittyhawks coming back with 'holes you could climb through...you could also overheat the engine and it would still keep going'. Its firepower was deadly, with bullets that could tear through metal and, at close range, even engines. Its six machine guns – when they did not jam – had a high muzzle velocity, which could put 1400 rounds into the air in a ten-second burst, though most bursts from a Kittyhawk were far shorter than this. It also carried a nice thick piece of armour plate just behind the pilot as well as an armoured windshield, and self-sealing fuel tanks designed to instantly plug up bullet holes with a rubbery substance that reacted to leaking petrol. Its Stromberg Carlson fuel-injected carburettor also meant the Kittyhawk could execute the favoured 'bunt' from a fight without its Allison engine missing a beat, whereas the Zero's conventional float system would see the engine cut out and not kick in again until it had resumed level flight.

How then were the Australian pilots expected to take on and defeat such a contrasting machine in the skies above New Guinea in 1942?

Claire Chennault, the American aviator and general in charge of the famous American Volunteer Group (AVG) dubbed the Flying Tigers, was one of the first Westerners to be given a close-up look at the Zero, watching it in battle both from the ground and in the air in the skies above China. So alarmed was he by what he saw soon after the Zero's deployment in mid 1940 that he wrote a report to Washington, along with a photograph of the Zero and its estimated flight characteristics, warning that disaster would befall any British or American aircraft that attempted to dogfight with it. The report was disbelieved and shelved. It would take the shock of Pearl Harbor and its aftermath to convince the rest of the world that Chennault was correct.

Chennault's pilots were all volunteers – mainly retired US army and navy pilots – lured to China by the astonishingly high wages offered by the desperate Chinese Nationalist government to assist in their losing war against the invading Japanese. Most had been trained in classic First World War dogfighting, and the first thing that Chennault told them upon their arrival was to forget everything they had learned. The only way to combat these new Japanese aircraft and their extraordinarily skilled pilots, he told his men, was to get above them, then, using the P-40's superior firepower and diving speed, plummet down on them in a slashing attack, then climb back up and do it again. Chennault's manoeuvre would likewise become 75 Squadron's mantra.

In the end, Chennault's pilots did not have to confront the Zero, as it was withdrawn from China by the time the AVG began operating a couple of weeks after Pearl Harbor. It would be over Burma encountering Japanese 'Nate' and 'Oscar' fighters that the American Volunteer Group did much of its fighting, but the principle of Chennault's 'dive and zoom' tactic was sound.

Arthur Tucker believed that John Jackson had seen, or was at least aware of, Chennault's suppressed report, and espoused it to his own men. It was Tucker's understanding that when being fired at from a Zero from behind, and 'those flaming cricket balls' – the Japanese tracer and cannon

– started appearing around your head, 'you just jammed everything into one corner and bunted away'. Whenever it could be achieved, 'dive and zoom' became 75 Squadron's standard practice. Later, when, for spurious reasons, the higher authorities in the RAAF ordered a change of tactics, the results were disastrous.

•

75 Squadron had begun the 44-day campaign well, with a surprise attack on the Japanese that destroyed a considerable number of their aircraft and put them on notice that invading Port Moresby was not to be the walkover they were expecting. After that first day of 75's deployment, much of the arrogance displayed by the Japanese pilots ceased. There were no more cocky displays of aerobatics by the Zero pilots over Moresby Harbour, nor imperiously unescorted bombing raids in which the pilots made some dummy runs over the target before dropping their bombs. From now on, the gunners aboard the Betty bombers would be nervous and on the lookout for these daring Australian pilots in their brutally armed machines. The Japanese formations also flew higher, around the more protective 20,000 feet mark, which drastically affected the accuracy of their bombing. For both sides, it would be a long and difficult battle.

Tuesday 24 March was a busy day for the squadron. Still stunned by what had happened at their aerodrome at Lae, and having failed to deliver any sort of knockout blow in retaliation the following day, the Japanese sent over another reconnaissance bomber, similar to the one shot down by Barry Cox and the now absent Wilbur Wackett on the first afternoon, to get some sort of idea of this new force they were up against. And in a similar scenario, the pilot of this aircraft showed no awareness he was being stalked until it was too late. Scrambled to the intercept, John Piper was still 5000 feet below the Japanese aircraft when he noticed it, but kept his distance, stalking cautiously. Thinking he'd maintained surprise, Piper was about to fire when the Japanese aircraft began turning towards him. He fired hurriedly, and missed. Hurtling past, he fired wildly again, as a stream of tracer spat out from the Japanese aircraft, missing him slightly below. Only on his third burst did Piper notice a small fire start in the bomber's port wing tank, before the plane began to roll uncontrollably. Two bombs were jettisoned, then the aircraft, like its predecessor, turned over onto its back and crashed into the sea. 'I was lucky,' said Piper years later. 'It was on its own, and I was on my own.' A couple of days later, he would be 'lucky' again.

Whether or not the Japanese recce aircraft was able to get a signal off before it was shot down, at mid-morning the squadron operations tent received word of a large incoming formation: more than a dozen bombers escorted by three Zeros were heading towards Seven Mile Strip to revisit the work started a couple of days previously. Only two machines could be scrambled in time to meet them, piloted by Ron Bailey and Les Jackson. The way the two groups of aircraft were positioned, there would only be a chance for one pass, and the confrontation would be head-on.

Somewhere in the confusion, Ron Bailey became separated from Les Jackson and failed to make contact with the enemy, leaving Les to take them on by himself. He was undaunted; displaying his characteristic courage to the point of recklessness, he faced three Zeros, closing towards them at astonishing speed. Firing his guns, trying to spray his bullets across them as best he could and particularly keen to find the Zero's undefended windshield, Les felt a jolt as bullets hit his wing. The Japanese formation passed in a flash. For his trouble, an aircraft was seen to plough into the jungle below. His action was no doubt a contribution to the Japanese bombing inaccurately that day, which scattered wide, doing little damage to Seven Mile Strip. This, thankfully, was often the case, due to the inaccuracy of Japanese bombing from the unfamiliar high altitude, as well as their G4M Betty bomber's modest bomb load of less than 2000 pounds (the Kittyhawk itself was rated to carry more than that in one of its later incarnations as a dive bomber, though it seldom did).

The Kittyhawk had an overall advantage over Japanese aircraft when employed in the 'dive and zoom' technique, but it was of little use without the advantage of height needed to execute it. As the pilots of 75 soon found, too often it was the Zeros that were 'diving and zooming' onto them. There was simply not enough warning given of an incoming Japanese raid for the pilots to get above their enemy, and as they raced for their Kittyhawks, the pilots knew that most of the time they were taking off into a position of considerable disadvantage. This was precisely the scenario that faced John Piper and his wingman Ron Bailey when, on the afternoon of 28 March, they heard the yell, 'It's on!', and scrambled to intercept five enemy aircraft bound for Port Moresby at 10,000 feet.

It had been a very eventful week for John Piper. Just the day before he, Jeff 'Pop' Woods and Ron O'Connor had been flying a standing patrol at 4000 feet when they encountered a formation of Zeros carrying out a similar exercise of their own, 30 miles east of Moresby. Woods had been able to get above the Zeros and zoomed down to attack. However, he then became aware of another Zero directly above and behind him and, in a tight 90-degree turn, attempted to manoeuvre to face his attacker. He was then confronted with the sight of two others he had missed, which then unleashed long-range bursts of cannon and machine-gun fire, puncturing Woods' Kittyhawk and wrecking his radio set before he could escape to the sanctuary of a cloud. When he emerged, the sky was empty, with no sign of his wingman, Ron O'Connor. Climbing again to 10,000 feet, Woods noticed a parachute a couple of thousand feet below him and a small fire in the jungle, which he presumed – correctly – to be O'Connor and his shot-down aircraft.

While this had been happening, John Piper and Ron Bailey went for a formation of bombers, managing to get up to 12,000 feet before attacking one of them. It took two passes, but on the second, Piper's guns hit the Betty's port motor, which burst into flame. Bailey then went for the starboard before the enemy dived for cloud cover. It crashed in flames to the jungle floor just east of Port Moresby. A few days later, a search party located the wreck, finding all eight dead Japanese crewmen onboard, and souveniring one of the bomber's 20-millimetre cannons. Between them, Piper and Bailey had accounted for a Japanese bomber.

Once again, the Japanese raid had failed to make an impact. Twelve bombs had been strewn across Seven Mile, but not a single parked aircraft had been hit.

Later that day, Pop Woods flew a search flight to try to locate O'Connor and his Kittyhawk, but it had been swallowed by the vast jungle. A patrol from the 39th Militia Battalion – soon to make a name for itself on the Kokoda Track – set out to search for him in the vicinity of nearby Mount Lawes, but found nothing but a wooden drop tank discarded from a Zero. Ron O'Connor, the sole survivor of those pilots who had come to grief on that disastrous ferry flight from Bankstown, had not survived his first week of combat.

A few weeks later, an RAAF corporal reported he had seen a Zero circling a parachute on that day, and had heard the ominous sound of machine-gun fire as it passed close by the descending pilot. Technically listed as 'missing', Ron O'Connor's grieving mother clung to the forlorn hope that he may be alive somewhere up until her death in 1968. Her son remained her sole beneficiary, and the Air Board was required to confirm his death before her affairs could be settled.

•

John Piper was taking off again – once more with Ron Bailey, Pop Woods and, in O'Connor's place, the very green Oswald 'Ozzie' Channon – rushing into the skies to meet another formation, this time approaching from the northwest over Redscar Bay. John Jackson was set to join them as well, to make it a force of five, but had misjudged a runway edge while guiding his aircraft to taxi – the Kittyhawk was notoriously hard to steer when on the ground – and, cursing with fury, bogged himself. Piper would have to go into the attack without his boss.

Ten miles in the distance, Piper spotted the Japanese: three Bettys in a loose V formation 8000 feet above. He willed his heavy aircraft to climb faster to meet them. Eventually, at 16,000 feet, he and Bailey were in position to attack from the less-than-ideal position of slightly below and to the side, and manoeuvred to fire. Suddenly, orange balls of tracer shot past his head. In a classic 'out of the sun' swoop, the bomber's top cover had dived onto the Kittyhawks, the two Zeros unseen by anyone but Channon who, due to faultly radio sets, was not able to warn the others. Piper felt his aircraft hit in several places but could not tell where. It was an amazing piece of deflection shooting from the skilled Japanese pilot, who was in an almost impossible shooting position – directly above his prey. Desperately, Piper wrenched his aircraft around to meet his attackers, but the big Kittyhawk dipped a wing and spiralled into a spin, losing contact with friend and foe alike.

Channon took up the attack, but in his inexperience, flew straight at the leading Japanese fighter and two of them opened fire as he closed the range. Avoiding their machine guns by yawing his aircraft into a side-slip, Channon noted another Zero below, right on the tail of a fellow Kittyhawk, and dived down to assist. The unwary Japanese aircraft seemed to pass right across Channon's gunsight as he rode the firing button but as he strained to see the effect, he too was suddenly under attack from behind, as the wingman of the Zero he had attacked a moment ago now jumped him. Bullets ripped into his rudder and elevator, then into his cockpit, one 7.9-millimetre round passing through his wrist. Instinctively, he jammed stick, rudder, everything, into a right-hand bunt and the Kittyhawk lurched suddenly over and fell away. Making it back to Moresby without further attention from the Zeros, Channon noted with dismay that his flaps could not be lowered as he approached the strip at Seven Mile. The Kittyhawk, he knew, landed at a high enough speed at the best of times, but without flaps, it could be perilous. In a testament to the aircraft's handling capabilities, not to mention Ozzie Channon's skill, he made a perfect landing.

John Piper also survived the encounter unscathed with only minor damage to his aircraft, but like the previous day, one of 75's rank was missing. When recovering from his dive, Piper had noticed a Kittyhawk plunging away, a Zero close on its tail. Some Papuan villagers later reported such an aircraft falling to the ground in a flat spin, and a search was again mounted, but as was the case with O'Connor, Sergeant Ron Bailey was never found. His aircraft was located three weeks later in a swamp, and a roundel cut from it and returned to the squadron in remembrance. Recently married and a champion footballer, Ron Bailey was just 21.

It had been a bad day for 75 Squadron. Another Kittyhawk lost along with its pilot, and all four of their attacking aircraft had suffered varying degrees of damage without being able to press home any attack against the Japanese. The escorting Zeros had carried out their tasks well, defending the bombers by dividing, isolating and then attacking the Australian aircraft in pairs.

By the end of the month, 75 Squadron had lost eleven aircraft: four to combat, four to ground strafing and three in accidents. Its strength was down to just five serviceable fighters. Also on this day, however, six replacement Kittyhawks left Townsville for Port Moresby, escorted by a Hudson bomber.

The crux of the problem for 75 Squadron throughout the campaign was proving to be time – time to gain height against their enemy and time to bring their 'dive and zoom' tactic to bear. As the pilots were discovering, there simply wasn't enough of it.

CHAPTER 9

Observation

Two years earlier, radar had been a crucial factor in deciding the outcome of the Battle of Britain. Time and again, the German airmen were dumbfounded at being met on the approach to their target by Spitfires and Hurricanes whose pilots seemed to possess a sixth sense in knowing exactly where they would be. Far from any supernatural power, the advent of radar gave the defenders the height, direction and rough numbers of the enemy they would be facing. Radar works most effectively when, like in Britain, there was nothing between you and your approaching enemy save a wide flat sea, but in New Guinea, 75 Squadron's early warning system had a particularly high range of mountains to contend with, the Owen Stanleys. And this was only one of their problems.

The RAAF's 29 Radar Station was the first such unit deployed outside mainland Australia, and the problems they had to contend with established this group of four radar mechanics and eight operators as pioneers in the true spirit of the word. Arriving at Seven Mile Strip the same day Darwin was bombed, 19 February, the official history described their subsequent tenure at Moresby as 'a constant struggle to exist'. Billeted in the town, the equipment they needed took an eternity to unload as the ship was required to leave the port during the day to avoid Japanese air raids. Then, due to either incompetence or the prevailing atmosphere of wartime secrecy, they found few of their crates had been labelled, or had been labelled incorrectly, making the task of finding anything in a hurry virtually impossible. One particularly irksome omission was anything resembling cooking equipment, which emerged as an egregious problem when taking up their assigned lodgings in Murray Barracks, as no-one was prepared to feed them. Nor, for that matter, was there any power, water, guards or sanitation.

Taking matters into their own hands, the radar men simply salvaged what they could from the virtually abandoned town, helped themselves to government stores without seeking permission, and made a connection to the live 240-volt power lines that ran overhead alongside the main road.

The agreed site for Seven Mile's radar, King Spur, rose 690 feet above sea level, two miles east of Moresby. Everything had to be done from scratch. Army engineers assisted in laying a concrete slab, but each piece of equipment had to hauled or winched up. No suitable transmission wire to carry the heavy current was available either, so the men resorted to stringing hundreds of feet of bare wire all the way up to the spur, supported by convenient trees. On one occasion, when some of those trees gave way, the radar's turning gear was nearly lost. It was then found that the town's mains supply could not cope with the equipment's load, leading to erratic power and damage to the components. Scrounging around the docks, the ever-resourceful radar men managed to purloin a dismantled power unit, which they put back together and somehow got working. However, when they turned on the big rotating radar aerial, the voltage dropped from 240 to 180. Giving up, the men reverted to rotating the aerial by hand. The power supply issue wasn't properly solved until the end of 1943. By whatever means they managed it, 29 Radar Station was on the air by 18 March, not long before 75 Squadron's arrival.

But setting up the station was only the beginning of more troubles. Air raids were a continual menace and slit trenches – covered over as protection from falling anti-aircraft shrapnel – were shared with millions of mosquitoes. The operators also realised that the set that had been rushed up to them in New Guinea was one of six experimental pre-production models, with which they had no operational experience and about which the mechanics knew very little. But much of the efficiency of radar at Seven Mile was moot, as from the north – the direction of almost all Japanese air attacks on Moresby and its airstrip – it was largely ineffective, due to the insurmountable barrier of the 14,000 foot mountains. Visual warning, it was decided, was the only means of at least attempting to give 75's pilots the time they needed to get above their enemy when they appeared.

It was recommended therefore that a series of observation posts be established along a series of concentric rings emanating from Port Moresby at intervals of 30, 60 and 100 miles. A Royal Australian Engineers officer, Major Donald Small, then established the New Guinea Air Warning Wireless Company, comprising 37 army signals volunteers drawn primarily from the 39th Battalion, then stationed at Moresby. Like almost every aspect of the nation's defensive efforts at this time, the formation of this group was rushed. The small teams were intended to be supplied with binoculars, aircraft identification material, a petrol generator and supplies to last a couple of months. In reality, the men often struggled to master Morse code. Their medical supplies consisted of little more than a 'beer bottle filled with liquid quinine' and they needed to forage and trade with locals to survive after their supplies quickly ran out. The depth of cover that would have been given by the manning of concentric rings was never achieved, the under-equipped and inadequately trained men instead being scattered mainly along the New Guinea northern coast in a line running west to east. Some posts were established further inland, but there were vast gaps through which the Japanese air fleets could pass, appearing over Port Moresby virtually undetected. Even in ideal situations, the outer post, at a distance of 100 miles – perilously close to the Japanese bases of Lae and Salamaua themselves – could only give the pilots back at Seven Mile a 30-minute warning, usually closer to twenty, barely enough time for them to scramble, gain height and meet their enemy on even terms.

This was the best that could be managed, and between the information gathered from the radar and the reports from the observers sending their frantic signals over open radio with the sound of Japanese aircraft already above them in the background, a system of sorts, evolved.

•

Number 4 Fighter Sector was formed about the same time as 29 Radar Station, its purpose being to coordinate the various elements of incoming information from Australian, and some American, radar stations, coast watchers and army observation posts, and guide the pilots of 75 Squadron to the interception of the enemy. Its various elements were spread over a wide area around Moresby, camouflaged and concealed from the air as well as they could be. It was based on the system that had worked brilliantly in the Battle of Britain, so what better person to run it than an Australian officer who had done just that with the RAF during that epic battle?

Brisbane-born Wing Commander G E Sampson had commanded an RAF Spitfire squadron earlier in the war, then worked as a fighter controller during the Battle of Britain. Brought back to Australia and charged with getting a similar team up to speed to face his own country's emergency, he would discover that Port Moresby was a far cry from the luxuriously organised structures of southern England, where there was a proper plotting room and table to mark out the positions of friend and enemy. Wireless Operator Mechanic Leigh Hoey, who served for seventeen months with 4 Fighter Sector, recalled, 'The receiver room was a small building constructed of galvanised iron on a small hill and set up so that we could work with lights on during air raids. There we operated AR7 receivers (one had a bullet hole from earlier action) while the transmitters were dispersed in huts protected by bunkers.'

Out at Seven Mile Strip, the set-up was even more primitive. When 75 arrived in March, the Fighter Sector was simply a tent at the west end of the strip with some telephones linked to a cave that had been discovered and enlarged in the side of a nearby hill overlooking the aerodrome. An RAF air commodore, S F Vincent, who was advising on fighter defence, stated in a report on Seven Mile Strip: 'there is, at present, only a very crude form of control in operation for the fighters'. He went on to detail a scene that would almost be comical but for the deadly seriousness of the context.

As Vincent observed, the fighter controller system at Seven Mile Strip operated via three phone lines running from its cave above the airstrip. The three lines – one back to Moresby, one to the airstrip operations tent and another to the ack-ack (anti-aircraft) batteries – ran across open ground or through the scrub. Unlike in England, there was no plotting table, nor any other visual representation of the information being received from the radar stations or observers, just a few battered tables and a bank of incessantly ringing telephones. As soon as information was received, a clerk would write it down in a log book then pick up a receiver and relay it to another phone nailed to a wooden pole next to the standby strip, where someone – usually Stu Collie – would pick it up, yell, 'It's on' and get the pilots airborne. From this point, it was even more bizarre, as Vincent described:

> The controller stays at the entrance to the tunnel until enemy aircraft are heard overhead and endeavours to control the fighters by R/T [radio telephone] from visual observation, and this method is frequently successful, although obviously, at times, clouds or distance prevent it, and the interception is left to the fighters. There is only one entrance to this tunnel and the ventilation is bad, and the danger of a direct hit from a bomb in the only entrance is a real one.

Added to this was the unreliability of the Kittyhawk's AT5/AR8 radios. The sets frequently broke down or were damaged, and with only two radio technicians to service all the radio equipment for the whole squadron, the fragile valve sets often didn't work at all. When they did, according to John Piper, there was often so much background noise it was difficult to hear anything anyway. Strangely, the pilots would often pick up the conversation of the enemy better than their own side. 'We didn't do much good with our own system,' he recalled, 'because we had a controller, an Englishman, who ran the control from a little hut. We could see him mainly but we couldn't hear him. We'd get Tokyo flat out but nothing happening from our local bloke at all.' The range of the pilots' sets was 30 miles, which meant that they were only good for the immediate vicinity of Moresby. When 75 took the offensive to the Japanese at Lae or Salamaua, there was limited communication between the pilots, and none back to the airstrip whatsoever. More often than not, the pilots would forget about their radios altogether, communicating instead in the same manner as the pilots of the First World War, via hand signals and wing waggles.

With radar intermittently useful, and blind to the vital direction of north in any case, the fighter controllers of Port Moresby came to rely more and more on the network of observers stationed at their lonely jungle vigils to give them warning of the Japanese approach. One of these men stands out: the quiet, unassuming, yet utterly heroic figure of Leigh Grant Vial.

The eldest of four sons born in 1909 to a comfortable middle-class family in the old Melbourne suburb of Camberwell, Leigh Vial was educated at Wesley College, then took up a commerce degree at the University of Melbourne. In 1932, for some extraordinary reason, Vial decided to apply as a cadet patrol officer in the Mandated Territory of New Guinea. Chosen from 1659 applicants, he was assessed as 'stocky, self-reliant, quiet' and, in June 1933, was sent to the Morobe District on New Guinea's north coast, incorporating the settlements of Lae and Salamaua. In 1936, he married a colonialist's daughter soon after his promotion to patrol officer. One might pity the young bride chosen by Leigh Vial. He was rarely at home, patrolling deep into the jungle for months on end, even penning articles on the many native peoples he came to know for periodicals such as *Walkabout* and *Oceania*.

When war came in 1939, Vial was approached by a fellow former patrol officer, Lieutenant Commander Eric Feldt. Feldt had been pulled out of retirement from the navy to set up the New Guinea Coastwatcher system, an observation network operating along similar lines to the army's New Guinea Air Warning Wireless Company. Japan, they knew, would sooner or later enter the war, and when it did, men like Vial would be greatly needed. Vial was the perfect candidate, but needed to be inducted into the armed forces. Feldt knew only too well the slowness of the navy system in acquiring for him the necessary commission, so instead pulled strings for Vial to join the RAAF, with the rank of pilot officer.

In early 1942, hauling his heavy teleradio set and accompanied by two locals, Vial headed into the jungle, and on 28 February, his 33rd birthday, began transmitting from an observation post he had constructed looking northeast over Salamaua and Lae. Vial was careful in his choice of location, later advising other observers that posts should be positioned in terrain that would confuse radio direction-finders, have well-concealed lines of withdrawal, offer cloud-free views and a good water supply. It was the perfect position to detect Japanese air movements, as many of their bombers took off from Rabaul, meeting their Zero escort in the sky before heading to Moresby.

Vial's presence during the 44 days was inspirational. Up to nine times a day, he broadcast details of weather, Japanese shipping and aircraft movements in clear, authoritative tones, and his identification moniker of 'Golden Voice' soon became legendary to the Australian, and later the American, forces in New Guinea. He lived almost entirely on yams, taro and nuts from the okari tree, occasionally snaring for himself a cuscus or tree kangaroo.

The Japanese became obsessed with Vial, tormented daily by his open-voice broadcasts, but were unable to find him, despite numerous close calls. Ted Church heard that 'Twice he escaped by remaining motionless in the fork of a tree infested with stinging green ants while a Jap patrol passed below.' The Japanese attempted to bribe local villagers to betray him, but Golden Voice Vial stuck at his solitary post in the dank jungle, constantly wet, beset by leeches and mosquitoes, at times suffering tinea so badly that he had to crawl to his set to crank it up and broadcast.

At one stage he suddenly went silent, and the men at Moresby feared the worst. Ten days later, a local appeared with a letter from Vial requesting radio valves to replace some that had failed. Another ten days later, Vial was back on the air.

Eventually he was moved, not further from danger but virtually overlooking Salamaua to get under the cloud cover and improve his view. It was extremely dangerous, but still the Japanese failed to find him, despite giving him a scare 'about once a week'. In the end, bad food, isolation and the blinding effect of constantly using binoculars saw Vial relieved of his post in August 1942. For two days he walked back through the jungle to Wau, then on to Moresby. His intelligence officer reported that with the exception of the time his equipment failed, 'not on any single occasion did he neglect to get his messages through'.

After writing a book on jungle survival, Vial perished in late 1943 in one of the many air accidents that were a feature of the New Guinea campaign, when the B-24 Liberator he was in crashed into the jungle, killing all on board. For his 'extraordinary heroism' he was awarded the United States' Distinguished Service Cross, that country's second highest bravery decoration and its highest for non-citizens. Curiously, however, his own country overlooked him.

Michael Butler at least appreciated the value of Vial's work. 'That fellow saved so many lives...he should have been given every decoration that was ever made,' he said after the war.

•

Late on the morning of 31 March, one of the more peculiar episodes of the campaign to involve the wireless operators of

75 Squadron occurred, when they intercepted and translated an odd series of signals from a Japanese aircraft to its base. The first began, 'Finished bombing. All bombs hit mark.' This in itself would not have been unusual, but for the fact that, over Seven Mile that morning, the skies had remained clear with not an enemy aircraft in sight. A little later however, at 10,000 feet, a lone Mitsubishi type-96 'Nell' bomber appeared, having approached unobserved. Watching its progress across the patchily cloudy sky were John Pettett and Peter Turnbull, who were off duty and down beside the strip. The bomber seemed to be making no indications of wanting to attack, so it was assumed it was heading back to Lae, having dropped its load somewhere else.

Somewhat irked by the prospect of the Japanese bomber heading safely back home without being so much as challenged, Peter Turnbull grabbed a stick, or possibly even a machete, pointed it with both arms extended in the direction of the aircraft, and 'went into a high-stepping, hard-stamping dance accompanied by incantations of the "Hi Booga Loo Booga Boo" variety,' John Pettett recalled. 'Pete Turnbull was a country boy – stockman, horseman, cattleman and a man with a great sense of humour...he also gave one the impression that he admired, respected and understood the Australian Aborigine.'

The aircraft immediately flew into a cumulus cloud over Waigani, but its disappearance did nothing to quell Squadron Leader Turnbull's performance. 'Within twenty seconds, we heard an explosion,' said Pettett, 'and pieces of aircraft began to fall through the cloud. I will never forget the look on Pete Turnbull's face. For one short moment, he was dumbfounded, but being the character he was, he recovered and, turning to us ordinary blokes, exclaimed, "Got the bugger!"'

At the crash site, seven Japanese bodies were discovered. A number of the squadron had watched the bomber enter the cloud, followed seconds later by the sounds of snapping metal, then, without a shot having been fired towards it or a fighter scrambled, saw it emerge, spinning out of the cloud base, its severed wing fluttering down like a leaf after the fuselage, its bombs detaching as it disintegrated. Looking at the wreckage, the men could only shake their heads, no-one more so than the man who had 'pointed the bone', Squadron Leader Turnbull.

The truth of the story, discovered years after the war, is no less strange. On 12 December the previous year, this Japanese crew had been involved in an attack on Clark Field, the American base in the Philippines, when their aircraft was hit by anti-aircraft fire in the left engine and crash landed. The crew survived and were captured. Their superiors posted them as 'missing' and, in accordance with Japanese tradition, each man was awarded a one-rank promotion.

Shortly thereafter, the Philippines fell to the Japanese and the men were liberated from an American prison compound. Having been steeled in the Japanese code of 'no surrender', their commander was aghast when this previously written-off crew turned up like a bad penny, complete with their recently awarded promotions. To prevent the supposed infection of cowardice, the men were segregated from the rest of the squadron – now based at Rabaul and operating over Port Moresby – and immediately sent on bombing raids against the Australians, their aircraft placed in the most vulnerable position to fighter attack. But they just kept coming back.

The situation eventually became intolerable, and Admiral Takijirō Ōnishi, who later distinguished himself as the 'father of the Kamikaze', issued an order that the bomber crew was to fly over Port Moresby alone, with no escort and explicit instructions of 'do not return'.

The reason for the crash, however, remains something of a mystery. Some speculated that the pilot deliberately flew into the cumulus to be torn apart by its notorious updraughts, but the weather that morning was not severe enough for this to occur. He may have twisted the controls in a particularly violent manoeuvre, but whether this could have snapped a wing is unclear. It's possible the aircraft may have been sabotaged, but the mystery will most likely never be solved.

The second radio message intercepted by the Australian wireless operators at Moresby fifteen minutes after the first reportedly laid clear the bomber's intentions: 'We will go in. All around is clear. Thank you for your kindnesses during our lifetime. Banzai for the Emperor.'

The men who died that day had the dubious honour of possibly being the first Kamikaze mission of the Second World War.

CHAPTER 10

The coming of the Americans

At the beginning of April, the Americans began to arrive, just as the Japanese extended their reach into the southwest Pacific, with particular attention now being paid to a troublesome airstrip seven miles from Port Moresby.

Though quick to get into the war after the shock of the Pearl Harbor attack in December, distances and logistics hampered the US Army Air Corp's initial deployment of air power to New Guinea, the only place left from which they could strike at their enemy after the lightning-fast Japanese advance across the Pacific. The first to arrive in Australia was the US Army Air Corp's 3rd Bombardment Group, consisting of four separate squadrons, one of which, the 8th Bombardment Squadron, arrived at Port Moresby on the last day of March.

Initially earmarked for the defence of the Philippines, the 3rd Bombardment Group sailed from San Francisco in the army transport *Ancon* in January 1942. But when the Philippines campaign – in reality a rout – went from bad to worse, they continued south and disembarked instead at Brisbane on 25 February, awarding the 3rd Bombardment Group the distinction of being the first US troops of the Second World War to arrive in Australia. The glow of attention from the Australian media was short-lived, however, as the men soon found themselves a long way from Brisbane – or anywhere else for that matter – on a large and lonely airstrip in Charters Towers, to the southwest of Townsville.

The young Americans probably should have been grateful, as being hurled into the maw of the Philippines would almost certainly have spelled their demise, and perhaps they would not have minded the isolation of Charters Towers if there was something there for them to do. Unfortunately much of their equipment, including their aircraft, had not yet arrived. Their ground crew were quickly snatched by other arriving squadrons, but the pilots could do little except admire what scenery there was and wait.

When their aircraft did turn up, they were found to be missing guns and other essentials, but after much frustration, by the end of March, the 8th Bombardment Squadron was ready to deploy to Port Moresby to take their fight to the Japanese in a dive-bombing campaign against their installations along New Guinea's northern coast.

The 8th was equipped, however, with a true 'Jekyll and Hyde' aircraft in the Douglas SBD Dauntless. Later, at places like the Coral Sea and Midway, this single-engine observation/dive bomber became famous as a carrier-based ship-attacker, but on land it was utterly woeful. Operating in this incarnation as the A-24 Banshee, it was slow, underpowered and, without fighter escort, suffered terrible losses against ground defences and Zeros, ensuring its career as a land-based aeroplane was brief.

The 8th's troubles started early. On 31 March, under the command of their leader, Captain Floyd Rogers, thirteen Dauntlesses left Charters Towers for Moresby via Cooktown and Horn Island. Here, three of them started guzzling dangerous amounts of oil and had to turn back to Cooktown, while two others became bogged in mud. The rest took a chance and set out on the 430-mile hop to Moresby. Someone, however, neglected to give the Americans a brief on local time zones, and as the sun went down, the pilots realised they would be landing at Seven Mile, an aerodrome they had never set eyes on, in the dark.

With fuel running low, they circled the airstrip, barely able to make out the runway's 'flare path' – a straggling line of hastily placed hurricane lamps – but just after nine o'clock, they came in. At this point it became apparent that another piece of information had not been passed on to the Americans: that some 300 yards of the runway they were now approaching was still under construction.

The first pilot touched down in the centre of the tarmac, but his relief in having actually found the place was quickly dashed by the sight of a large piece of construction equipment looming out of the gloom directly in front of him. He slammed into it, wrecking his aircraft's mainplane. The second Dauntless was following close behind and crashed into him. Both aircraft were written off, although the pilots and gunners were not injured. Several other arriving aircraft swung into violent ground loops on the unfamiliar airstrip. It was almost an arrival as inauspicious as 75 Squadron's. From starting off with thirteen aircraft, Captain Rogers was now down to just six.

It could, however, have been disastrous – due to shipping limitations, the Americans had been required to ferry their own 500-pound bombs all the way from Australia, then land with them in their racks under the fuselage. This virtually unheard-of practice, which could easily result in the untimely detonation of bomb, tanks and aircraft, was under normal circumstances forbidden.

Frayed nerves or not, the very next morning, those six A-24s were in action, flying with 75 Squadron on a bombing mission once again to the Japanese airstrip at Lae. Taking off at six am and meeting up with the Kittyhawks fifteen minutes later, the Australian pilots must have been warmed by the idea that, along with their own machine guns, bombs were now part of their arsenal against the Japanese. But their efforts over Lae were thwarted by low cloud, so the aircraft instead turned their attention to the Japanese secondary airstrip at Salamaua. This was used primarily as a refuelling point, and no aircraft were sighted, but the dive bombers attacked anyway, landing five of their large bombs perfectly along the Japanese runway, blowing apart some buildings and setting others on fire.

Without even being challenged by the Japanese, all aircraft made it back safely on this spectacular start to the Americans' tenure at Seven Mile, but the euphoria would not last. Tropical diseases soon began to exact a toll on the American airmen and their ground staff. One of the first casualties was Captain Rogers, and soon a long line of men were evacuated back to Townsville suffering dengue fever. Their aircraft too, were proving unsuitable to the conditions, and the American mechanics cried out for proper machine shops and maintenance facilities that would never arrive. The Australian crews could only shake their heads and concur, having had to put up with this already for more than a week.

There were several more successes with the American dive-bombers. On 7 April, the combined squadrons set off to once again attack Lae, this time appearing just above the Japanese airstrip at dawn, catching a combined force of Japanese bombers and fighters preparing to embark on a similar attack on Seven Mile. Seven 500-pound bombs and over a dozen incendiaries were dropped with great accuracy and nine aircraft were caught on the ground, including five Zeros, destroyed just as they were refuelling. Several bombers were also claimed as damaged and one Zero pilot fell victim to the A-24's rear-gunner. Another American bomber claimed a Zero destroyed on their way out for the loss of one American aircraft that crash landed, the crew of two captured and later executed by the Japanese.

But with long periods of downtime, and a rotating sick list of personnel, the 8th's morale suffered badly. It hung on at Seven Mile for several weeks after the 44-day period, until one catastrophic attack in July when seven of its aircraft set off to find an eight-ship Japanese convoy 50 miles off Buna, along New Guinea's north coast. The US Airacobras detailed to escort the bombers became lost over the Owen Stanleys, but Captain Rogers elected to press on. The squad was pounced upon by over twenty Zeros and all but destroyed, with only one aircraft making it back to Seven Mile, badly damaged. The 8th Bombardment Squadron had had enough and was withdrawn, its aircraft deemed unsuitable for land-based use without escort.

The Japanese were busy in early April too. Despite 75's daring and success in at least denting some of Japan's previously unstoppable ambitions, on 7 April, the same day as the Americans' successful attack on Lae, they seized Buin, a strategically important village on the southern tip of Bougainville, then Lorengau on Manus Island, extending their ring of control across the Bismarck Sea.

Over on Rabaul, Japanese reinforcements were also arriving, to deal once and for all with this meddling group of Australian airmen in Port Moresby flying their lumbering, clearly inferior machines. Japan was now preparing to introduce to the battle for New Guinea the finest, most experienced airmen of the Imperial Japanese Navy, the already famous Tainan Kokutai, the Tainan Air Group. As Arthur Tucker put it, 'the people we were to find in Moresby were some of their very top men'.

CHAPTER 11

The Jacksons

With American air power starting to make its presence felt in New Guinea, one afternoon in late March, Les Jackson found himself at 18,000 feet protecting the arrival of a B-17 Flying Fortress four-engine bomber. It had been a frustrating morning; he had taken the early patrol, then at nine-thirty was scrambled to make contact with reported enemy aircraft, which they failed to find. Now he sighted below him two Zeros turning to attack the Fortress and he put his Kittyhawk into a steep dive to assist. Descending from such a height, the dramatic shift in temperature in the warm tropics caused his windshield and canopy to fog up, and in a few seconds he was completely blind, hurtling towards the ground at tremendous speed.

As he wound his canopy back to let in air, he nearly rammed an enemy aircraft, then turned in a half-circle as he struggled to see ahead of him. Behind him, suddenly, was a Zero, which he twisted and turned to evade. Their attack on the Fortress had been thwarted, but when Les returned to Seven Mile, a quick inspection of his aircraft revealed that the radio aerial mast on the back of his fuselage had been torn away.

Les Jackson, John's younger brother, was already establishing for himself a reputation as a true character of the squadron. An excellent pilot, and undoubtedly courageous, he frequently led head-on attacks against Zeros in which he seemed completely devoid of fear. During a fierce engagement on 6 April, seven Japanese bombers and their fighter escort were engaged over Moresby by nine Kittyhawks and two Airacobras of the visiting 36th Pursuit Squadron. Five of these problematic American aircraft – described by author Peter Ewer as 'the most exotic operational fighter to fly in World War II' – had arrived the day before, as had seven sorely needed replacement Kittyhawks, which had come up from Townsville. 75 was therefore able to meet the Japanese in strength. Just as well, as the Zero pilots this day defended savagely, falling on the Australians from height as they attempted to attack the bombers. Making things even more difficult, the Bettys now flew in 'steps' in order to maximise the defensive power of their machine guns and cannon.

The Americans had been able to gain height with their lighter Airacobras, deploying this aircraft type for the first time in the southwest Pacific theatre, attacking the bombers from 24,000 feet. However, when they attempted to fire their enormous 37-millimetre cannon – so large that the Airacobra's engine had to be positioned behind the pilot to make room for it firing through the propeller hub – they found their much-vaunted 'one-shot' bomber-destroying weapon resorted instead to its usual habit of jamming up immediately due to a faulty breech mechanism.

Ozzie Channon and Peter Masters, again without the luxury of height, made climbing attacks on the bombers but came under withering fire from the Japanese gunners shooting from the Bettys' defensive blister positions. Masters saw tracer hurtling past his cockpit and dived away to safety. Channon too had a fighter on his tail.

John Pettett was already struggling with an oil weeper valve that was seeping onto his windshield, partially obscuring his view, but he managed to line up a bomber. Just as he was about to fire, he heard a terrible thump somewhere behind him and his aircraft was thrown into a spin. He managed to get out of it, but then found he was alone. 'I didn't know where the squadron was, they were gone. I was flying number two to John Jackson, I think, and I could hear him calling but I didn't know where he was. But when I looked back it was like a can opener had been through the leading edge of the tailplane on the starboard side.'

Not knowing the true extent of the damage, Pettett gingerly manoeuvred his aircraft, first turning one way, then a little more steeply the other. To his relief, the robust construction of the Kittyhawk was living up to its reputation and the aircraft appeared to be flying along quite well despite the damaged tail. 'It didn't make much difference – I couldn't say that it made any difference actually. I did some steep turns and lifted the nose and dipped the nose. I didn't do anything terribly violent!'

But half blinded by an oily windscreen, all alone with the enemy somewhere in these same skies, Pettett felt particularly vulnerable.

> The first thing to do is to find out where Moresby was and I was almost right over it. Having levelled out and seeing the damage, I then started working out whether I should stay up with the cloud, just in case the Zeros who had been accompanying these bombers had chased me down...the imagination can take over and when you are on your own you think you are the only person in the world.

Despite a tailplane that appeared to be 'busted open', Pettett landed safely. Inspecting the damage close up, he was amazed that it seemed to be the result of a single explosive shell. When he mentioned the oil leak at the debrief, he was angrily asked why he didn't engage the hand pump, designed to squirt away just such a mess. 'I don't think they believed me when I said I'd never heard of it,' he later said.

Another pilot who found himself in trouble that day was Flying Officer Edmund Johnson. He too had made a climbing quarter attack on a bomber but was also fired upon almost immediately by a Zero at his rear. His engine began to falter, then finally gave out 2000 feet above the ground. Looking around for somewhere to put his crippled aircraft down, he decided on a swamp some fifteen miles from Moresby, into which he made a reasonable wheels-up landing. Racing from the cockpit as it began to smoke, he waited for it to explode but after 30 minutes, the fire, to his relief, petered out. A further adventure awaited when locals challenged him with knives, initially believing him to be Japanese. When he managed to convince them of his identity, they offered to canoe him back to Port Moresby. Unfortunately, the flimsy vessel attracted the attention of some Australian army machine gunners, who opened fire momentarily, causing the locals to abandon ship, and Johnson began drifting away to places unknown. Vigorous hand signals eventually persuaded his rescuers to return to the helm, and he was back at the squadron in a few days.

Les Jackson had the third lucky escape of the day after finding himself on the receiving end of one of his own preferred tactics, a head-on attack. Taking it in turns, the Zeros positioned themselves in line astern to subject Les to a series of frontal firing passes. He fired back, and some of his tracer appeared to enter one or more of the Japanese aircraft but to no apparent effect. His engine, meanwhile, was hit and began to smoke. Like Ed Johnson, Les was forced to crash land, choosing to come down on a coral reef just offshore, which he managed to land on without mishap, even climbing out on the wing and performing a short dance to demonstrate his good health to his fellow pilots passing overhead before he was picked up and taken to shore in a canoe. One of those flying above Les was John Pettett, who was coming in to land his own damaged plane.

> Yes. I can still remember I saw that when I was coming back into land…the aircraft was in shallow water over the reef. The nose had dipped down into the water, with the wings and tail high and dry – but Les was sitting up, I think on the tailplane, and dancing up and down to indicate that he was okay. I can remember John saying, 'Oh, there's a fellow down on the reef. He seems to be all right. Seems a happy sort of chappy.' He didn't know it was his own brother.

Les Jackson was nothing if not tough. Early in the campaign, he would begin racking up kills that would see him become 75 Squadron's highest scorer in the Port Moresby battle, and an ace. But, as one of 75 Squadron's flight commanders, he nonetheless seemed to operate as something of a loner, a reserved, often surly, man who never let the fact that the beer was warm put him off drinking his grog ration, nor, occasionally, that of others.

Bill Deane-Butcher remembered a day soon after the arrival of the American Aeracobras when Les noted the large stock of beer the always better equipped Yanks had with them, and concocted a plan to relieve them of some of it. The standard air raid warning at Seven Mile at that time was three cracks from a rifle, which would make everyone within earshot quickly seek cover. One afternoon, Les created an 'air raid' of his own while the Americans were at rest in their quarters. Letting go a volley of three shots, he waited until the squadron's guests had sought shelter in slit trenches, then helped himself to sufficient bottles to furnish the next round of his regular 'parties'.

On another occasion, he managed to bring a beer-filled drop tank from Townsville (hopefully it hadn't already been used for petrol). Deane-Butcher recalled being expressly told by Les to handle some medical cases with great care, only to discover that one of them was half filled with beer bottles. However it was acquired, Les was nonetheless generous with his booty, and reportedly enjoyed nothing more than 'drinks with the boys'. How his older brother looked upon this sort of behaviour remains unclear.

Later, in the squadron's most challenging hours, it would not be Les Jackson's skills as a flyer that would be questioned, but his role as a leader of men.

•

Peter Jeffrey was correct in his early assessment of John Jackson as a man who would not hesitate to put himself in harm's way looking for a fight – and he was always looking for a fight. Like his brother, John conveyed the sense of a man quite free of physical fear, an attitude he was keen to impart to others. In one of the squadron's most difficult times, when only a handful of aircraft were available to once again climb up and attack the ever-increasing numbers of Japanese, Ted Church remembered Jackson cheerily commenting, 'It's a bit harder, that's all, but we like it tough – if the game's too easy we shall all get soft.'

Never was Jackson's courage more in evidence than when it came to taking the attack to the enemy. He seemed to be almost drawn to the Japanese aerodromes, as if they were only just out of sight over the 'hump' of the mountains to the north, and itched to get at them. It was also a practical response to the situation: the disparity in the respective flying characteristics of the Kittyhawk and Zero meant that shooting them up on the ground was a far easier way to reduce their numbers than battling them in the air, but this in no way diminishes Jackson's extraordinary personal bravery. Every strafing raid against the Japanese was preceded by a reconnaissance flight, which Jackson invariably carried out himself, alone. Then, when the potential rewards were realised, and the risk assessed, he struck. It could be argued that, as Jeffrey feared, Jackson was reckless. After all, he broke the cardinal rule of ground strafing the morning after their arrival on 22 March, when he turned and came in for a second run at the line of parked Japanese aircraft, an action that may have cost the life of Anderson and very nearly of Wilbur Wackett. But the opportunity to inflict great damage on the enemy was a reward he thought worth the risk.

At dawn on 4 April, Jackson was in the air again, flying alone into the maw of the enemy, determined to bring back to his men the most up-to-date picture of the Japanese positions. Back at Seven Mile Strip by eight am, Jackson rushed into the pilot's standby tent, enthused by what he had just seen, and wanting to get away again as soon as possible. But at eleven, three shots rang out. Four enemy aircraft were sighted, but no contact was made, so it was not until three-thirty that Jackson took off, leading a group of five towards Lae. Barry Cox became disoriented in cloud and turned back, but Jackson led his remaining fighters down to sea level after descending from the mountains, crossing the coast then swinging left to cross it again a few miles to the west.

John Pettett was flying with Jackson that day, and remembered vividly that last turn. 'It was tight – but, when John eventually straightened up and I was able to see what lay ahead, there was the Lae airstrip with a string of bombers down the left and a string of fighters down the right! Half the flight followed – John strafing the bombers, and the other half did their best to get the fighters without also getting me.'

Just one pass was made – the pilots tilting their aircraft down, then up again to maximise the streams of bullets tearing up everything underneath them. The attack only lasted seconds, barely time for the defenders on the ground to realise it was happening.

Flying with Jackson that day was Squadron Leader Jim Wright, seconded to 75 from 22 Squadron for some actual combat experience. Wright was being mooted to take over the squadron after John Jackson. He and Wright attacked the bombers, setting two alight. Les Jackson set his sights on a line of nine Zeros parked conveniently down the middle of the runway, and the third in line burst into flame. On their run, Pettett and Channon were nearly blinded by the smoke from the first blazing bomber, but fired anyway. Re-forming out to sea, the group then proceeded to Salamaua to cause damage there, shooting up radio huts and, according to John Pettett, narrowly missing the antenna towers. With great satisfaction, the pilots noted that the blaze they started back at Lae was still visible nearly 25 miles away.

Jim Wright had received a couple of hits from what was thought to be anti-aircraft fire, and was wounded by glass fragments embedded in his back. Historian Anthony Cooper has subsequently come to believe that it was in fact fire from Les Jackson's aircraft that the inexperienced Wright received as a result of straying into Les's path. All around, however, it had been an excellent day's work for 75 Squadron, with four bombers and three Zeros left blazing as well as many others suffering various degrees of damage. The Japanese were also apparently caught unawares, as they failed to show up, leaving Jackson and his men, for once, unmolested.

The next morning, 5 April, Jackson led a force of seven Kittyhawks to attack seven bombers and their escort in an intense air battle that rivalled the fiercest engagements of the Battle of Britain. Les once again turned into his favoured attacking position, dead straight on to the enemy in a frontal attack. Men fired at targets that flashed across their gunsight for an instant, sometimes cursing that the angle was not quite right. A Zero Les was shooting at caught fire, chalking up another kill for him. Sergeant Bill Cowe fired into the belly of a Japanese bomber, as did John Pettett, who got off a five-second burst. 'It was just a great mess in the sky,' he recalled years later. 'If you had a chance to shoot at something that had a red roundel on its side rather than the white and blue, that's what you did, and that was exciting.' Once again, 75 had inflicted losses on the enemy – a fighter and a bomber – for no losses of its own. John Jackson and his raw collection of pilots were putting on a performance of flying and fighting that would have seemed unimaginable a fortnight earlier.

That day saw even better news with the arrival of seven new fighters and their pilots, who had come up from Townsville. It was an enormous boost to the strained and isolated pilots and crew, who perhaps now felt a little less abandoned in this desolate corner of the tropics.

Writing to his wife in his typical style, Jackson said:

> We've seen a lot of action since we arrived, practically every day. The boys already have five scalps and have destroyed a lot of aircraft on the ground. Les had three Jap fighters after him the other day and managed to shoot one down. A nice bit of work. I think we'll hold the yellow bastards here. We've already given them a few decent cracks.

But there would be many more days in this long and intense battle, and on one of them, John Jackson would begin the ordeal of his life.

CHAPTER 12

Keeping men and machines going

If the dismal conditions at Seven Mile made life uncomfortable for the pilots, for those charged with keeping their aircraft in the air, it was almost impossible. 75 had 111 ground staff toiling constantly on the aircraft under the command of the squadron's engineering officer, William Irwin Matson, a permanent pre-war warrant officer who, before the war, had worked primarily on the wooden airframes of less sophisticated aircraft such as Tiger Moths and Ansons, hence his less-than-flattering nickname among some of the pilots: 'the wood butcher'. When war came, Matson accepted a commission as flying officer and the role of 75 Squadron's engineering officer, in some of the most challenging circumstances imaginable.

On a daily – as well as nightly – basis, Matson and his team worked minor miracles on 75's Kittyhawks, performing tasks in mere hours that in peacetime would have taken days. There were no workshops nor even hard standings nor proper revetments for the aircraft: the ground crew's facilities amounted to a series of open tents and tarpaulins with crude improvised rope pulleys and block and tackle attached to the stronger-looking tree trunks. There was a chronic shortage of tools and other equipment and, amazingly, even the Kittyhawks' essential maintenance manuals had failed to arrive. By day, the tropical sun made the aircraft almost unbearable to touch; by night, the men strained under oxy-acetylene floodlights. Dust was a constant enemy, difficult enough to work in, but which also found its way into sensitive engine parts, requiring them to be constantly, painstakingly cleaned. Equipment officer Ted Church said of Matson that he 'monotonously achieved the impossible'.

In this way Matson and his men would toil, undertaking everything from repairing battle damage to performing an engine change. The day John Piper returned from Lae with a damaged main spar after striking the parked Zero, for example, his aircraft required a new wing. 'We didn't have a workshop,' Piper recalled, 'we had a bit of a tarp and a tree and we had Bill Matson, and he performed, oh, real miracles. Kept things going absolutely. He kept the morale of his troops up and was sitting with the thing hooked up in a tree and a couple of boxes to get an engine out and people breaking them as fast as he got them put together. No, he was fantastic.'

Bill Deane-Butcher remembered him similarly. 'Matson was a very solid, plethoric sort of man who was never seen unless you went out at night specially to find people working on the aircraft, and they had engines chained to the branches of trees, trestles built from logs and so on with engines and parts lying around and floodlights and working all night to get them going, or keep them going.'

The ground staff would sometimes not be seen for days at the mess tent, electing to stay out at the dispersal areas to continue working on the aircraft, fending for themselves the best way they could.

There was also, of course, the enemy to contend with. Deciding to dig their slit trenches alongside the 'nice and safe' bomb-proof walls adjacent to the aircraft dispersal bays, Matson soon discovered that this subjected him to Japanese bombs. As he recalled later: 'After a number of bombs had fallen within 30 feet of our trenches, we came to the conclusion that sooner or later, one was going to fall in one of the trenches.' Understandably, this concern began to affect the morale of the men, particularly during the hours at most risk from an air raid: ten in the morning to two in the afternoon. Said Matson, 'the chaps had one eye on the sky, and the other on the job, as we nearly always had a raid between those times'. At the sound of the warnings, therefore, the ground staff began to take shelter further into the bush from the dispersal areas, but this in turn wasted more time in getting them back to the vital tasks at hand after the all-clear had sounded.

Eventually, Matson decided to move the aircraft needing major work to a spot he'd found 'almost on the side of a steep hill'. Aircraft were towed to the new location at dawn or at dusk, then carefully hidden from the air with branches and palm leaves. This presented its own set of problems. 'At times it appeared that we would do more harm to the aircraft getting up this hill than they would have received from the bombing.' The ruse worked for most of the 44 days until eventually it was spotted by Japanese reconnaissance and bombed with anti-personnel daisy-cutter bombs, on a day Bill Deane-Butcher would remember for the rest of his life. But by then, said Matson, 'we had so few kites that it did not matter anyway'.

Starved of proper equipment, the understaffed ground crews frequently had to perform acts of improvisation that would have been deemed unacceptable in less urgent times. The Kittyhawk's complicated illuminated reflector gunsight had given problems from the outset, primarily because of the specialised bulbs, which blew frequently in the tropical climate and for which there were no replacements. Instead of a ring of lights projected onto the windshield indicating the precise amount of deflection needed to bring down an enemy aircraft, the pilots were usually presented with a blank screen, and could only sight their guns by watching the tracer. 'I'm convinced that had it been possible to obtain these spare bulbs, or a more suitable type of sight, the results of 75 Squadron would have been more than doubled,' said Matson. However, one of his resourceful crew, Flight Sergeant Seward, knocked together more traditional ring-and-bead sights from lengths of three-inch water pipe, and fitted them to the sides of the pilots' windscreens. Not surprisingly, they found them 'awkward to use in high speed combat', particularly as they required the pilot to lean to one side of the cockpit to see them, putting his head dangerously outside the protective zone of his armour plate, but it was something at least.

John Piper remembered being particularly impressed by one example of Matson's improvisation, after a particularly unmemorable day when, taxiing to the service area having air-tested a Kittyhawk following a wing repair, his wheels went through a loose piece of metal runway matting and the aircraft went over on its nose. The bent propeller would usually render such an aircraft unflyable, and in for a long wait for spares. Instead, Matson decided to cut four inches off each tip to even up the damage, and sent Piper on his way to Townsville to pick up a replacement prop. Cautiously testing the aircraft at cruising speed, ready to throttle back if the engine started to vibrate off its mounts, Piper made it to Townsville, found a prop, then – while he was about it – picked up a brand-new wing at Amberley, and was back with a fit aircraft at Seven Mile within a few days.

•

A proper engineering or Repair and Salvage unit were not the only facilities denied 75 Squadron at Seven Mile Strip. No provision was made for proper catering or even a decent mess and its associated recreation activities to ease the tensions of daily combat. But it was the lack of adequate hygiene and its associated illnesses that presented perhaps the most potent threat to the men's well-being as well as 75 Squadron's ability to perform as an effective fighting unit. To no-one was this daily reality more acute than the squadron's redoubtable medical officer, Bill Deane-Butcher.

On his arrival at Seven Mile, he began straightaway, from a medical point of view, to get an idea of the overwhelming problems that confronted him. 'I noted with dismay,' he wrote in *Fighter Squadron Doctor*, 'the overflowing grease traps and kitchen waste. There were insufficient latrines in the camp and where men were working on aircraft there were none at all. It was a hot climate and there were flies. As expected we soon suffered an outbreak of gastroenteritis.'

He also noted there was no way for the men to keep clean. Even if there had been a canteen where items such as soap could be acquired, there were not showers in which to wash, just a single hanging water pipe left over from the strip's pre-war days, still awaiting the installation of a shower head.

No sooner had the squadron arrived than the men's health began to deteriorate. 'We had a dengue fever outbreak as soon as we arrived and dengue was a nasty condition,' recalled Deane-Butcher. 'It's mosquito borne. Its other name is "break bone fever" because it's associated with so many aches and pains and distress...a lot of people got that and were confined to tents.' The squadron seemed to be spared from a wide outbreak of malaria, which was more a summer wet season occurrence, but by far the greatest medical scourge to the men of 75 throughout the 44 days was gastroenteritis. It had already taken its toll on the workers who had constructed the airstrip the previous November, and continued unabated after 75's arrival. A combination of open latrines, flies and poor food that could not be protected, meant that almost everyone who passed through the place would get sick. The effect of gastro on anyone on the ground was awful, but in the air it was far worse. In the 1993 ABC television documentary *44 Days*, Deane-Butcher explained:

> Gastroenteritis will produce, as most people know, not only liquid stools but also gas in the abdomen. If it's a bubble of gas and you go from ground level to 20,000 feet, that multiplies in size. If it can be passed at either end of the alimentary tract, that's good news, but if it can't, it causes distension and gets blown up in pain. And it's not easy to fight for your life if you have a severe pain in the gut.

Often sick to begin with, the pilots would throw up on the ground, then suffer 'at both ends' once airborne, pulling their oxygen mask to one side to vomit lest they foul it and run the risk of having no oxygen, while liquid faeces ran down their legs. 'Fortunately,' said Alan Whetters, 'we had a good set of flying boots. Practically all pilots had this problem. One could not, or was not, relieved from his duties unless it was absolutely essential. As a consequence men did fly in an unfit condition.'

Arthur Tucker also remembered what it felt like.

> The baked beans would blow up in your stomach, you already had gastroenteritis, there was nowhere to wash your clothes, so you'd take a spare pair of shorts down to the strip and when you landed you'd clean your aeroplane up, wash your shorts, put your other wet ones on, and so we lived in wet clothes...there were no latrine trenches dug and so our only hygiene was a shovel and a roll of paper in the nearby kunai around where we had to be on standby from before dawn until after dark. Now this is no exaggeration, that is the truth. We were all suffering acute gastroenteritis the whole time. We were nearly defeated by it.

Having trained to treat battle wounds, Deane-Butcher instead found himself primarily fighting the effects of tropical disease, but again was hampered by a lack of sufficient supplies. Not only were tropical drugs such as quinine and Atabrine in extremely short supply, simple insect repellent never seemed to be available, and even the mosquito nets were inadequate. 'We were issued with nets but it's pretty hard to tie one up in a tent and if you've got six people in a tent and six mosquito nets, they tend to drape down and trail on your legs and arms anyway. Mosquitoes used to laugh at them.' There were also the permanent complaints of rampant tinea and other forms of fungal infection, exacerbated by lack of personal hygiene and suitable supplies to treat them. To add to their woes, the men were dressed almost exclusively in tropical kit: shorts and short-sleeved shirts.

In contrast, however, there were some supplies that were never used at all, such as several large boxes with rope handles containing surgery equipment that Deane-Butcher never recalled getting around to unpacking as 'there was no place to use them'.

He was not entirely alone in his care of the sick. Four orderlies were at his disposal: Jack 'Dr Mack' McIntosh, a former St John's Ambulance officer from Queensland, was accompanied by Bill Topping and Pat Walsh, a First World War veteran who had worked in New Guinea. A fourth fellow, a young man Deane-Butcher referred to only as 'Willie', found the conditions of Seven Mile almost intolerable but carried on regardless. 'The care of the sick,' he wrote later, 'by its very nature, inspires compassion and dedicated service by most people who work in the field of health. The medical orderlies of 75 Squadron were no exception.'

Deane-Butcher and his orderlies would conduct a daily morning sick parade to which anyone could report, or friends could report for those too ill to leave their tents. The orderlies treated minor conditions, but anything more serious was referred to Deane-Butcher. 'Usually I couldn't do much anyway.' In retrospect, he believed he probably delegated far too much to his medical orderlies. 'In doing sick parades in the morning and following up the troubles of many of the men who had to stay in their tents, my medical orderlies did a marvellous job and I felt perhaps I should have given them a little more support.'

John Pettett recalled his experience with dengue fever, caught soon after his arrival:

> Two days after we got to Port Moresby I got dengue fever, which I had obviously picked up at Townsville. I think the incubation period is seven days...So we arrived there on the Saturday, we had the Lae raid on Sunday, I was on an intercept on the Monday, but Monday night, I finished up in hospital with dengue fever, and it was terrible. The most shocking illness of sore eyes and body and every muscle in your body hurts. I was in hospital, I think, for ten days in Moresby then back to the squadron. I can remember Les Jackson saying, 'Oh, good, he's back, he can go on tomorrow,' and then Bill saying, 'Like hell he will. He's got a day off tomorrow.'

It was one of many such disputes Deane-Butcher would have with Les Jackson, and not all would he win.

With the facilities at hand, Deane-Butcher was not equipped to deal with serious cases, especially when the limited number of beds at Seven Mile were full. There was, however, a larger RAAF hospital in Port Moresby, but that too occasionally became overloaded. In such cases, he was told to make his way to a new army hospital at Rouna Falls, sixteen miles from Moresby.

When warning of an air raid came, Deane-Butcher and most of the ground staff usually had time to seek shelter. His routine was to collect men in the squadron ambulance and drive up to the safety of the dispersal areas on higher ground established by Bill Matson to protect his men and the aircraft. From here, Deane-Butcher could watch the raid unfold below like a macabre piece of theatre. However, one day in mid April, the Japanese finally discovered the sanctuary and directed their attention towards it. 'On this occasion,' recorded Deane-Butcher dryly, 'the bombing raid was directed at us…and we got the lot.'

After terrible *krumps* of explosions and vibrating earth, Deane-Butcher and orderly McIntosh emerged from shelters they had quickly found. Looking around, they saw trees and foliage had been sliced to pieces by horizontally exploding fragmentation daisy-cutter bombs. Nearby, the groans of soldiers could be heard. 'The two men writhed on the ground. They both had extensive ragged wounds to their abdomens and legs. It was obvious that there was little chance of their survival. They were both soldiers and I didn't know their names.' Deane-Butcher's and McIntosh's only hope was to get them quickly to the new, well-equipped hospital at Rouna Falls. The trouble was, neither Deane-Butcher nor McIntosh had ever been there. The trip turned out to be 'a rather unpleasant undertaking'.

Deane-Butcher himself was suffering the dreaded gastro at the time, and the rough trip over a treacherous road made things worse. Giving the two shocked men as much morphine as he dared, Deane-Butcher could only treat their myriad wounds with 'dressings and towels and anything we had'.

Off they set in their civilian two-wheel-drive ambulance, wholly unsuited to the terrain. Every fifteen minutes, Deane-Butcher needed to stop to relieve himself by the side of the road. In the driver's seat, Dr Mack found the mountain road a challenge. Climbing up a cutting into the side of a mountain, it became worse: water flowed over the road, causing the wheels to slip, and endless slimy potholes rocked the vehicle from side to side, causing agony for the men in the back, despite the morphine. One of the young men lapsed into unconsciousness and the other was rambling about his wife and children. 'The amount of pain they experienced, I really don't know, but I certainly gave them high doses,' Deane-Butcher recalled.

When they finally arrived at the army hospital, it had all been for nothing. The men soon died, and Deane-Butcher collapsed and had to be treated there himself. 'Eventually, we found our way back.'

Later in the battle, when Les Jackson was in charge, Deane-Butcher was told, 'I'll look after things in the air, you look after the ground.' Deane-Butcher's role evolved into an integral factor in the fabric and running of the squadron, in some ways more important than the commanding officer himself, who remained a divisive figure. A doctor displaying empathy towards a patient in an operational squadron in wartime is simply not sufficient; as much as it may have run against peacetime codes, one of Deane-Butcher's elementary roles was to keep the pilots in the air. 'It was my responsibility to ensure that they were fit to fly. A pilot who cannot, or will not, press home his attack on the target is a risk to others as well as himself…I tried to support morale and help to sustain the will to fight.' This entailed not just the physical but emotional, even moral, capabilities of an individual.

A man whose reaction to the fear of combat flying was excessive would display recognisable symptoms of nervous collapse – tremor, agitation, loss of bowel and bladder control, panic – and should be regarded, in Deane-Butcher's opinion, as sick and be relieved of his obligations, as such an attitude was usually infectious. On the other hand, a man who was 'malingering', that is, simply attempting to evade his responsibilities though perfectly fit, was harder to spot. In wartime, it seemed, the normal standards of doctor/patient confidentiality occasionally broke down and, years later, Deane-Butcher reflected on the inherently invidious position of a military doctor.

> It was difficult to exercise vigilance and at the same time be a trusted friend. A medical officer's in a strange position in a squadron. He swears that he will do what is necessary for the service…yet his whole training as a doctor is to the patient and any doctor who divulges a patient's confidences is not likely to have many patients, and so there was a clash of interest. I very soon made up my mind that my responsibility was to relate to the patient, otherwise I would have no trust placed in me. I became something of a confidant, and

> the only person in the squadron who had no-one to talk to was myself. Perhaps that's an angle which is sometimes overlooked, that even a doctor can be sick or can feel threatened or can have his personal problems and he's rather alone.

Later, the notion of 'malingering' or more bluntly, cowardice, would become one of the deepest and most controversial of wounds in the entire 44 days.

Years after the war, Deane-Butcher recalled a conversation in the mess one evening after a young pilot had been killed. Another young flyer facing his own mortality took the doctor aside to enquire whether he believed in God. Although he replied that he did, Deane-Butcher harboured similar doubts to the young man, and could think of no reason why any higher power looking over them would not be doing the same for the Japanese. Typically hiding their emotional reactions to the perils they faced on a daily basis, the pilots would make light of the dangers, and Deane-Butcher took it on himself to watch for the cracks.

> Bob Crawford, for example, a very fine young pilot, got a bullet through his throat microphone which left a graze across his throat. Now he didn't show any particular reaction to that…but I'm sure there was a lot of suppressed concern. They tended to cover it up and there was a lot of joking about it all.

Deane-Butcher found himself becoming an expert in some unusual areas. 'The range of my medical duties extended in the most unexpected directions – sometimes downwards,' he recalled. 'My medical life veered a little from the expertise of suturing and surgical knowhow to a rather intricate knowledge of how to build a latrine and find lice in pubic hair and that sort of thing.'

In overseeing the construction of the squadron's new toilet facilities, Deane-Butcher would make some interesting discoveries. A 'six-holer' latrine was easier to construct than a one- or two-holer, and the regular visits evolved, he said, into a social event of sorts. 'This was a social place, yes. The kunai grass in parts was fairly high, maybe two or three feet high, and little tracks went from the tents around the place down to the mess and of course to the six-holer. It wasn't a very attractive place but people had to go there anyway.'

It was discovered that a judicious amount of kerosene and a lighted match could at least keep out spiders, scorpions and other everyday nasties of the tropics. 'Practical jokes in this context were definitely out as serious burns [could] have been inflicted. Too much kerosene entails the risk of spectacular fire. Once our keen young medical orderly, Willie, put in petrol by mistake and blew up the whole works.'

Hygiene issues associated with these inadequate facilities remained a serious problem, and were eventually one of the reasons 75 moved their camp to neighbouring Twelve Mile Strip in late April.

In other areas too, Deane-Butcher had to learn fast. Vermin and local wildlife, water purification, laundry and washing facilities plus many more topics of a non-medical nature were soon crowded into a repertoire of knowledge which needed to adapt quickly to an unfamiliar environment.

Boredom, and its associate, erosion of morale, also became an area of concern for the squadron doctor. With nothing for the men to do in the mess by day, evening singing sessions provided one of their few social activities, and Deane-Butcher unexpectedly found himself in the role of squadron composer. The mess tent was fifteen yards long with a dirt floor, furnished only with a few folding wooden chairs and benches ('certainly no tablecloths or anything like that'). Guy ropes and pegs stuck into the ground and had to be loosened when it rained. 'It had quite a number of holes in it, I must say, and there were areas where water dripped through.' At night, with nothing but a few kerosene lamps, reading was difficult so singing evolved into something of a ritual. 'I took part in this and finished up trying to compose a couple of songs.'

Beside the mess was the cook's galley, a small tent where the cook, usually stripped to the waist, sweated away over boiling pots of bland fare, which was announced with the crudely bawled, 'Come and get it, fuck yas!' to all within earshot.

CHAPTER 13

John Jackson's triumph

Thursday 9 April was a busy day for 75's commanding officer, John Jackson.

Having flown in an army-cooperation role in the Middle East, John Jackson knew the value of good reconnaissance, as well as how to get it. Although a very different place from the open flat plains of the desert, here in New Guinea, the principles were the same: fly in at zero feet to avoid detection, read from the map on your knees, keep your eyes open, take notes and, if possible, watch out for the enemy before making a quick run home. After completing another successful reconnaissance circuit of Lae and Finschhafen, he headed back to Seven Mile to attend a conference at RAAF HQ in Moresby on the progress of the battle thus far. Striking the Japanese hard and regularly and on the ground was, it was agreed, the best chance of blunting their superiority in both equipment and numbers and overturning their timetable of taking Moresby by early May. The squadron would, therefore, be keeping up the pressure and making attacks on the enemy bases of Lae and Salamaua at every opportunity.

It should have come as no surprise that, upon Jackson's return to Seven Mile at eleven that night, orders awaited for another reconnaissance flight to the Japanese strongholds at first light the next morning. Jackson insisted on carrying out these solo recce trips himself, and arranged that an aircraft be made ready before dawn. How he slept that night will never be known; perhaps in his mind there was a nagging misgiving, knowing that a dawn flight offered an inquisitive pilot and his aircraft little cover, unlike those taken in the afternoon when the tropical cumulus had built to great cathedrals in the skies. But HQ were eager to get at the Japanese again, and soon. The information gathered by Jackson would go towards planning another attack.

At six am, the squadron's flight controllers in their dugout above the strip were informed that Jackson had taken off, and was heading north. Perhaps he was reassured, as Ted Church recalled seeing 'his tiny aircraft silhouetted against the background of heavy cumulus clouds'. A short time later an army observer post noted his progress towards the northwest.

It should have been another quick run for Jackson, who was due back at Seven Mile by eight. He had not returned by eight-thirty and a sense of alarm began to creep through the squadron. As nine o'clock ticked over, the time by which his petrol would have run out, alarm was replaced with dread.

Then a slow and peculiar Morse transmission was picked up. The signal was unclear, but one of the words being slowly repeated was thought to be 'Lori', the name of a village roughly 50 miles to the northwest. It was enough to go on, and an American A-24 dive bomber from the neighbouring US 8th Bombardment Squadron was loaded up with emergency supplies and prepared for take-off.

Australian pilots were keen to join the search for their boss too, but almost as soon as he was posted missing, three shots rang out to warn of another Japanese air raid. If the pilots were feeling dismay at their missing leader, they did not show it.

Helped by Leigh Vial's golden voice, nine Kittyhawks – the largest formation 75 had so far been able to make ready – took to the air to meet a force of seven bombers and six escorting Zeros. By putting on power in a steep climb, this time some of the Australians were able to get above the Japanese, and they made them pay. It was a particularly auspicious debut for a young pilot from Launceston, Tasmania, Geoff Atherton, of whom John Pettett said, 'he was the only person who ever said to me that he wasn't scared, and I believed him'. Michael Butler concurred: 'He was a cool, calculating fellow; an extremely fine fellow, wonderful pilot and there's nothing he seemed to enjoy more than a scrap and honestly he just didn't know what fear was.'

On this, his first combat, Atherton, in a former life a quiet accountant, attacked from 24,000 feet, swooping down on a Betty that had dropped out of formation. Firing into it repeatedly, smoke began to stream from its belly. It went into a spin, crashing into Mount Bellamy, not far from the village of Efogi. Atherton would go on to a stellar career in the RAAF, accruing five more claims or part claims of Japanese aircraft over Moresby before the end of the 44 days finishing the war as a Wing Commander with a DFC and bar.

Two more bombers were damaged that morning, both victims of John Piper, who was able to execute several 'dive and zooms' during which he pumped hundreds of rounds into the Bettys. To his frustration, he was rewarded only with smoke and fuel vapour as they flew off, for which he blamed the squadron's paucity of incendiary ammunition. Luck was with Piper that day, however, when two of the escorting Zeros jumped him, taking out his cooling system. Shutting his Allison motor down before it overheated and seized, he instead elected to 'windmill' without engine power back to Seven Mile, where he landed safely after executing an excellent glide approach.

Back at base, the celebrations were short-lived, as the reality of 75's missing leader sank in. A little before midday, the American Dauntless finally took to the skies, although by now the weather had rolled in, cutting visibility to almost nothing. Another attempt to find John Jackson was made later that afternoon, but again it drew a blank. Barry Cox had a go on his own, but by then the weather was so bad he could barely locate the search area. The pilots returned with no news, and along with the rest of 75 Squadron, spent a grim and depressing night without their beloved leader.

Without wishing to give the enemy time to recover, another raid was mounted on Lae at first light the following morning, 11 April. The slow and mysterious Morse broadcast of 'Lori' had resumed, further confounding the radio operators at Seven Mile. Just about everything that could fly was thrown at the Japanese base with six Kittyhawks and seven A-24s attacking the airstrip, then flying in a wide search back towards Moresby. The A-24s had the benefit of an extra pair of eyes searching from an open rear cockpit and one American gunner believed he glimpsed an aircraft on the ground far away in the Cameron Range, but again the weather closed in, preventing a follow-up flight.

Jackson's brother, Les, also conducted a search, flying low through the valleys to the north where an aeroplane could have come down. More searches were conducted over the next two days, but there was no sign of John Jackson.

The squadron, said Alan Whetters, was in shock, sentiments echoed by Ted Church: 'It was as though the life's blood of the squadron had been drained away. For two days the squadron lay like a rudderless ship at the mercy of any wind that blew.'

The day before his flight, word had come through that Jackson had been awarded the DFC for his services in the Middle East.

•

> 12/4/42.
>
> Dearest Betty.
>
> Went off to Lae about 06.00 on 10/4/42 to do a low reconnaissance flight. Just as leaving Lae, three Japanese fighters surprised me and shot my plane to bits.

With these characteristically straightforward words penned to his beloved wife, John Jackson began the long and careful account, kept in a daily diary, of his extraordinary two-week ordeal in the jungle. In many ways, his was a similar experience to that of Wilbur Wackett, shot down over Lae a fortnight earlier. Both airmen endured sagas of survival that beggar belief. With Jackson as commander, however, the stakes for the squadron as a whole were higher.

Having made it to Lae at low level in the early morning light, Jackson zoomed in over the Japanese aerodrome as planned. He got his bearings, made his notes, counted the numbers of aircraft parked along the runway – bombers and fighters – and was, in an instant, heading out to sea. Next he would make a long slow turn to head south again to Seven Mile, where he would gleefully inform his pilots of just what an attractive target the Japanese were presenting of themselves, relishing the idea of a return visit – this time with company – later that day. On that occasion, however, nothing would go Jackson's way.

Preparing themselves for just such an incursion, three Zeros were already warmed up and ready to go as the pale underside of Jackson's Kittyhawk thundered overhead in the soft morning light. Whether he noticed them as he passed overhead is not known. And it wouldn't matter, because soon they would be right on his tail.

'When I first saw them I didn't attempt to fight them as it was essential to get the information back and I relied on my extra speed to get away,' he recorded in his letter.

Indeed, at low level in the thick air, the Kittyhawk was a match for the Zero in a flat-out chase, but for some reason – perhaps it hadn't been quite properly tuned in the challenging conditions at Seven Mile – Jackson simply could not coax what he needed out of the big Allison engine. Skimming low over the ocean, his hand jammed against the fully opened throttle, Jackson glanced repeatedly up to his rear-view mirror. The three pursuing Zeros, distant specks at first, now began to close in on him. Jackson knew what was to follow. In a three-against-one fight, he would be at the mercy of the undoubtedly skilful Japanese pilots, and mercy, he believed, was not likely to be afforded. So, doing the only thing he could, he turned to fight.

As his brother, Les, had demonstrated, the Zeros' lack of armoured front windscreens made them particularly vulnerable to a head-on attack from the Kittyhawk's thumping half-inch guns. The Japanese pilots no doubt braced for a storm of fire from the small outline of the aeroplane rapidly hurtling towards them as Jackson wheeled hard around to face his pursuers. Jackson himself had three targets looming ever larger, but knew his six guns – each packed with two hundred rounds apiece – had a wide arc of fire, their impact amplified further by the aircraft's speed. He squeezed the firing button on top of his control stick, and the guns spluttered momentarily, then went silent. On this of all mornings – whether they had already been hit, or had been affected by the tropical conditions or just bad luck – his guns had jammed. Unable to either outrun or outgun his opponents, he looked down at the water and waited for the inevitable. An avalanche of machine-gun and cannon shells tore into his aircraft, shuddering against wings and engine, and the Perspex and glass cage surrounding him disintegrated. Smoke poured up into the cockpit from the engine as he lurched towards the sea. 'The aircraft was a mass of holes, windscreen all shot away and on fire. Crashed into the sea about three quarters of a mile off land near village.'

Jackson did not record how hard he hit the water. It would have happened in a flash, but he managed to unstrap and leap from the cockpit in the seconds before the Kittyhawk began to sink. So fast did he make his escape that he realised he was still attached to his oxygen tube, which he quickly unplugged before he was dragged under the water as the aircraft headed to the bottom.

Inflating his life jacket, Jackson could see the shore clearly and headed for it. Then he looked up, watching helplessly as the three victorious Zero pilots – perhaps contemplating the bravery of this mad Australian pilot who had ventured alone into the hornet's nest – circled overhead, wingtips pointed to the sea, the aircraft's pale grey and red circle markings – and the pilots themselves – clearly visible.

'I had a few anxious moments waiting for them to strafe me. After what seemed an eternity they went away.'

Now it was the turn of nature to torment Jackson. Close to shore, a crocodile broke the surface in front of him. He initially thought it was a log and went towards it, but stopped himself when a snout arose from the water. It seemed to sniff him for a moment, before deciding, in his words, 'it didn't approve and turned away'. An equally serious threat however, awaited him when he staggered ashore. Arriving in front of a village not too distant from the Japanese bases of Lae and Salamaua, Jackson soon gleaned that some of their number did not seem at all pleased to see him. In fact, many looked frightened – 'bluffed by the Japanese', he wrote. To be fair, the villagers knew already the ferocity of reprisal that would descend if they were found to be harbouring a downed Australian airman. Like Wilbur Wackett, however, Jackson would discover that two of them had spent time at the mission station on Duke of York Island off Rabaul, and were willing to help.

These 'two good lads' – Edmond, who was Church of England, and Arthur, a Methodist – offered to guide Jackson to safety. He readily agreed, but was told by Edmond, who spoke some English, that they had to leave immediately. Grabbing a small bag of belongings, the men quietly hurried away along a jungle track, almost pulling Jackson in their wake. And for good reason. A little way out of the village, they looked back to see two Japanese boats appear off the beach. Jackson now reflected on the Japanese reasons for not finishing him off in the water: better to pick him up from the village, where he might prove a useful source of information about the audacious group of airmen at Port Moresby.

As Wilbur Wackett had done, Jackson too had jettisoned his heavy flying boots to make better headway in the water, a decision he would likewise regret – already his feet were in agony.

Edmond and Arthur plunged into a shallow creek and began walking downstream. Jackson recalled going 'down to my waist in slime and mud'. At one stage, one of the men looked back again to see some of the villagers leading the Japanese along the path they had just travelled, but the small party managed to evade them until darkness.

Emerging onto a beach, Jackson was tempted by a fire that had been lit previously as well as a night in a reasonably comfortable looking hut, but 'decided to push on though nearly done'. Amazed at how his guides could find their way along six-inch-wide jungle tracks that Jackson could not discern even in daytime, they plunged on into the jungle, Jackson at first holding onto one of the men's sarongs, then, when his feet became bad, holding onto his shoulders. 'When we came to a stony river crossing my feet wouldn't work at all and they had to carry me across.'

Another hut in the middle of the night, and a dawn feed of roots and coconut, and they were on the move again. A single rifle shot, heard soon after they left their camp, quickly dispelled any notion Jackson had that the Japanese had given up the pursuit.

At some stage a pair of old sandshoes was found for Jackson, but fitted so poorly he could not keep them on his feet. Soaked by 'tropical deluges', Jackson limped on, now up a mountain where the men took turns in basically pushing him up the treacherous razorback slopes. At midday, some 'toasted green bananas – pretty tasteless' provided a meal, and time enough for Jackson to reflect on his remarkable good fortune thus far. If nothing else, he still, against all odds, had his liberty: 'Providence alone has saved me. My aircraft was shot to ribbons. The croc turned away and I have two wonderful helpers.'

Insisting he rest up a day in a deserted village to give his feet some chance of recovery, Edmond and Arthur fashioned for Jackson a pair of crutches and cut up a bag for his feet, using vines for twine. He also discovered the men had come relatively well equipped with quinine, plaster, scissors, a razor and toothbrush. 'His toothbrush,' wrote Jackson, 'is the only thing I haven't borrowed so far.'

Merciful too, was the apparent lack of mosquitoes and a sarong and jersey, which offered Jackson protection from the cool nights and to gain some rest, but his feet were still in terrible condition. 'My feet are the trouble – this morning they felt like two pulps and I could hardly bear to touch them with my hand let alone stand. I will have to go very easy.' After a further day's recuperation in their mountain eyrie, Jackson decided to push on into rough country where there was 'barely a goat's track over high mountains and valleys'.

As they progressed, Jackson was rejuvenated to see his squadron at work high above escorting American Dauntless dive bombers on an attack on Lae. 'My two boys here cheered as the bombs were falling.' He had no way of knowing that he was witnessing some of 75 Squadron's fiercest battles of the 44 days. Then to his wife, he added, 'I'm constantly wondering if you've heard I'm missing. I trust not.'

Jackson's angels of mercy eventually managed to fashion the ill-fitting sandshoes into something he could use, transforming his progress. After a day or so the swelling was going down, and he was almost 'getting used to it'. It was decided they would make for the large village of Marpos, further into the mountains in the Buang Valley. It was thought contact with the outside world would be easier from there. Getting to the village, however, was a nightmare. Although assured by villagers they came across that Marpos was 'just ahead', Jackson found everyone to be 'tantalisingly vague about time and distance'. Hours of slog seemed to bring them no closer.

> Struggled all day. Seemed to be an endless climb up and up. What a track! I really never have put in a more hellish day. Leeches by the billion on the men's feet. You could see the patches of blood on them all day. They didn't worry me. I was past caring. Could have been snakes sucking at me and I wouldn't have felt them, my feet were so sore.

His diary also noted his intrigue at the people and the cultural life he witnessed. Every place he travelled through it seemed 'sing-sings' would start around him. He assumed, from the endless beat of the kundu drums and the male dancers dressed in nothing more than painted ochre and head dresses fashioned from bird of paradise feathers, that it must be some kind of festival season. Despite the war, and the trials of his physical condition, one senses the fascination of this uncomplicated man from rural Queensland with the villagers, assuaging, perhaps just a little, the harshness of his circumstances. 'All the girls wear nothing from the waist up and look most alluring. They are friendly and sympathetic and gave me two sweet potatoes but couldn't provide any coconuts or water to drink. I was about done in for a drink.'

At Marpos – finally – Jackson was given something resembling treatment for his feet, and the morning after their arrival, the second in charge of the village brought him tea, and even some Australian Sunshine condensed milk. The luxury was appreciated. More importantly, he was told a detachment of the New Guinea Volunteer Rifles (NGVR) was in the area. Jackson hastily wrote them a note, which, he was assured, would be delivered.

An anxious day was spent on 15 April wondering if his message had got through, even as he rested and bathed his battered feet in a basin. Then early on 16 April, shouting was heard in the village, announcing the approach of two white men.

'About 9am…in blew Sergeant Stuart Fraser and Rifleman George Kerr and it was great to see them.' Jackson's relief had arrived. Issuing him with some army boots, their intention was to head to Wau where a larger outpost could transport him by air back to Moresby. Looking at Jackson's feet, however, it was decided he was not up to the journey on his own, and a stretcher party from the village was organised to assist his passage down the mountains. Along the way, Jackson observed the cultural lives of the New Guineans, noting, 'In some cases the people yodel or call out in a musical sort of chant the story of my arrival', and beat the 'hollowed drums with lizard or snake skin stretched across one end'. And as Wilbur Wackett had similarly observed: 'You can walk all day in New Guinea, and in the afternoon, see no distance away, the place you left in the morning.'

Arriving at Wau, Jackson impressed the seasoned men of the NGVR with the story of his survival, and the signal was sent to Seven Mile that their leader, John Jackson, was safe. Back at the strip, it was wonderful news to hear.

The next day, a mission was mounted from Seven Mile with the two-fold purpose of delivering supplies to the Wau post of the NGVR, and to bring back John Jackson. One of the Dauntless dive bombers, piloted by Lieutenant Schwab, took off with a three Kittyhawk escort but bad weather separated the formation, and prevented all but one of the escorting pilots, John Piper, from finding Wau at all, and that, he later said, was more by chance than anything else. Piper was all alone, though, and simply had to turn around and go back.

The next day, 23 April, Schwab and Piper took off again, this time locating the airstrip at Wau where a relieved John Jackson was waiting for them. The two pilots were lucky. Twenty minutes after leaving Seven Mile, the strip was struck by eight Japanese aircraft, a mixture of bombers and fighters. Six Kittyhawks took to the air in its defence, but were too late to be of any effect. Bombs once again hit the strip.

At Wau, John Jackson was given a quick lesson in how to operate the Dauntless's twin rear-mounted machine gun. He was not expecting to use it. On returning to Seven Mile, a proud Lieutenant Schwab, who had himself searched for Jackson in the days after he had gone missing, buzzed the airstrip at low level to announce the imminent return of 75's leader. It was a mistake. Unbeknown to the American, the Japanese fighters were still lurking in the area, and his actions alerted three of them to his presence. Seeing an American Dauntless flying at level and apparently slowing down, flaps extended and intending to land, they banked sharply towards it.

In his escorting Kittyhawk, John Piper was also on circuit to land, but saw the Zeros too late. One Japanese pilot pounced on the lone Dauntless, and John Jackson, not even returned from his two-week ordeal, found himself already under fire.

A single 20-millimetre cannon shell hit the aircraft as Jackson attempted to fire back, a fragment slicing off the tip of a finger on his left hand. Schwab quickly diverted the Dauntless's approach and put her down at nearby KilaKila, or Three Mile Strip. Piper, arriving before the Zero could follow up its attack, chased the Japanese plane off. Schwab and Jackson chose to call it a day. In closing off his letter to his wife, Jackson typically downplayed the drama.

'Yesterday had a hot reception. Was about to land when three Japanese made a surprise attack. Aircraft I was in got full of holes. Had tip of my finger grazed. Just a mere scratch. Providence surely guided and protected me all through. Tons and tons of love sweetheart to yourself, Patricia and Arthur. From your ever-loving husband John.'

A single image exists of Jackson moments after his landing at Three Mile Strip. About ten men crowd around the Dauntless, their eyes directed towards the man with the hulking frame who has his back to the camera. Little imagination is needed to hear his deep voice making light of his ordeal to his delighted men hanging on his every word. Although his back is facing the camera, his demeanour is palpable. John Jackson had returned, to the delight of his squadron.

CHAPTER 14

Hard days for the Japanese

Strung out at the edge of a vast and rapidly conquered swathe of the southwest Pacific, the Japanese never felt their hold on their bases along New Guinea's northern coast to be a firm one. At Lae and Salamaua, little attempt was made to secure anything much beyond the airstrip and its tiny associated settlement, enabling watchers like Leigh Vial and the patrols of the New Guinea Volunteer Rifles (NGVR) to operate successfully. At one stage in late March, an NGVR unit was able to get close to Lae airstrip, where it even recorded the numbers on the Zeros' tails as well as measured the Japanese fighters' take-off distance before slipping silently back into the jungle.

Supply lines were stretched and, like 75 Squadron at Moresby, the Japanese at Lae struggled to keep their aircraft airworthy, with the backlog of damaged and unserviced planes always outnumbering those fit to take to the air. The job of holding Lae was initially given to the newly formed Imperial Japanese Naval Air Service's 4th Naval Air Group, a mixed unit of bombers and fighters that was itself part of the larger 24th – and, later, 25th – Naval Air Flotilla. Deployed to Rabaul on 17 February, their bomber force was almost wiped out three days later when all but two of their seventeen Betty bombers fell to the guns of radar-guided American naval aviators in an action off Bougainville.

In order to step up attacks on Moresby, in preparation for the invasion planned for early May, the 4th Air Group began arriving at Lae on 11 March. If, for the Japanese airmen, Rabaul had appeared a tough posting, it was luxury compared to Lae: no decent food or creature comforts, no power but for dim kerosene lamps, and not even proper revetments for the protection of the aircraft, as John Jackson and his pilots would discover when they found them lined up in very shootable rows along the runway. Lae was not even particularly well garrisoned, with just seven Zeros comprising the initial force, a number that had barely doubled by the beginning of April. While unopposed, however, they nevertheless proved a formidable force as demonstrated in their numerous undefended attacks on Moresby and Seven Mile Strip in the weeks prior to the arrival of 75 Squadron. Such was the Japanese airmen's confidence, believed pilot Michael Butler, that they flew without parachutes, knowing their chances of being shot down were virtually nil. Once the Australians began fighting back, their arrogance in the skies of New Guinea diminished rapidly. On the very next raid in retaliation for Jackson's daring first attack on 23 March, the Japanese could muster merely four Zeros to escort a force of nineteen bombers.

However, the Japanese had plans for Lae. A few days after the arrival of 4th Air Group, ground units appeared to begin repairs on the runway. This little airstrip, it was decided, would soon form a major part of the upcoming seaborne invasion of Port Moresby and the ranks of the 4th Air Group at Lae were to be reinforced by one of the most famous fighter units of the Imperial Japanese Navy, the renowned Tainan Kokutai. Even before Pearl Harbor, this elite unit was already battle experienced, formed in Tainan on the island of Taiwan in October 1941 from specially selected veterans of the Sino-Japanese War. When Japan attacked in the Pacific, the Tainan was everywhere, wreaking havoc on the Americans in the Philippines, then, following Japan's lightning conquest of the Dutch East Indies, stationed at Tarakan in Borneo, and supporting rampaging naval units from bases at Balikpapan in Borneo and Bali.

Given the special marking of a black V and a three-digit number on their tails, the Tainan pilots flew the Mitsubishi Zero almost exclusively and were masters of it. In a short time they boasted more aces than any other unit in the Japanese navy. The press, naturally, loved them, with the exploits of their young pilots providing fodder for the public at home in faraway Tokyo. Among their stars was Hiroyoshi Nishizawa, a pale and sickly son of a sake brewer who went on to become possibly Japan's top-scoring ace of the war. Japanese fighter kills are notoriously difficult to determine, but some sources have put Nishizawa's tally at well over a hundred aircraft. Taciturn, solitary and seeming to shun companionship on the ground, it was in the air that Nishizawa came alive, his fellow pilots nicknaming him 'the Devil'. His skill in a Zero, particularly in aerobatics, was described by those who witnessed it as 'unpredictable…breathtaking'. In contrast there was Toshio Ota, a young and exuberant chief petty officer who accounted for 34 enemy aircraft before meeting his own end at Guadalcanal. Tall and charming, it was said he was more at home in a nightclub than a combat airfield.

Most dominant of all was the remarkable Saburo Sakai. Born into an ancient but now impoverished family of Samurai, Sakai failed high school and had no choice but to join the navy in 1933 at age sixteen, subjecting himself to the horrendous traditions of Japanese military training. Writing after the war of his experiences in his book, *Samurai!*, Sakai stated, 'It is difficult, if not altogether impossible, for Americans and other westerners to appreciate the harshness of the discipline under which we then lived in the Navy.'

As the navy's lowest form of life – a cadet – the slightest breach of discipline or error in training invoked the wrath of the dreaded petty officers – 'sadistic brutes of the worst sort,' said Sakai – who would ritualistically beat the young recruits with wooden planks till they were virtually unconscious, at which point a bucket of water was hurled over them, and the punishment would resume. 'After such treatment it was impossible to lie on our backs on our cots.' Any audible groaning would result in the entire hut being given the same treatment. 'Within six months the incredibly severe training had made human cattle of every one of us...we were automatons who obeyed without thinking.'

Upon graduating and being sent to sea, Sakai found life inside the turret of a battleship to be just as bad, so, in 1937, he applied to the naval aviation school at Tsuchiura near Tokyo for pilot training, and was surprised to be accepted along with 70 other successful applicants from 1500 hopefuls. First experiencing combat over China, Sakai's victory tally climbed into the dozens before being badly wounded and sent to instruct, thus becoming one of the few of his colleagues to survive the war.

On one occasion, he was ordered to attack a civilian Dutch DC-3 over Java, but seeing women and children on board through the window, he simply waved to the pilot and left it in peace. He did not report the incident to his commander. In May 1942, he and his fellow aces, Nishizawa and Ota – who together had earned the nickname 'The Clean-up Trio' – decided to put on an aerobatic display over Seven Mile, executing perfectly coordinated, wingtip-to-wingtip loops over the harbour and the town. The watching Australian army ground defences were apparently too awed to open fire. A short time later, a lone American bomber appeared at Lae and dropped a message tied to the end of a long piece of ribbon.

It was written in English by Seven Mile's commander and addressed to his Japanese counterpart. He apparently thanked the gentlemen for their display that afternoon, but assured them his anti-aircraft gunners would pay them far more attention should they choose to repeat the performance. The three pilots were rebuked, but all agreed it had been worth it.

Sakai's autobiographical *Samurai!* remains the only detailed narrative of the 44 days from the Japanese point of view. Remarkably, today his Zero, V-173, is on permanent display in the Canberra War Memorial. His arrival at Lae however, was one he would rather have forgotten. 'I groaned when I circled the field,' he wrote of his first impressions on 8 April. 'Where were the hangars, the maintenance shops, the control tower? Where was anything but a dirty small runway?'

As glamorous as the Tainan Kokutai may have been, their new home at Lae was not. Having fought in the Chinese, Philippine and Dutch East Indies campaigns, the pilots of the Tainan could not help the feeling that every posting – further out towards the perimeter of Japan's new conquests – was progressively worse. Bali had been a dream posting, but then Sakai received his orders for Rabaul. Far from being sent there in style, the pilots, to his amazement, were packed into the hold of a flimsy old freighter called the *Komaki Maru* for a ghastly two-week journey to the new posting. The fumes and paint smell made him sick in both mind and body. Nor was there any relief upon reaching Rabaul, situated as it was beside an active volcano that shook the ground beneath their feet and 'hurled out stones and thick choking smoke' every few minutes. However, even this compared favourably to his next posting, Lae.

Noting that the strip was hemmed in on three sides by mountains and butted up against the sea on the other, Sakai felt as though he was landing on an aircraft carrier. Upon touching down, he was greeted by a fellow pilot who had arrived a day or two earlier. 'Welcome home, Sakai,' said his friend, 'the world's most wonderful place greets you!'

The view was similarly dismal from the ground. There was but a single small, bullet-riddled hangar, the wrecks of scuttled Australian transport aircraft, and a still, unwelcoming little harbour, where a bombed merchant vessel lay sunk at a weird angle, broken and abandoned in the mud. Sakai rapidly concluded that this 'forsaken mud-hole' was the most wretched base he'd ever seen.

The Japanese garrison at Lae comprised 200 sailors manning the flak positions, 100 ground and maintenance personnel and 30 pilots. If anything, conditions here were harsher even than for the Australians at Seven Mile. Sakai's billet was a simple bush hut raised a few feet off the damp ground and measuring six by ten yards, which he was required to share with over twenty other NCO pilots. 'A handful of candles provided our only light,' he wrote. 'The men cut an empty fuel drum open and shaped it into an impromptu bathtub.' The camp's only electricity, provided by battery, was restricted to powering the telephones.

With their accommodation situated half a kilometre from the runway, the pilots at Lae walked or ran to their aircraft, or, if scrambled, were picked up by the dilapidated old Ford that had been left behind by the Australians, and taken to their dispersal or the command post, which Sakai said, 'failed to deserve even the name "shack" for it had no walls!'.

Like the Australians' diet, the Japanese menu was monotonous and unvarying: a dish of rice and soybean-paste soup with dried vegetables and pickles. Their flying routine was also comparable, the pilots also awoken before dawn, though in the Japanese case, at the even earlier hour of three-thirty. They would then force down a miserable breakfast and either be called to one of six Zeros warming up at the end of the runway poised to take off to meet a dawn attack, or wait at the command post for further instructions. When not flying, days were filled with chess and checkers until bed at nine.

Apart from being encouraged to swallow impossibly bitter quinine tablets to help prevent malaria, little else in the way of medical precautions seems to have been available to the Japanese at Lae to prevent the ravages of tropical illness, although at five each afternoon, a compulsory session of gymnastics was organised to supposedly keep the men's minds and bodies sharp.

For a prize as important to the Japanese as New Guinea, it is curious that their air strategy was so haphazard. Their bombers, too large to be properly dispersed into the bush a safe distance from Lae's feeble airstrip, were repeatedly lined up along the runway, presenting easy targets for the strafing and bombing attacks of the Australian, and later American, airmen. But as Sakai pointed out, throughout the entire period of the Japanese occupation of the Lae airstrip – which lasted until 1943 – no attempt was ever made to upgrade or improve its capacity.

The Japanese resources were also spread thin, with their Betty bombers required to undertake not just offensive actions over Moresby, but maritime reconnaissance and convoy protection, particularly above the sea lanes around their other great prize, the Solomon Islands. This diluting of resources resulted in little more than a squadron's strength of Japanese bombers being available to attack Moresby at any one time.

The Tainan Zeros were similarly stretched throughout the campaign. Although on paper their arrival at Lae in early April boosted the number of fighters there to 36, due to a chronic shortage of spare parts, this figure usually dropped to no more than twenty. These were required to operate across a number of other airfields including Rabaul and Gasmata, performing not just bomber escorts to Moresby, but also fighter sweeps, convoy escort duties and the air defence of other aerodromes besides Lae. Hence the Australians' surprise when the enemy did not appear at Seven Mile at all on some days.

Nor did the Japanese seem able to properly follow up their victories over the Australians, the higher command of the 4th and 1st Air Groups suddenly pulling their stretched air resources away from Moresby to conduct operations elsewhere, thereby easing the pressure. For example, after fierce defences against 75 Squadron attacks on Lae on 11 and

13 April in which two Australian pilots, Sergeant Ally Davies and Sergeant David Brown, were lost, the Japanese were not sighted for another four days. During this time 75 Squadron flew security patrols and absorbed the reinforcements that were gradually trickling in from the south. Men like Sakai found that just when they felt the enemy was close to being on their knees, the Australians would be given the hiatus they needed to recover, appearing once again over Lae aerodrome a few days later for another gruesome low-level attack.

Nevertheless, despite the discomfort, the privations, and the completely unexpected tenacity of the Australian pilots, the morale of the Tainan Kokutai remained high. They were, after all, men bred – even brutalised – into the bushido warrior culture, highly trained and blooded in battle, and motivated for one thing: fighting their enemy.

Interviewed for the 1993 television documentary *44 Days* – still the only televised depiction of the campaign – a charming, somewhat dapper Saburo Sakai spoke freely of his war, as well as his initial impressions of the Australians he met for the first time over Lae.

> When we were first attacked at Lae, I could tell by the emblems on the plane that it was Australians who were attacking us. Until we got to Lae, we had fought a number of battles, but we had always been on the side of the attack. This was the first time we were being attacked. I felt at the time, 'Gosh, this is going to be some fight.'

•

The fate of Sergeant David Brown on 13 April was particularly tragic. Flying wingman to John Piper, the two provided top cover to a group of Dauntless dive bombers making a successful attack on a large fuel dump at Lae. When Brown was hit not by Zeros but by anti-aircraft fire, which appeared to knock out his cooling system, his aircraft exited the combat area, but made it only as far as Salamaua before his engine began to fail. The 24-year-old Brown, from Castlemaine in Victoria, force landed on a beach. Australians of the NGVR watched Brown's descent but reported also that Japanese troops were soon on the site, poring over the aircraft.

Hoping to perhaps replicate the lucky escape of Wilbur Wackett, the unharmed Brown had collected his knife and service revolver and taken off up a nearby hill. But luck, that day, would not be with him: a squad of Japanese infantry were in the area and he was soon cornered. When machine guns were turned towards him, Brown elected to surrender rather than be killed on the spot.

After being searched for papers and equipment, Brown became visibly upset only when relieved of a picture of his fiancée, an act of contemptible weakness in the eyes of the Japanese. The officer in charge nonetheless regarded the quiet, intelligent-looking young airman as a potential source of information and, later that day, handed him over to the commander of the Japanese garrison at Lae. Brown was sent to a prison cell at Rabaul, and the Australians officially posted him as missing.

A large file exists in the National Archives of Australia on Sergeant David Brown, and its nearly 150 fading pages of typed and handwritten notes, letters and official forms make for melancholy reading – a testament to a long journey of suffering endured by his tormented parents. For years, from their home in the leafy suburb of South Yarra in Melbourne, they searched desperately for any trace of their son, assisted by the various officials from the Casualty Section of the Department of the Air.

Rumours of Brown's fate circulated for years. At war's end, a face that may have been his looked out from a *National Geographic* photograph of recently released prisoners, convincing his parents there was still hope of his return. Stories that he had been incarcerated in the notorious Ofuna and Omori POW camps were put about, only to be dismissed by other men who had been there, and who had no recollection of the quiet Australian pilot.

In the late 1940s, two US airmen – Sergeant Lutz and Corporal Reid, themselves shot down in a B-26 Marauder on 18 April – were identified as possibly being Brown's fellow prisoners at Rabaul and were contacted. Reid took the time to reply in detail. Indeed, he remembered Brown, having last seen him on the dock at Rabaul Harbour on 26 May, as part of a group of prisoners being loaded onto an aircraft carrier to be taken to Japan. Brown however, was separated from the group and Reid did not see him again. After that, the leads went cold.

It was to take the work of Squadron Leader Keith Rundle, an asthmatic who had spent the war behind a desk in the Casualty Records section, to close the chapter. At war's end, Rundle was awarded the field job he had so coveted, recovering the mortal remains of some of the missing men he had catalogued for so long. After uncovering a number of airmen's remains in various locations of the Pacific War, Rundle acted on a local tip at Rabaul and, in 1950, found a mass grave close to the volcano of Matupi, alongside Simpson Harbour. In all, fifteen Australians, twelve Americans and an unknown civilian were exhumed and identified by their dental records and dog tags. One of those bodies belonged to Sergeant David Brown.

Disturbingly, Rundle also discovered the men had been buried with personal items, such as cooking gear, suggesting they had believed they were simply being transferred to another camp. Upon this grisly discovery, a large number of Japanese who were known to be in Rabaul at the time of the deaths were interrogated – or re-interrogated – by Australian investigators to piece together what had happened.

It was discovered that the men had been led away from the wharf at Rabaul to an open grave and decapitated by the stroke of a sword; some were wounded and lying in stretchers, and were murdered where they lay. It was also reported that the officer in charge – who, according to a furious Rundle, was still walking the streets of Tokyo a free man – addressed his men, expecting them to display the same level of bravery shown by the Australian and American airmen, should they be required to give their lives for their country.

Finally, after years of false hope, Mr Leslie Brown, David's father, received an official Air Force letter informing him that his son had never left Rabaul, and had indeed been killed on or about 26 May 1942 and that his status had been adjusted from 'missing' to 'killed on active service'. It was added that 'It is realised that your sorrow in the loss of a gallant son will be added to by the fact that he was the victim of a crime against all the laws of warfare and humanity but it is considered that you would desire to know the true facts.'

On 18 July, according to the letter, Sergeant David Brown was reinterred into the Bita Paka War Cemetery, Rabaul: 'Plot H, Row C, Grave 8, to be cared for in perpetuity by the Commonwealth War Graves Commission.'

CHAPTER 15

Fighter pilot reality

> My general feeling which, along with the gastro, built up rather quickly, was that I genuinely felt that I would not survive Moresby.

An intelligent and sensitive man, Arthur Tucker described eloquently the experience of being a fighter pilot during the trial of the 44 days. 'I felt strain,' he recounted in his post-war interviews, 'but I didn't feel fear.'

In the archives of the Australian War Memorial exists the gun camera footage taken from Tucker's Kittyhawk as he shoots down a Zero over Port Moresby. 'How did you feel?' a family member who had viewed it once asked. Tucker had to think before answering, aware that his response may disappoint. 'Look,' he said earnestly, 'would it be unbelievable if I said I didn't feel anything, because it was a sort of technical thing?' The short snippet of grainy film, he said, gives more detail than he can ever remember seeing at the time. 'I was flying around…doing something I was trained for, it was a long way away, and I was concerned that somebody would get on to me. I had all the anticipation of danger, but I didn't have any feeling of it. That came at night and at other times.'

Arriving just as the enemy had been reinforced by the aces of the Tainan squadron in early April, Tucker was thrown into the thick of almost daily air fighting, debilitating illness, poor food and – as he refers to the consequence of his less-than-deferential attitude towards the more pig-headed aspects of military authority – 'people treading on my toes'.

When asked how the strain affected him, he recounted one particular incident that stayed with him the rest of his life. When on standby the pilots would wait, sometimes from dawn till dark, for the unmistakable crack of three quick rifle shots that would see them bolt to their aircraft. 'You'd get in and people would hand you the straps while you plugged yourself in, and then you'd just wait,' he said. Over the radio, which on the ground usually worked, would then come 'Okay, take off!' Tucker would open his throttle and his training would kick in. A false alarm was indicated by the controller declaring. 'Scrubbo!' At which point the men would stand down. The first time Tucker heard this, he threw off his straps, climbed down onto the Kittyhawk's rather high wing, pushed himself onto the ground and collapsed in a heap, unable to stand up, his legs apparently paralysed.

'Now, you've heard of people going at the knees,' he said later, 'well it's an actual physical thing.' Gaining feeling eventually, he pretended to his armourer to have simply slipped off the wing, but vowed he would never let it happen to him again. In a false alarm, the adrenalin build-up in the anticipation of flight, combat and danger simply had nowhere to go. Hence when subsequent 'Scrubbos!' were called, he would make a point of remaining in the cockpit, chatting to his ground crew until he could once again feel his feet.

In August of 1942, Tucker would take part in the decisive Battle of Milne Bay, where he would come his closest to being killed. Emerging from a low cloud ceiling one afternoon, he found two Zeros directly behind him. One immediately put a cannon shell in his starboard wing, jamming his ailerons completely, though thankfully in the neutral position. With nothing but his rudder to manoeuvre, Tucker headed out along the long passage of Milne Bay, being pursued by the Zeros, who no doubt sensed the easy kill of a lame duck. But Tucker was an excellent pilot: dodging in and out of clouds, using the rudder to lower one wing, then the other, waiting for the tracer of the Japanese machine guns to whizz past, then dodging the cannon shells that inevitably followed. He flew as low as he could to the surface of the water, daring the Japanese pilots to line up on him, and risk clipping the water with their wings as they did so.

The pursuit lasted all the way down the bay and then back again until the Zeros' modest supply of ammunition was exhausted. Then, to his horror, three more joined in the chase almost to the threshold of his airstrip, where he landed, amazingly, without the use of ailerons. 'I mean, looking back on it now,' he recalled, 'it wasn't a bad bit of flying, but no-one took any notice of the fact that I'd managed to get it down in one piece with jammed ailerons – but that night, I really had the shakes.'

The fact that he'd almost been killed meant absolutely nothing to anyone but himself. Tucker's tent mate – and subsequent friend for life – Alan Whetters, thought Tucker's shattered nerves 'a great joke. You can ask him what sort of a state I was in.' But the next day he might be called to do it all over again, and perhaps not be so lucky. Such was life on an active fighter squadron taking casualties. The fear, Tucker said, hit hard, 'but very, very slowly. The next day, you're back on the job again, you see. You get quite numb to it.'

In fact, Tucker suspected that even at the time, many of the pilots, himself included, were 'terribly depressed'. After a particularly intense week of action in the middle of April, three or four pilots were lost from his tent in a matter of days. 'The beds had been sort of turning over,' he said, and the atmosphere around the base was particularly morbid. After the evening meal one night, Tucker returned to his tent to see fellow pilot Flying Officer Dave Ellerton, a Middle East veteran and one of 3 Squadron's '1940 originals', reading a letter by the light of a kerosene lamp. It was on blue paper, which Tucker knew to be from Ellerton's wife of just five weeks, Judith, a nurse he'd met while recovering from a dose of scarlet fever contracted in North Africa. At that moment, thought Tucker, Ellerton probably regarded his chances of seeing her again as particularly slim.

Noticing his friend walk in, Ellerton looked up. 'Well, Friar –' with his surname being Tucker, the nickname stuck, '– I wonder which of us it'll be tomorrow, you or I?' It was a logical sort of question, but Tucker couldn't recall offering an answer.

An hour or so later, the acting CO, Les Jackson, whose brother, John, was still missing, came down to the tent to speak with Ellerton. 'Look, Dave,' said the boss, 'I think it's time you had a bit of a rest from combat flying. There's a Fortress which will be going out at about five o'clock. Go down to Bankstown, there's a couple of aeroplanes there, bring them back and after that, okay, you're off combat duty.'

Ellerton being one of the pilots Les actually liked made him aware perhaps of Ellerton's state of mind, which, Tucker believed, was fragile with battle fatigue after his extended service in the desert. The news from his CO no doubt came as a surprise, perhaps relief, as he could now look forward to seeing his new bride.

Rather than the Fortress, Dave Ellerton flew out of Seven Mile on 21 April in a Kittyhawk in need of some repairs, a journey that took him as far as Townsville. He spent nearly a week there before starting the return trip in a replacement Kittyhawk, no doubt contemplating it might have been his last trip to the remote and difficult Port Moresby strip.

Unknown to Ellerton, the previous morning, fifteen P-39 Airacobras of the US 8th Fighter Group's 35th Squadron had taken off from Cairns bound for Horn Island, the final leg of their journey to Seven Mile as one of the early vanguards to the tide of American air power soon to arrive in the Pacific. In a story that mirrors 75 Squadron's own tragic experience when flying north from Bankstown a month earlier, the American pilots, despite a reasonable forecast, similarly ran into a wall of black, impenetrable weather. Radio communication broke down, and some turned back to Cooktown while others attempted to fly through the torrential rain. In all, eleven of the fifteen Airacobras ran out of fuel and crash landed, the aircraft damaged beyond repair. Two pilots vanished forever around the Cape Grenville area.

One of the luckier ones, Lieutenant William McGovern, was forced down at a place called Murdoch Point, 50 miles north of Cooktown, landing successfully on the beach, where he spent a lonely night.

Dave Ellerton, heading north along the coast the following day, 27 April, noticed the odd sight of a waving American pilot beside a stranded Airacobra on the beach.

McGovern watched the Kittyhawk circle, then, to his surprise, it lowered its flaps and wheels and appeared to be coming in to land, right there on the beach.

Being a veteran of the desert, Ellerton was unperturbed by the idea of landing in sand, and according to some of his fellow pilots, would have been quite happy to 'drop in' to offer what assistance he could to the American. It was a fatal error. Some reports state that his wingtip hit an unseen dune, others that the sand was simply too soft to take the aircraft's weight, but McGovern watched helplessly as the Kittyhawk's wheels touched briefly before the aircraft lurched forward at the nose, flipping over on its back and coming to rest just above the line of breakers rolling in on a fast tide.

McGovern raced the quarter mile from his own aircraft, but saw instantly there was nothing he could do – water was already lapping around the partially submerged aircraft. With a feeling of utter helplessness, he watched, impotent, as the tide overwhelmed the inverted Australian airman and he drowned in his cockpit. What Ellerton himself must have gone through can scarcely be imagined.

The memory of Dave Ellerton, particularly on his last night in the tent at Moresby where he seemed to experience a premonition of his own death, remained with Arthur Tucker. Even amid the awful waste of war, Ellerton's end seemed particularly pointless, even perplexing; what he thought he could have achieved landing on the beach that day remained a mystery.

'I can't imagine what purpose there would have been in it,' said Tucker. 'He landed just where the surf rolls up on the beach, turned over, and drowned, trapped in his cockpit. You know, it always seemed to me to be a paradoxical sort of situation.'

Ellerton's body was later recovered and buried in the Townsville War Cemetery, one of the handful of 75 Squadron's pilots from the 44 days interred on Australian soil.

For all his experience of air fighting, Tucker emerged without a scratch. The closest he came to a combat injury bordered on the comical. While on patrol a few days after his arrival, he was surprised by a Zero and started taking hits in his port wing. 'So I headed straight down at full power and the needle "off the clock",' he recalled. Such a violent bunt almost inevitably resulted in the pilot's lapsing momentarily into semi-consciousness from 'red out' as the extreme gravity forced blood into the brain. When Tucker woke from this dive, he had a terrible pain on the left side of his head and thought he'd been hit but 'no blood, no hole in the head. After landing with a major headache, I found that I'd failed to secure the straps of my full army water bottle inside my parachute harness. Under the negative 5G, it had swung up, limited only by my seat belt, and clocked me over my left ear.'

Tucker never viewed what he or his fellow pilots achieved during the 44 days as particularly heroic, at least not in the traditional sense. From where he was, it all seemed a far more scrappy affair.

> It wasn't the heroism of individuals, nor the actions attributable to any individuals. We were up against aeroplanes that could out-climb us and they were always on top, and then there'd be a fight, and we were mostly tangled up with their fighters. Now, this wasn't terribly effective with respect to knocking down bombers, or probably even knocking down a lot of fighters. But it only needed an aggressive response, however pitiful, for the squadron defence to be effective. I think there's a big lesson in this – that if you

respond and you're sufficiently aggressive about it, people will back off no matter how small that response is.

Tucker noted the change of tactics of the Japanese soon after his arrival, which coincided with the deployment of the Tainan squadron. From mid April, staggered groups of fighters arrived over the base, the first designed to lure the Kittyhawks into the air, others, arriving later, to strafe them as they came into land. 'I got strafed in landing on one occasion,' he said. In the late afternoon of 29 April, at the end of a busy day that had already called Tucker into the air in two scrambles of half an hour and an hour's duration, he and John Piper discovered six Zeros flying in formation at around 6000 feet. 'To my great surprise, they sheered off.' After searching for them for another couple of hours, fuel was running low, so Tucker broke off and headed along the coast towards the northwest, having been warned they were still in the area. 'They clearly were hoping to pluck us off, gear down, as we went in to land. Now, this is the silly part,' he said. Realising that the next day was to be his first day off in a week, Tucker decided to risk coming back to Seven Mile rather than put down somewhere else and waste his day finding his way back to the base. His day off, he decided, 'was not to be missed'.

Flying back low and dodging in and out of the hills behind Port Moresby, Tucker slid down quietly on the southeast end of the strip. As he came to a stop, a voice announced over the radio, 'They're coming!' Tucker swung his aeroplane to the left and leapt out onto some grass as a Zero zoomed overhead, firing its guns and putting a hole into his rear fuselage behind the cockpit he'd just vacated. 'I'd really had nowhere else to go, but the triviality of my priorities still shakes me.'

The tactics of the American Airacobras beginning their war against Japan out of Seven Mile differed from those of the Australians and, for some, the tactics did little to engender respect. Rather than fly up and face the enemy directly when scrambled – admittedly often from a position of disadvantage – the American practice was to head due south out to sea in a straight line towards Australia to gain altitude, then return to the fray with the advantage of height. The trouble was, by the time they joined the battle, the Japanese were often already on their way home after attacking Port Moresby. Nor did the Australian Kittyhawks have the luxury of gaining height as quickly as the American aircraft by adopting their straight-line approach. Flying straight in a combat zone, as every fighter pilot knew, was tantamount to suicide.

According to John Pettett, the American pilots 'were intending to gain height and then come back to the area of operation, but very often not arriving back in time. The bombing was all over by the time they'd got back.' Perhaps unfairly, the Australians quickly disparaged the Airacobras as 'the fishing fleet'. 'If we'd done what they did,' said Tucker, 'Moresby would have been clobbered well and truly.'

Not that his own squadron's tactics consisted of much more than forming a kind of gaggle – if they could – then scattering and acting alone once the Japanese planes appeared, at which point individual levels of flying skills – and luck – came into play. Ultimately, however, 'there weren't enough of us to do more than just fly up and cop it when they came down'.

Never a man to offer a typical view, Tucker also believed the standard idea on just what sort of person made the best fighter pilot differs from the norm.

> There was a belief, widely spread among people, that fighter pilots should be harum-scarum wild men, you know, care about nothing at all and rather be upside down than right-side up. But the error with that is that if you don't fly smoothly and instinctively, when you get into combat you'll be slipping or skidding, and when you press the tit the bullets don't go where you're aiming, they get thrown off to one side and you won't hit anything.

Perhaps this was easy for Tucker to say, as he was regarded as one of the finest shots in the squadron.

•

For his part, Peter Masters believed adrenalin was an essential element of combat flying. A week after his arrival, escorting American dive bombers in an attack on Lae, he noticed his friend Pop Woods being followed down by a Zero, turning tight to bring his guns to bear at a short and deadly range. Masters dived, speeding down on the attacker, and also turned, pulling the big heavy Kittyhawk around to line the Japanese aircraft up in his own sights. It was a superhuman effort, but still the Zero was too far to his starboard for him to fire and any moment would begin to blast at Woods. 'I had everything on,' he remembered, 'stick full back and all my strength – you get extra strength when adrenalin runs heavy.' Then, for some unaccountable reason, the Zero made a very high, very sharp left turn. 'Suddenly he was just sitting there in my sights and I started pulling the trigger.'

Managing what he estimates to have been about an aeroplane-length's lead in deflection, Masters saw his bullets hit the Zero, then its wing begin to detach and 'bits come off the cowling'. Still the two aircraft turned together, Masters employing exactly the manoeuvre the Zeros usually made on the Kittyhawks. The Japanese aircraft began to crumple, topple over and go down, vanishing into the jungle canopy not far below. There was no parachute and the pilot, unquestionably, was killed.

Asked years later in an interview about his feelings on this occasion of his first kill, Masters replied, 'In retrospect if feels horrible, but at the time, elated.'

John Piper similarly felt little emotion when, in quick succession, he brought down two Zeros over Lae. As he fired at one of them, he noticed the Japanese pilot pull back his hood and climb out onto the wing to bail out. With the man clearly in his gunsight, Piper had no hesitation in pressing the firing button. 'I was able to shoot him on the wing, which gave me some satisfaction. Looking back, I suppose it isn't very nice.'

Arthur Tucker believed true emotion was always cloaked in self-protection, with the death of colleagues often being explained, almost justified, by some supposed error of judgement on their part. 'If somebody pranged,' he said, 'he was always "looking for it", or "asking for it", or something like that; you didn't have any friends.' On one occasion, his mate Alan Whetters went missing for a day after a morning sortie. Tucker was one of those who went looking for him but said he couldn't 'remember it touching me at all, and he was the closest I had to a friend. I think we must have been quite dreadful people.'

•

John Pettett remembered the moments just before take-off to be the most difficult. When on standby, sitting around the operations tent playing cards, writing letters or just waiting for something to happen, one could perhaps block out the reality of why one was there. Then suddenly, the adrenalin rush as the rifle shots or the voice of Stu Collie yelling 'It's on!' or 'Pilots!', acted as a switch, throwing you into a frenzy of activity:

> You generally had your throat microphone and your Mae West on anyway and you would hop into the aircraft, sit down and the crew would throw the straps around your shoulders and grab them from down below and start to get those connected together while you got your helmet on and strapped that on and plugged it into...your microphone and

> earphones into the intercom thing and your oxygen mask too. That's when it was really scary.

The engine would then start and roar into life, then the short taxi down the slight slope from the dispersal bays to the runway. 'That was the worst time of all,' he said, 'because it was the moment of truth. Then, once airborne, a tremendous feeling of excitement of course, and not being any bravado here at all, but there's no fear – too busy to feel fear.'

For Pettett, fear came only when he could not see his enemy.

> If you could see them and there was a plan, well then the fear was replaced by some sort of excitement. I can't describe it really but certainly I didn't feel fear when I could see where they were. The fearful thing is your imagination and if you're flying particularly alone and you know that there are enemy aircraft in the vicinity but you couldn't see them, you are going to be – well, I was anyway – scared stiff.

Bob Crawford remembered the fear too, but said it vanished once he opened the throttle and the aircraft became airborne. 'I used to think awful things on the ground but felt a lot better once airborne. Then when things happened, you were too busy to worry about it. After you got back you just thought to yourself how lucky you were again.'

CHAPTER 16

Dramatic days

The last fifteen days of April were arguably 75's most dramatic, with furious actions taking place virtually every day. The battle of 17 April remains unique as the only combat to be described in detail by the Japanese ace of the Tainan squadron, Saburo Sakai, flying his first bomber escort mission. Although his recollections differed somewhat from those of the Australians, he nevertheless gave a vivid account of such aspects as the effectiveness of the 'dive and zoom' technique from the enemy's point of view, as well as the destructive power of the army's anti-aircraft guns, the other aspect of Port Moresby's aerial defence during the 44 days.

At around three-thirty in the afternoon, 75 Squadron, led by Les Jackson, managed to send nine Kittyhawks into the air to meet a large formation of eighteen Japanese bombers and seven fighters. The Bettys and their escort made their approach to Moresby at 16,000 feet, when suddenly, according to Sakai, the

Australian anti-aircraft fire opened up like 'angry blossoms of flame and black smoke bursting into being below the bombers'. On this day, some of the Australian pilots had managed to gain height, and raced down onto the Japanese from above. Sakai described the Zeros as climbing up into them, splitting their ranks and 'spilling them away from the lumbering heavyweights'.

Also flying with Sakai was Yoshio Miyazaki, an experienced airman, but who probably should not have been flying at all. Like the Australians, the Japanese were subject to the debilitating rigours of gastroenteritis, and Miyazaki was unwell. Sakai had done his best to discourage him from flying, but Miyazaki had insisted on taking part and initially, Sakai's fears seemed unfounded as Miyazaki kept his usual perfect formation.

The bombers pressed on to execute a long, slow, left-hand turn over the harbour on their run in to the target. Then, said Sakai, more flak barrages 'exploded thunderously above us'. Closer to the target, the Japanese formation was hit again by some of the Kittyhawks, which had managed to climb up a second time and fall onto their victims. Sakai was ready to meet them and 'hauled back on the stick, standing the Zero on its tail'. This attack broke open the tight formation of escorting Zeros, forcing them to abandon their protective 'weaving' manoeuvre around the bombers. Below, fierce individual combats erupted with both Cocky Brereton and Bill Cowe involved in twisting, turning fights with Zeros on their tails.

Sakai observed with alarm that Miyazaki was flying erratically, way out of formation and, along with two other fighters, appeared to have 'gone crazy, swerving down, below the bombers' and placing himself in a position of extreme vulnerability.

But there was no time to worry about the others. Another barrage of fire from the ground appeared to swallow up the formation of bombers with 'bursting shells which spewed out thick smoke. For a moment it looked as though the shells had struck dead centre.' The Bettys, however, emerged 'from the boiling smoke with bomb doors open…and their black missiles tumbled through the air. I watched them curve, picking up speed; they erupted in fountains of smoke, the blast waves from each bomb bursting outward in a flash of light as it struck.' Now suddenly lighter, the bombers immediately picked up speed and wheeled hard over to begin their run home. At this point, the flak began to die away and Sakai sighed with relief as Port Moresby fell behind. Then, nearly a mile above him, he noticed the incredible sight of a single Kittyhawk begin a near-vertical dive towards the formation.

> He came down so fast I could not move a muscle. One second he was above us, the next the lone plane plummeted like lightning into the bombers. Six hundred yards in front of me, I watched the fighter – he was going to ram! How that plane ever got through the few yards' clearance between the third and fourth bombers of the left echelon, I shall never know. It seemed impossible, but it happened. With all guns blazing, the P-40 ripped through the bomber formation and

poured a river of lead into Miyazaki's plane. Instantly, the Zero burst into flames.

Sakai watched, mesmerised, as Yoshio Miyazaki's Zero exploded.

Confusion has long clouded the identity of the Australian pilot who made the daring plummet onto Miyazaki's aircraft that day. The pilots' gun cameras were empty of film, and the only witness to the event itself was, ironically, Saburo Sakai.

The Tainan wing reported the loss of another Zero pilot for 17 April, Petty Officer Second Class Yoshima Sakai – no relation to Saburo. Again no witnesses came forward to vouch for his demise, but Les Jackson submitted a combat report that was only one of two for that day to survive. In it, he described shooting down a Zero that was chasing Alan Whetters. 'I chased this Zero for approximately 20 miles and delivered a stern attack, opening fire at 100 yards...I saw tracers entering at rear of the cockpit...engine immediately poured out dense black smoke...engine cowling shot away...aircraft last seen diving from stalled position still smoking heavily...'

Had he any recollection of the incident, Alan Whetters would surely have been grateful to Les for his timely interception on his behalf, but for the rest of his life, Whetters was adamant it did not take place. He maintained he was neither pursued nor attacked by a Zero that day, but did remember keeping a close eye on one aircraft following at a distance for a considerable period after the initial engagement, and which landed right behind him back at Seven Mile Strip without incident. That aircraft turned out to be Les Jackson's.

Some publications speculated that Les was in fact the pilot who dived through the Japanese formation that day onto Miyazaki – an idea Les himself was keen to perpetuate – but his own combat report bore little resemblance to Sakai's description of the events. He also placed his position – 25 miles northwest of base – nowhere near the incident, and at entirely the wrong altitude.

On balance, it was more likely to have been Arthur Tucker who made the fateful plunge. Returning to altitude after an initial and inconclusive attack on some of the bombers, Tucker remembered seeing far below a Zero on the tail of Sergeant Cowe, and diving down towards it. Almost incidentally he passed through the formation of Japanese bombers. To his surprise, the Zero reared up in front of him in a classic 'split-S' manoeuvre, but for once, the Japanese pilot had mistimed. Tucker later recounted that the Japanese aircraft 'pulled up suicidally in front of me. I stitched him down the middle and passed under him, leaving him hanging on his prop.' In fact, Tucker's guns virtually tore the Zero in two, which then fell in flames and exploded.

This description tallied closely with that of Sakai, although Tucker claimed that, if anything, the Japanese pilot was exaggerating the drama. He remembered diving down through the bombers, but not in a near-vertical dive, and missing the Bettys not by inches but tens of yards and hardly thought he presented the awesome spectacle that Sakai so breathtakingly described. Indeed Sakai's memoir, while undoubtedly fascinating, is prone to incidences of outrageous exaggeration, particularly when it comes to combat kills against the Australian and American aircraft. In one such incident, he claimed four Australian Kittyhawks were shot down by the Tainan pilots in a single encounter. Needless to say, no record of any such slaughter exists.

Whatever the truth in who accounted for who that afternoon, it was a torrid and confusing engagement. Brereton's and Cowe's aircraft were hit as well as Tucker's, returning peppered with Japanese bullets. Brereton's aircraft in particular was a mess, having been struck by two cannon shells in its starboard wing, with the panels covering the guns and wing underside either hanging open or shot away. Tucker collected nine Japanese-made holes, but as he could provide neither a witness nor gun camera to back up what he had stated, his claim was disallowed at the time.

•

One of the few surviving contemporary diaries of the time, penned by 26-year-old Flying Officer Alan Hill Boyd from Quirindi in New South Wales, has only recently come to light, and gives a sense of the intensity of life as a fighter pilot. An original 3 Squadron desert veteran, Boyd had acquired the rare distinction of becoming an ace flying biplanes. In his Gloster Gladiator fighter, he accounted for six Italian aircraft destroyed, two probables and a couple more damaged in just a few weeks at the end of 1940. Arriving at Seven Mile Strip in the first week of April to serve with 75 as a flight commander, the desert must have seemed a long way away. His dramatic descriptions of the Moresby air fighting were penned generally within a couple of days after they took place.

Alan Boyd recalled taking off from Seven Mile at dawn on 19 April to fly a standing patrol, while myriad American Mitchell and Marauder bombers came and went below him. He also gave a description of the previously unrecorded visit, in a B-17 Fortress, of a number of senior RAAF staff officers and dignitaries, including the former aviation minister under the recently ousted Menzies government – and future caretaker prime minister – Sir John 'Black Jack' McEwen.

> Geoff Atherton and I had a yarn to him just after we landed and I didn't waste the opportunity to tell him what we wanted. I hope something comes of it. While we were talking and waiting for the B-17 to get ready, we said something about it being too bad we couldn't turn on a decent raid while he was here.

With exquisite timing, the telephone nailed to the pole near the standby tent rang with news that sixteen enemy aircraft were on their way. Even McEwen's famous six-foot-plus ramrod frame swayed a little when he heard that. 'It rather rocked McEwan,' said Boyd, 'and he was rather nervously walking about while pilots ran to their aircraft.'

Thus scrambled, Boyd took to the air again, leading six Kittyhawks up to 18,000 feet. 'We sighted 8 bombers first of all approaching the aerodrome and then I saw 2 Zeros swinging just behind them – all about 5000 feet above – the bombers then letting all their bombs go.' The Japanese target that morning was not in fact Seven Mile, but Three Mile, the neighbouring home to the American Dauntless dive bombers, closer to the beach. Their bombing was inaccurate, and Boyd remembered most of the bursts – he counted about 70 – occurring along the beach or in the water. His response? A succinct 'Lovely!'

Boyd's battle was not over yet. Chasing some bombers down the coast, he came across a combat between a Zero and P-40 at 22,000 feet, 'so into it we sailed'. It was John Piper's aircraft, which had made a head-on attack into a bomber, only to be assailed by two Zeros.

> Well we got stuck into them with a vengeance. I saw Geoff Atherton pouring lead into a Zero which flicked and went down a bit, then pulled out – I promptly got stuck into him and according to reports from locals, finished him off and also had another good shot at another Zero, which someone else finished off.

Boyd was correct in his assessment, and was credited with a shared kill of a Zero, bringing his wartime tally to seven. During the engagement, Boyd described himself

> throwing his aircraft into some lovely spins – one was about one turn of an inverted spin, all of which are very hard to get out of. I also fired a pretty accurate burst into a Zero while inverted, with dirt and stuff falling from the floor. All of which doesn't mean I'm particularly keen on air fighting – not at all in fact.

On 23 April, Boyd was in action again, leading six typically outnumbered Kittyhawks to intercept eight bombers and seven Zeros:

> …but they were too high and going too fast – we were about 17,000 feet when we sighted them ahead and doing their bombing run across 7 Mile, and they were then about 25,000 feet. The Zeros were spread out widely and above the bombers. We followed them, watched them unload a great stick and cut off the corner as they turned for home – we got a lot closer and up to their height eventually, but about 4 miles away…So I tried by swinging across their rear to draw the fighters – sure enough three detached themselves, and came towards us, but wouldn't follow us, as I tempted them. They were doing steep turns around each other about 5000 feet above us – some of the same ones that attacked Johnny [Jackson], no doubt, in the Dauntless. I did about 4 hrs flying that morning, but I can't remember what else happened that day. It was generally exciting anyway.

Despite their best efforts, it was one of the increasing number of occasions in which the Australian pilots failed to intercept the Japanese bombers, now being protected by ever larger numbers of Zeros. The next day, 24 April, was one Boyd described as 'several times more exciting'.

Shortly before midday, four Kittyhawks led by Les Jackson and flying standing patrol at 5000 feet engaged another superior force of a dozen Zeros descending on Seven Mile in an intensive sweep. Only a few minutes before, six American B-26 Marauder bombers had landed after an aborted attack on Lae and, hearing the alarm, scrambled to take off again as quickly as possible rather than risk being strafed where they stood. Four made it out to sea and safety under cover of the standing patrol up at 5000 feet, but a fifth Marauder was dived upon by several Zeros as it flew low out over Port Moresby Harbour.

Observing from a rare position of height, Les descended with Bob Crawford to attack, but their advantage was wasted as both pilots missed their targets and the Japanese pulled up to meet them head-on in a climbing attack. The initial aim of getting them away from the B-26 was, however, successful. Soon Bob Crawford was in the extremely unhealthy situation of dogfighting with a Zero. From behind, bullets tore into his aircraft, severing his left rudder cable and puncturing his fuel tank, which caused petrol to enter the cockpit and begin sloshing alarmingly at his feet. In the nearest of misses, one bullet even carried away his throat microphone, grazing his neck. Having found the range, bullets were followed by cannon shells, which exploded around him, wounding his unprotected arms and legs with shrapnel.

With his aircraft barely controllable, Crawford had no option but to exit the battle. In the hope that his superior diving speed would save him before being incinerated in his mortally wounded aeroplane, he threw his stick forward in a bunt. A Zero tenaciously followed him down to sea level, but its shooting was inaccurate. At perilously high speed, bracing himself against the gunsight, Crawford hit the water of Moresby Harbour in a spectacle of white spray. Caught by his radiator scoop, his nose went down and his tail went up, but Crawford was protected by his harness, and he managed to scramble out of his submerging cockpit, shaken but not hurt. Discovering he was in just six feet of water, he even managed a wave to Les Jackson as he zoomed by overhead. Crawford was soon collected in a launch.

Meanwhile, four more Kittyhawks became airborne. Climbing in pairs, Ozzie Channon led Arthur Tucker alongside the less experienced sergeants Bill Cowe and the lad described by Bill Deane-Butcher as 'a quiet, tough country boy', Michael Butler. Climbing hard, the pilots took time to attain the almost unheard-of altitude of 25,000 feet, the threshold of the Kittyhawk's effective ceiling. They would not remain there long. Realising the Japanese were far below them, they peeled over in a dive to attack four of them. From that frigid altitude, however, the Kittyhawks' windscreens quickly fogged up as they entered the thick tropical air, blinding the pilots and causing them to lose contact with one another. This same alarming phenomenon had happened to Les Jackson a week or so earlier, nearly resulting in his demise.

At 7000 feet, frantically wiping the Perspex with his hand to restore some vision, Tucker fired into the fleeting fuselage of a Zero that passed just a few yards to his front, then quickly climbed again to 9000 feet where he sprayed some shots at another over the water before opening his hood to restore his view. Where his wingman Ozzie Channon had got to, he had no idea.

The Zeros had seen them coming and quickly reversed the situation, employing their standard tactic of turning into the attackers and breaking up their formation. The inexperienced sergeants neglected to avail themselves of another opportunity to climb away, and tried to fight the Zeros on their own terms. Soon there were enemy aircraft firing on their tails. Butler himself recalled the incident clearly: 'It was just, you know, bog in and I got mixed up with some Zeros so I dived into the one and only cloud in the sky.' The tall cumulus turned out not to be as big as Butler had first thought, and no sooner was he hidden inside it, than he emerged out the other side. Frantically re-entering the cloud several times, Butler 'skidded' his aircraft from side to side to put the Japanese pilots off their aim. 'But then, all of a sudden, there's hell let loose and black smoke started pouring out from behind the spinner…I had full control of the aeroplane but the temperatures were getting a bit hot.' His oil cooler fatally damaged, Butler's engine had seconds before it would begin to falter. 'I thought, "oh, they're going to come and finish me off."' In these frantic seconds, Butler remembered seeing a diving Kittyhawk, similarly under attack from a Zero. Below him, a clear patch of green presented what looked to be a suitably makeshift airstrip about six miles from his base. Wheels up, he descended into the six-foot-high kunai grass, cutting a swathe before swinging into a vicious ground loop. Closing his eyes and praying to both providence and the Kittyhawk's sturdy construction, Butler felt his tailplane being wrenched in half by a hidden anthill but as it slid to a stop – the tail section 300 yards behind him – he realised he was shaken but unhurt. 'Fortunately, for me, it remained upright, didn't overturn or twist or ground loop, it just went straight ahead...I was just terribly lucky.'

Overhead, he was spotted by a searching John Piper and decided, sensibly to sleep the day off on the wing and wait to be picked up rather than trek back to Seven Mile on his own. He was picked up by an army patrol and was back in his tent that evening, flying again the next day.

Channon, however, did not survive the encounter. Most likely blinded by his fogged-up windscreen like Tucker, he was pounced upon as he attempted to climb, possibly not even seeing his attacker. It was his aircraft Butler had noticed diving down, pursued, and it crashed near a village called Porabada. From Manly in Sydney, Pilot Officer Oswald John Channon was 24 years old and was buried at the Bomana War Cemetery, Port Moresby.

CHAPTER 17

'Dive and zoom'

Anzac Day proved to be a particularly busy one for 75, not least for the fact that it was on that day the squadron's camp was relocated – with just 36 hours' notice – further inland to Twelve Mile Strip, still under construction. Here, it was hoped, some respite might be gained from the relentless low-level attention of the Tainan pilots, as well as a chance for the men's health to improve in a dryer, less mosquito-infested position. The squadron would still fly, however, from Seven Mile.

Determined both to interrupt the move and deny the American bombers a second escape, the Tainan pilots again appeared, fifteen in number, over the airstrip just after eight am. Their persistence paid off. Two of the American aircraft that had become stranded overnight on a boggy patch of the increasingly unserviceable airstrip were shot up severely. One of them, full of fuel, went up like a torch, and while the other did not burn, it was still a write-off. One of the Marauder's ground crew, who had camped overnight under its wing in a slit trench, returned later to find his blankets and belongings cut to pieces by Japanese bullets. A parked B-17 Fortress was also struck, starting a small fire aft of the cockpit. Without proper firefighting equipment, it was left to a soldier of the local 39th Battalion to attempt to extinguish it, but his efforts were foiled by the aircraft's locked door and the Fortress was lost.

The squadron had planned to make the move to Twelve Mile quickly and quietly without the enemy noticing. The plan failed. In his diary, Alan Boyd remembered it as the day the Zeros 'did the place over properly, starting huge fires and... doing steep turns all over the place'. He did not mention whether he was one of those caught in a strafing attack as they moved to Twelve Mile, forced to abandon their vehicles and seek shelter in the bush.

Four Kittyhawks were airborne, but once again the skilled pilots of the Tainan turned to meet them head-on as they dived to attack, out-manoeuvring them and turning the tables. One of those pilots was Alan Whetters, who had an extremely lucky escape, for which he had to thank the Kittyhawk's designer. 'I was probably at about 4000 feet, and suddenly felt a series of shocks on the rear of my armour plate at the back of my seat.' A Zero had latched onto his tail as he flew, oblivious, over Moresby Harbour. Immediately recalling the old World War One flyer's adage, 'Beware of the Hun in the sun', he felt a brief pang of annoyance at having allowed himself to be thus surprised, before instinctively throwing the Kittyhawk's nose down in a bunt, forcing the Zero to overshoot. He would forever recall the sound of the Japanese pilot's machine-gun bullets hitting his armour plate as akin to 'piano notes without the music'.

On 26 April in another torrid encounter, both Whetters and Michael Butler again experienced more high drama and miracle escapes. Despite his crash landing in the kunai, Butler was still expected to take his place in the battle order. 'If you were still standing up well, that was it, 'cause we didn't have the pilots,' he says.

The day began as the two pilots joined Bill Cowe and Geoff Atherton in a standing patrol at 11,000 feet, 10 miles south of Port Moresby. This increasingly used tactic chewed up not only fuel but often hours of flying time, but as the reinforced Japanese began appearing in ever-increasing numbers in late April, at the same time as 75's strength was waning, it was seen as one of the only ways to gain the height to at least present an aggressive defence.

At about eight-fifteen am, four Zeros were spotted going in to strafe Seven Mile Strip as a precursor to an incoming bombing raid. The always aggressive Atherton wheeled over first, planning to fall on the Zeros as they came up from their run over the field. On this occasion, however, his fire was ineffective, as the Zeros spotted the Australian's descent and turned to meet him.

Tearing through the Japanese formation, he wheeled around again to have another go, firing at a Zero at close range, which rolled onto its back and, using its manoeuvrability, dived away. The rest of the Australian formation joined in, followed by two more Zeros that had been unseen at a higher altitude. The action quickly became a melee.

To avoid a dogfight situation with the superior Zero, the Australians used their 'dive and zoom' tactic in a series of spirited swooping attacks. At one point, Cowe missed a collision with a Zero by inches, then stalled his aircraft, putting it into a spin that removed him from the fight. No sooner had Butler fired at one Zero ahead of him than he began taking hits from another to his rear. He dived immediately, but was pounced on again. 'So then,' he says, 'I headed off.' This time, however, it would be much harder to shake off his assailant. For their part, the Japanese pilots seemed determined not to let Butler escape.

Having only two days earlier survived his crash land in the kunai grass, Butler must have wondered how much luck he had remaining, but over the next twenty minutes, he would need it all. Chased now by not one but five Zeros, Butler at first headed for the protection of a cloud, but then turned flat out in a northeasterly direction along the coast of the Huon Peninsula in an attempt to escape his pursuers. The Kittyhawk could match a Zero in a straight chase, and try as they may, the Japanese could not quite close the distance. Whenever they came close, however, Butler saw a white eruption of machine-gun and cannon shells tearing up the water below him.

Using his boost, which gave the motor extra power in short bursts only, Butler managed to put some distance between himself and the Zeros, but sooner or later, he knew he would have to turn back towards the safety of Moresby or run out of fuel. This meant making a turn that would both slow him down and expose him to their gunfire. He also ran the risk of over-boosting his big Allison engine, igniting the fuel before it reached the cylinders, effectively killing it, and most likely himself. Fearing for his life, but keeping cool, Butler worked the throttle gingerly, attempting to find the balance between enough power to outrun his enemy while at the same time keeping his engine from failing. He recalled:

> They were firing at me every now and again and the bullets would go into the water, just missing the wings. So then I'd bend the throttle a bit more. I didn't think it was possible you could get so much boost out of an engine. I can't remember but it was something in the vicinity of about seventy inches.

Careful to make the shallowest turn possible, Butler pointed his nose to starboard, taking him out to sea. Cursing, he saw the Japanese pilots follow. One can imagine their frustration at having their quarry in their sights and opening fire, only to watch the Kittyhawk edge away again, all the while keeping an eye on their own fuel gauges. For 125 miles across the Gulf of Papua, Michael Butler was chased, drawing the Japanese slowly around in a wide circle back towards the defensive protection of the aerodromes of Port Moresby. Eventually, they pulled away.

In his book *Samurai!*, Saburo Sakai cited one of those Zero pilots as being the Devil himself, Hiroyoshi Nishizawa, who he described as chasing a Kittyhawk 'all over the sky' but not quite being able to bring it down, despite his skills. In fact, it was discovered that, in all the fire directed at Butler's Kittyhawk, not a single shot landed true.

Believing the Zeros would make an attempt to bounce him while landing at Seven Mile, Butler instead chose to evade them by getting down as quickly as possible at the smaller Three-Mile strip, now being occupied by the Americans.

> I just did a tight circuit straight in and landed at the Three Mile and I was absolutely stonkered. I got out of the aeroplane; I couldn't talk. A Yank came up to me and...I think I smoked about a half a packet of cigarettes before I could be sensible. I've never been so scared in my life and I was really in a mess.

So too was his aircraft. Earlier that day, his Kittyhawk had been a brand-new machine. Now its smoking Allison motor was spent, pushed beyond its limits and unfit for combat flying.

Later that evening, his nerves severely frayed, he begged Les to be taken off the following day's battle order. The request was refused. His replacement aircraft not yet ready for battle, Butler would take off nonetheless in his exhausted machine, heading out to sea to avoid an incoming bombing attack on the strip, therefore saving his precious Kittyhawk from possible destruction.

Alan Whetters, meanwhile, was having troubles of his own. After several dives and zooms at full power, his fuel gauge was reading dangerously low. With enough left in his tank for a single approach, he headed back to Seven Mile, but soon doubted he had enough even for that and began looking for a suitable place to put down and be refuelled safely. Near Fly River, not far from the strip, he noticed a smooth, cultivated-looking green field.

According to Whetters, Les Jackson, made temporary commander of 75 during his brother's absence, had 'complained bitterly' about Mick Butler damaging his aircraft in the kunai grass in his crash two days earlier. Whether he was oblivious to the perilous position in which Butler had found himself, or simply unconcerned, is unclear, but with serviceable aircraft now a diminishing commodity, Les had insisted pilots attempt to bring their aircraft home. Les was in the habit of forming vehement dislike towards some of the pilots, and Butler would bear the brunt of his bitterness for years.

Mindful of this piece of advice, and anxious not to risk damaging another precious fighter, Whetters extended wheels and flaps and began to come down in the field. Only when he was a short distance above it did he realise it was precisely what he was trying to avoid – kunai grass, with all its hidden dangers. But he was now committed to the landing and could only pray that he was not, like Butler, about to break the aircraft, as well as his own neck, in two.

His aircraft's propeller hit the grass first, sending a cloud of kunai grass into the air. A terrible, slithering, scraping noise tore past him as his wheels descended into the green. By sheer luck, the ground beneath his wheels was smooth, and he came to a quick stop, both he and his aircraft unharmed.

Only by standing up in his cockpit could he see above the tips of the grass, and he decided to make for the coast, where he believed he would have more chance of being spotted. After a few steps, however, the aircraft – and pretty much everything else – disappeared from view, and he elected to return to the Kittyhawk to contemplate his next move.

His landing had not gone unnoticed, and Whetters soon saw local men 'stealthily creeping through the kunai'. Standing up on the wing to attract their attention, he learned they were in fact the guides for a detachment from the New Guinea Volunteer Rifles (NGVR) who had observed his descent from an adjacent hill.

Inspecting his fuel gauge again, Whetters began to think that perhaps there was more in his tanks than he had first thought. After a brief discussion with the Australian commander of the NGVR, he decided to try to take off and attempt the short trip back to the strip. To clear a makeshift runway, help from the guides and the population of a nearby village was enlisted, all of whom brought their machetes to cut a swathe through the tall kunai. Alan started up again and opening the throttle, took off. 'But, as soon as I became airborne and checked my gauge again, I had further misgivings, and decided to land once more on my original path, as I knew I would not expect any obstacles.'

This time, the soldiers arranged for fuel to be brought up and, after a few hours, Whetters was off yet again, enough in his tanks to make it back to Moresby by that evening.

In his absence, a search had been undertaken by Arthur Tucker and others, and Whetters' aircraft had been spotted down in the kunai. It seems to have simply been assumed he was unharmed and would soon be back with 75. 'It was just accepted that I had been indeed fortunate, I was back again with the squadron. It was just accepted as routine I suppose.' In the background of the high drama of an operational fighter squadron, little was made of the incident, nor was any appreciation offered for him from the CO for bringing the aircraft back in one piece, as he had requested. Bill Deane-Butcher at least was impressed, describing Whetters' actions as 'a risky and skilful performance, but he got off and returned, thereby saving a valuable plane and a valuable pilot'.

Whetters' Kittyhawk was examined and marked fit for operational flying. It would prove however, to be a less than thorough inspection, as Arthur Tucker found to his detriment when taking it to the air a few days later.

•

One of three squadrons created with the same pen stroke, 75 Squadron would forge a unique association with its stablemate, 76 Squadron, formed on 14 March 1942 and based at Archerfield in Queensland. In order to circumvent the often long and cumbersome air force training and replacement system, something of a private arrangement developed between the two squadrons whereby new pilots were posted, with minimum fuss, straight from 76 to 75 as the need arose. While not officially condoned by the higher echelons of the air force, the practice was seen to work well enough under the circumstances and was left for the squadrons themselves to manage as they saw fit.

It was this arrangement that saw the recently named CO of 76, Squadron Leader Barney Cresswell, an officer with enormous flying but no combat experience, arrive as an attachment to 75 to gain some knowledge of what life was like in a front-line fighter squadron. On 17 April, accompanied by Flying Officer Pop Woods, Cresswell took off just after dawn for a reconnaissance flight over Lae. It was to be his first experience of flying into a battle area. After passing a small island off the northern coast, the pair turned west towards Lae in a wide, right-hand arc, then continued 30 miles to its west before heading through a long valley to Wau.

No Japanese activity had been encountered over Lae, but approaching Wau at low level, three Zeros suddenly descended on them from high above. Just a few days before, the Tainan squadron's numbers had been considerably reinforced with the arrival of twenty replacement Zeros being flown by pilots eager to get into action. As their luck would have it, Woods and Cresswell had crossed paths with a flight of seven Betty bombers and their six-strong fighter escort, heading out on an early attack to Moresby.

The more experienced Woods saw them pounce at the last second, but with their radios not working, he could only waggle his wings desperately to warn Cresswell, who was following 150 yards astern. Cresswell did not appear to notice. With the Zeros almost on top of them, Woods banked away into cloud, dodging a stream of cannon and machine-gun fire. He lost contact with Cresswell and was pursued by Zeros over the jungle canopy for the next fifteen minutes. Another Zero had latched on to the unsuspecting Cresswell who, perhaps stunned at the split-second realities of air fighting, took hits at close range.

Observing the action from below was an NGVR detachment – they often seemed to be everywhere – who reported seeing a Kittyhawk emit a long trail of smoke as it lost height, apparently seeking a safe place to crash land. Without warning, it keeled over and plummeted straight into a hillside near the junction of the Watut and Bululo rivers. Also watching the engagement, in the midst of his great trek home, was John Jackson, who unknowingly witnessed the death of his friend and 76 Squadron counterpart.

Barney Cresswell's remains were buried, with full military honours, at the local Bulwa Cemetery. Peter Turnbull, in Cresswell's place as the new boss of 76 Squadron, departed for Townsville.

CHAPTER 18

'I'm going to show you how'

In the 1993 television documentary *44 Days*, interviewer Geoffrey Robertson – whose own father, Frank, flew Kittyhawks with 75 Squadron later in the war – discussed various issues of the campaign with the ageing but dignified figures of Alan Whetters, Arthur Tucker, Bob Crawford and other former members of the squadron. At all times these wonderful old gentlemen were polite, circumspect, even occasionally coy about their achievements during the dramatic and terrible weeks of the campaign. Only at one point did the strain of 40 years previously come close to breaking through: when discussing the celebrated return to the squadron of its leader, John Jackson, following his ordeal in the jungle after being shot down over Lae a fortnight earlier.

Even without his arrival on 23 April, it had been a hectic couple of days for the squadron. Wilbur Wackett had ended his epic month-long odyssey just the day before, but the celebrations of his return were well eclipsed by the outpouring of relief at John Jackson resuming his place at the helm of 75. And his near demise when attacked suddenly by an unseen Zero in the last seconds as he came in to land at Seven Mile Strip, were almost too much for the nerves of the men to bear.

'Well, boys, I'm back again,' was the way he greeted them after things had settled down. In half an hour, the base was buzzing, and an air of revelry took over. Ted Church remembered the feeling well. 'Gone was the fatigue and utter weariness of the long days, forgotten the hopeless struggle against increasing odds – the CO was alive and back with the squadron, all was well again.'

The pilots interviewed before the camera for Robertson's documentary also remembered him well. Though thinner, Jackson's characteristic big grin remained undiminished. After a shave and a shower, he would only make light of his trial to his pilots, and announced he would be putting himself on the dawn patrol for the next morning. After some howls, and promises the whole squadron would personally tie him to his bed if he tried, reason intervened, and Jackson decided that, under the circumstances, a day off was probably not such a bad idea after all. Perhaps he quipped about the locals, or the food he'd had to digest, or ribbed one of the pilots about how much they would have enjoyed such an impromptu holiday. A truck headed into Moresby to load up on extra beer from the air force canteen.

War correspondent Osmar White also saw Jackson that night when, quite unexpectedly, he turned up with a bandaged hand to a dinner being hosted by an American general for the Moresby pressmen to informally discuss the evolving military situation and the impending arrival of American air power. White's impression of Jackson was telling.

> 'I owe you an apology, sir', he told the general with a faint, dry smile. 'I'm exactly a fortnight late for dinner.' He told his story willingly. One could see he was amused by it and more than a little wondering. He did not mention his personal feelings. His big body was thin, but his complexion was still ruddy. His hands and eyes were still rock steady. Yet – and this is not wisdom after the event – whoever looked at the man with friendly eyes that night saw one weary in soul. Too long in shadows had etiolated the strong stem of his resolution to live. I have never seen a man who needed more desperately some gentleness to make him feel again, as living men should, that the face of death is terrible and to be feared. He had done more than conquer fear – he had killed it.

The next morning, after a decent night's sleep, Jackson sat down and penned the long tale of his adventure to his wife. John Piper remembered him in typically cheerful demeanour, talking only of getting back into the air and fighting the Japanese. 'Yes, he was breathing fire,' said Piper in the television interview. Only when Robertson, with a note of incredulity, put it to Piper that it seemed unlikely, after all he had been through, that Jackson would have really wanted to go straight back to the fighting, did Piper's steady exterior seem to crack, just a flicker, as he rubbed the back of his neck in irritation. 'Oh, well how am I to know?' he replied in a voice that spoke of a lifetime spent contemplating that very question. 'Look, if I were he, I don't think I would have wanted to get back very much at all, not with a wife and family.' Then, just as quickly, he resumed his bearing and continued, 'But he was back, and he was determined to go back.'

Even the unflappable Bill Deane-Butcher (who still appeared wondrously fit in the early 1990s) bristled just slightly at Robertson's question of whether, after fourteen days slogging through the jungle, Jackson was in fact even capable of flying. 'Well, he didn't front up at my tent to ask me whether I thought he was fit,' he managed to say through a stolid patrician's smile. 'I had no say in the matter. I think his determination was such there was no way of stopping him.'

The general sense however, was of a group of men whole again upon the return of their leader. 'The squadron was back again to what it was previously,' said Alan Whetters. 'We were sort of leaderless after he had not returned.'

It is difficult to pin down exactly how John Jackson spent the few days following his return, but it is known that some considerable attention was given to examining what the squadron had been through in his absence. It is not difficult to imagine his shock in learning that four of his pilots – Sergeants

David Brown and Ally Davies, 76 Squadron commander Barney Cresswell on his first ever mission, and just the day before, Flying Officer Dave Ellerton, drowned bizarrely in an upturned Kittyhawk on a lonely Queensland beach – were all either killed or missing. 75 Squadron was down to just six serviceable aircraft. Added to this was news that both the strength and aggression of the enemy had increased considerably, to the point where 75 Squadron's meagre handful of pilots and aircraft, always outnumbered, were now being overwhelmed.

According to both Arthur Tucker and Alan Whetters, each of 75 Squadron's pilots were summoned in turn to Jackson's tent for a private meeting. Spread before him on a makeshift table were the sheaves of combat reports that had been submitted by the squadron's intelligence officer, Stu Collie, and countersigned by the acting commander, Jackson's brother, Les, who was suddenly absent. Having appeared in robust health, Les, to the surprise of some, had apparently checked himself into the base hospital at Moresby with a bout of gastro on John's return – the first occasion, it was noted, he had felt compelled to do so.

With a form in his hand, Jackson spent some considerable time grilling each pilot in turn on the details of the combats that had taken place in his absence, and to ascertain whether what was stated in the reports was accurate. Arthur Tucker noted also that many of the forms appeared to have had black lines through them, indicating that alterations had at some stage been made after the initial pilot interview.

The issue of combat reports during 75 Squadron's 44 days in Port Moresby remained contentious for many years after the war. Compiled as soon as was possible after returning from a flight, the reports were an essential way of recording exactly what had taken place in the air before a pilot's adrenalin and memory began to fade, and his recollections became skewed by doubts and other influences. It was also the point at which a formal claim for a kill or damage to an enemy aircraft could be made. In later years, said Arthur Tucker, the reports were a more free-flowing affair, with the pilot being asked to write what had happened in his own words, or to have the squadron intelligence officer simply transcribe them. But in April 1942, the pilots of 75 Squadron had yet to be afforded that freedom.

'We didn't write our own combat reports,' recalled Arthur, 'we were interviewed by the intelligence officer who wrote what we said down on a form, then we were given it to sign.'

Alan Whetters similarly stated, 'I cannot recall ever actually completing a combat report by writing the details myself.'

The pilots, according to Tucker, were not given the opportunity to describe combat in their own words but were instead 'interviewed' by the intelligence officer, who he said would 'sort out our impressions according to his mind'. This then went to make up the official record. Nor, for that matter, did it seem to matter if the pilot signed or not. Alan Whetters recalled viewing one of his own combat reports from the 44-day period a few weeks later when the squadron had withdrawn to Townsville, in which he not only recognised little of what he read but noted that it was unsigned by him.

Sometimes, the men were simply disbelieved. Early in the campaign, pilots attacking the still unfamiliar Japanese Betty bomber reported coming under attack from a gun situated under the aircraft's large tail. John Pettett even recalled being holed by cannon shell which also appeared to have been fired from this position. On both occasions, their reports were disallowed by Stu Collie, as it was not believed that the Japanese Betty possessed a rear gunner. It was assumed the pilots, in their confusion, had been hit by Zeros, and that was what was entered into the report. A number of the pilots felt obliged to mention that Stu Collie, a successful Melbourne lawyer, had no flying experience whatsoever.

Later it was discovered that the Betty did indeed possess a rear gun position, armed with a powerful 20-millimetre cannon, but by then, the record had been set. Tucker had to wait decades for his vindication, when, at a squadron reunion in the 1980s, a Japanese photograph taken from within a formation of Bettys was passed around, and, behold, there was the rather prominent Perspex rear gunner's compartment, complete with protruding cannon.

It is not known what John Jackson made of the combat reports that had been written in his absence, nor the meaning of the lines and alterations he discovered when he went through them. Unfortunately, most of them were placed in a large Gladstone bag and given to the care of Alan Whetters, who, along with most of the squadron personnel, was evacuated to Cairns by ship when 75 was ordered to withdraw and regroup a week or so later. Struck down with a severe fever onboard, Whetters awoke in a Cairns hospital a few days later to find the bag missing. Neither it, nor the reports, were ever seen again.

Another incident following John Jackson's return, one of the most important in the squadron's history, is now equally murky.

In his diary, Boyd recalled the brief visit of the chief of air staff, Air Marshal Charles Burnett, to 75 Squadron's base just outside Port Moresby, but most of the other pilots could not recall a single appearance by any senior RAAF officer. Alan Whetters, who was present for most of the 44 days, could not recall anyone of senior rank present at Seven Mile Strip: 'It has been known for certain officers to do this, and they were highly respected because of this attitude...but to my knowledge there had been nothing of this nature at Moresby. As a matter of fact I never saw the senior officers at any time.'

Arthur Tucker insisted flatly that no senior officers ever graced Seven Mile with their presence, at least during his time there. In fact, throughout his long subsequent service in the RAAF, such a visit occurred only once, later in the war, but is worth mentioning if only to illustrate prevailing attitudes among some senior officers towards fighting men in the field. In 1944, when flying with 86 Squadron based at Merauke in southern central New Guinea, Tucker was among a group of pilots being given an informal address by no lesser figure than the visiting chief of air staff, Air Marshal George Jones. If the pilots thought their courage was to be congratulated, however, they were in for a rude shock. Far from praising the men on their successes in the most trying of circumstances during their country's hour of need, Tucker remembered Jones 'scratching noughts and crosses in the dirt with the toe of his shoe' while he rebuked them for their appearance. How disappointed would their mothers be, he asked, to see them so unkempt in these scrappy pieces of uniform? They were upbraided also for the 'kind of language' he had overheard in his brief time spent around the Merauke airstrip. The address went on in this manner. At no point, insisted Tucker, did Jones manage to look any of them in the eye.

It was not the neglect of senior commanders that proved most damaging to 75 Squadron during the 44 days – but interference from men who could not be dismissed as desk-bound staff officers with no concept of the realities of combat. At the end of April 1942, 75 Squadron's darkest chapter would be brought on by two of the RAAF's undoubted heroes.

•

By 1942, Wing Commander Charles William Pearce had already enjoyed a stellar career in the RAAF. Just before the outbreak of war, Pearce, already a renowned pilot, was sent to the United Kingdom, where he helped form Coastal Command's famous 10 Squadron, with which he flew Sunderland flying boats on submarine patrols across the slate-grey wastes of the North Atlantic. For his efforts, he was the first RAAF officer in the Second World War to earn a DFC. When given command of a Catalina Squadron in Port Moresby in January 1942, Pearce implemented a series of air raid precautions, which resulted in virtually no losses in human life despite over 50 Japanese air attacks.

Pearce's overall commander in Port Moresby was a fellow 10 Squadron veteran of distinction, Wing Commander William Norman Gibson. In 1940, Gibson had chalked up the RAAF's first U-boat of the war, sinking it with depth charges before overseeing the rescue of its crew. Both Pearce and Gibson went on to long and distinguished post-war air force careers that stretched well into the 1960s. It could also be said, however, that both had a history of denigrating junior commanders in the field, in whose direction they readily – and falsely – levelled accusations of cowardice.

Author Mark Johnston, in his excellent one-volume history of Australia's entire Pacific air war, *Whispering Death*, cited an incident in 1941 when Pearce took aim at one of the pre-war Qantas pilots then under his command, and who had volunteered to fly the Catalinas of 20 Squadron at Port Moresby. Although acknowledging Flight Lieutenant Godfrey Hemsworth as a competent pilot, Pearce felt obliged to complain about what he called Hemsworth's 'Quantas [sic] outlook in that he will not take the slightest risk in flying in case it will jeopardise his position with Quantas Airways after the war.'

Johnston also noted that 'three of the first four Qantas pilots who signed up for active duty with flying boats in 1939 would be dead within six months of Pearl Harbor', including Hemsworth himself, who, while being disparaged by Pearce, had earned himself the Air Force Cross and demonstrated extraordinary courage in bringing back a badly damaged Catalina – the craft bore over a hundred bullet holes – to Moresby after a nightmare 24-hour ordeal evading multiple Japanese fighters over Rabaul. He would be lost on a reconnaissance patrol later in 1942, having extended his search far beyond what was asked of him.

Pearce had also apparently labelled as 'scared' Flight Lieutenant Bill Pedrina, a 24 Squadron Lockheed Hudson pilot whose name was synonymous with courage, having already won a DFC in February after being badly shot up in a daylight reconnaissance flight against overwhelming Japanese defences at Gasmata on New Britain. Pedrina would die in December 1942 while executing a low-level supply drop under fire to troops in Buna. His memory – as well as the injustice dealt him by Pearce – was evoked in a moving poem penned by another Hudson pilot, David Campbell. Its publication in the mid 1970s stirred bitter memories in some of 75 Squadron's surviving members.

For his part, Wing Commander Gibson was heavily criticised later in the war by a number of senior officers who believed he had directly contributed to a severe drop in airmen's morale. A subsequent enquiry cited his attitude to operational commanders as 'indifferent and on occasions high handed'. Gibson was sacked from his position as head of the First Tactical Air Force, although later reinstated.

These are the men who decreed, at the end of April, that 75 Squadron was just not doing enough. The insufficient impact they were having on the ever-strengthening Japanese apparently had nothing to do with lack of training, inferior aircraft for which there had been few replacements, poor diet and the most gruelling of living conditions, but the character of the men themselves, and particularly the man leading them, John Jackson.

The exact circumstances are unclear, but it seems these opinions may have been fomented during the extremely brief visit to Seven Mile Strip on 22 April by the outgoing chief of air staff, Sir Charles Burnett, finally on his way back to the United Kingdom after his disastrous tenure at the helm of the RAAF.

At the first opportunity following Jackson's return, Pearce and Gibson summoned him to Moresby HQ for a private meeting, for which there are now no records. It is understood that Pearce and Gibson insisted Jackson and his men were not pressing their attacks hard enough, not getting close enough and not getting results. The pilots, they said, were acting like 'dingoes' – a common colloquialism of the time for cowardice – and it was Jackson's fault, having instilled in them his lily-livered, hit-and-run notion of 'dive and zoom'. This, they insisted, would all have to stop. From now on, Jackson and his pilots would adopt a policy of direct engagement with the enemy, using their P-40 Kittyhawks to deliberately dogfight the Japanese Zeros.

Much has been made of this encounter between Jackson and his commanders over the course of the long history of 75 Squadron, and the bitterness it engendered rankled many of the pilots for the rest of their lives. In his documentary, Geoffrey Robertson forthrightly labelled Jackson's superiors as 'stupid', and even the normally circumspect Alan Whetters spoke of the encounter thus: 'He had been told by higher authority that we were not doing the job we should be doing and the pressure was on him to show what should be done. The whole thing was erroneous, of course. These men had high rank, but they'd never fought the Japs.'

In a practical sense, it could be argued that Pearce and Gibson were simply espousing the tactic used by the pilots much of the time anyway. The notion of 'dive and zoom' was all very well, but as we have seen, the opportunities the squadron had to employ it were few. Alan Whetters struggled to recall a single instance during the 44 days when he and his pilots enjoyed the crucial advantage of height at the outset of a contest, although in fairness, some others could. Most of the time, however, it was almost unarguable that the Kittyhawks simply did not have time to climb above their enemy. In the majority of cases, the pilots attacked from below then pulled up to meet the Japanese fighters head-on. But it was never their preferred method.

Whether they actually set foot on Seven Mile Strip or not, Pearce and Gibson did not like what they knew – or saw – of 75 Squadron. Perhaps they observed that 75's tactics were loose and scatty, with few briefings or discussions on the matter, the men simply behaving – both in the air and on the ground – as a group of individuals. Perhaps they were appalled by the lack of saluting, the highly informal uniforms and little apparent distinction between officers and other ranks. Perhaps they were disgusted by the food, the prevalence of illness, the smell of the makeshift latrines or the general squalor of the New Guinea airstrips. Perhaps they regarded what they saw as alarmingly 'unmilitary'.

Pearce and Gibson had flown in combat, but in a very different war and under very different circumstances from the one being fought in New Guinea. However, in a crisis such as the one faced at that perilous time, with the arrowhead of annihilation bearing down on Australia and seeming to hover above Port Moresby and its airstrips, it is perhaps understandable that a certain level of panic began to set in among the upper echelons of command. The Japanese, despite 75 Squadron's valiant efforts, were in the ascendancy at the end of April 1942, and the Allies had very few ideas about how to stop them. In wartime, the lives of young men are tragically, necessarily, expendable, and the pilots of 75 Squadron were no exception. For generals to exhort fighting men to further effort and further sacrifice is simply the stuff of war. But for experienced men in positions of command to exhort a tactic known to be not only impossible to perform, but profligate in both lives and aircraft, while at the same time having little hope of impacting on the enemy, borders on the incomprehensible, and gives weight to Geoffrey Robertson's blunt comment: 'stupid'.

We cannot know Jackson's reaction to Pearce's and Gibson's criticism, if he fought them hard or meekly acquiesced. Who could know the true state of his mind and body after the unimaginable ordeal of the previous fortnight? Late on 27 April, however, after his meeting with Pearce and Gibson, Jackson returned to the camp at Twelve Mile Strip and called his pilots to the mess tent. What transpired was regarded by Intelligence Officer Stu Collie as sensitive enough for him to record it only cryptically: 'tactics were discussed and advice was given…for the future guidance of the squadron'. For the men who were there, however, there was nothing cryptic in what Jackson said at all, merely disbelief. A letter written by Arthur Tucker to an enquiring friend in the 1990s, and which has only recently come to light, is one of the few documents that can illuminate the atmosphere of that meeting with John Jackson in the mess tent at Port Moresby:

> John told us they had complained that we were 'dingoes' because we did not directly dogfight the Zeros. This occurred in the mess after evening meal a couple of days after his return by air from Wau. Mine was one of the voices raised in protest: 'Hadn't he told us not to try to tangle with the Zeros in a turning contest – couldn't be done!'

He also added pointedly, 'If Pearce had complained of other features of the command of 75 Squadron after John failed to return from Lae, they might have had some justification.'

Accounts from other pilots reported that Jackson repeated what was said by Pearce and Gibson, that they were failing to 'press the enemy', that they were opening fire from too great a distance, and that, in the opinion of the officers, they were frightened of the enemy. Many of the men must have looked around the tent at the thinning, exhausted faces, recalling those no longer there, and shaken their heads in disbelief. From now on, continued Jackson, you must forget what you have learned – the hard way – about fighting the Zero. From now on, the policy will be to meet them on equal terms, to take them on, to dogfight with them. A howl of bewildered indignation rose up.

Peter Masters recounted that 'I don't think there was any doubt that he did what all of us swore we wouldn't do, because we knew that we couldn't do it and live. Because a Zero could eat you up.'

Another pilot thought that he (Jackson) would have had to have 'gone soft in the head during the period of his tramping back to decide to dogfight Zeros'.

How? Jackson's men cried. How can we fight like this when you told us yourself it could not be done? Jackson's reply, the exact meaning of which has come under much reflection, was uttered quietly. 'Tomorrow,' he said, 'I'm going to show you how.'

The following day's entry in Alan Boyd's diary read: '28th of April. A very bad day for 75SQN – we lost John Jackson and Barry Cox.'

CHAPTER 19

John Jackson takes on the Zeros...

The last day of John Jackson's life dawned wet and windy. For the first time since his return, he was on dawn standby along with Bill Cowe, Peter Masters, Barry Cox and Cocky Brereton. It was a quiet morning, and with the weather the men could be excused for raising their hopes that it would remain so. The only break in the monotony were the sounds of the aircraft being started, on the hour, to keep them warm and ready. As usual, while Jackson busied himself with the paperwork that constantly beset the commander of any fighting unit, the men played poker in the mess tent with an overly thumbed deck of cards and listened to one of the few records that could still play on the wind-up gramophone.

At around eleven am, the atmosphere changed abruptly when the telephone mounted on the wooden post near the standby tent rang loudly. A sudden silence fell as Stu Collie leapt up to grab it off the hook, and the men scrambled a split second later, following Collie's shout of, 'It's on!' Peter Masters recalled that Jackson's aircraft was the closest to the tent and 'although he left last, he got there first'.

As the men hurriedly clipped on their throat microphones, Jackson is reported to have shouted something. Masters claimed it was a hurried direction of tactics: 'We'll fly in a V formation, Masters, you're my number two.' While Ted Church remembered it as more of a cavalry cry: 'It's on, boys, now or never!' The already warmed engines turned over quickly, and the Kittyhawks made a short taxi to the runway. 'As always with Jackson,' said Masters, 'once his motor started, he was off.'

Five Kittyhawks took to the gloomy sky and kept close formation, climbing as steeply and with as much power as the Allison engine would give. Soon, however the formation began to disintegrate as Brereton's and Cowe's older, exhausted machines struggled to keep up. Regardless, Jackson swung to the north to face whatever was heading towards him. After fifteen minutes of climbing, Jackson attracted the attention of the closest aircraft without breaking radio silence by indicating furiously ahead and above. Masters reckoned the formation of Japanese aircraft were about 8000 feet above them.

Sources agree that eight Bettys came over the range that day, but estimates on their fighter escort vary between eleven and fifteen Zeros. Even at the most conservative estimate Jackson's men were outnumbered four to one. It was by no means the first time they hurled themselves against such odds and, as was usually the case, the half-hour warning they had received was insufficient to gain any height advantage above the enemy formation.

Once again finding themselves in the disadvantageous position of climbing to the attack, Jackson reached the Bettys from below at about 18,000 feet, but only after the bombers had done their work, dropping their load of nearly 100 bombs widely across Seven Mile Strip. As usual, some holes were left in the runway and a good deal of bush and scrub came off the worse for wear, but aside from the destruction of an already unserviceable P-40 and the starting of a small fire, the damage was relatively benign.

Jackson, with Cox on his left and Masters on his right, then led a firing pass on the Japanese formation. Peter Masters claimed to get so close to one of the bombers that he could clearly make out the grimacing face of the blister gunner in his Perspex 'glasshouse' along the fuselage. 'I was at my maximum climb and almost at dead stop with everything on, pointing at the sky,' he recalled. 'When I fired the guns, all hell broke loose.' Shooting from below, Masters saw his bullets begin to punch holes along the underbelly and rear fuselage of the Betty, until the recoil of his six powerful guns dragged back his already slow climbing speed to the point where his Kittyhawk stalled, flopping over nose-first like a breaching whale, then throwing itself into a long, flat spin. Thousands of feet below, he emerged under the cloud base and over the sea, where he later claimed to have seen and attacked a Japanese submarine with a single strafing pass.

Cocky Brereton was the first to be hit, finally arriving at the height of the bombers, but his slow machine presented an easy target for the Bettys' defences. The 20-millimetre cannon of the rear gunners – which Stu Collie had refused to believe existed – tore into Brereton's wings and fuselage, wounding him and forcing him to spin and retire from the battle. Bill Cowe's aircraft also spun out, and he too recovered control at low level, playing no further part in the fight.

This left Barry Cox and John Jackson at about 18,000 feet to face the onslaught of the defending Zeros. As the experienced pilots of the Tainan Squadron fell on them, they were obscured by clouds from the remainder of 75. At one stage, however, Masters and Brereton looked up and, through a break in the thick grey ceiling, saw that 'in the distance a fight was going on'.

Unusually, it was also claimed that Jackson broke radio silence, and the few words he uttered indicated he had stayed true to the pledge he made both to his superiors and his men, that he would – despite the disparity in numbers, despite the superior skills and experience of the Japanese pilots and their aircraft – deliberately attempt to 'take on' a Zero in a dogfight. The engagement was, almost certainly, brief. In the midst of a steep turn, Masters claimed that he could hear John Jackson cursing that he couldn't get himself in a position to fire. He and Cox would have pulled up to meet the descending Zeros, then most likely turned onto the tail of one of them. One can only speculate that in a matter of moments, a Zero had flicked up into a half roll and a turn and was now the pursuer, with Jackson in his sights. Perhaps it was a second or a third Zero Jackson had missed, or which had simply overwhelmed and outmanoeuvred him. Masters heard John cursing 'as only he could do', then heard nothing.

As had already been proven on scores of occasions, a nimble aeroplane like the Zero, particularly in the hands of an experienced and battle-hardened pilot of a unit such as the Tainan Kokutai, could turn quickly inside a heavy P-40 Kittyhawk and, in the words of Peter Masters, 'eat you up'. It had not needed to be proven again.

On the ground, John Pettett stood with a group of pilots and watched the battle above as best they could through breaks in the cloud. 'I was at the strip as part of the standby group. One aircraft crashed about seven miles west of the strip and a small fire could be seen on Mount Lawes.'

War correspondent Osmar White also observed the high-level combat. 'There were 17 Zeros, so high that they looked like small translucent insects,' he recalled in his classic, *Green Armour*. 'The sun shone brilliantly on the silver wings of the bombers, running below them in two deep Vs of seven and nine. The bombs came away. Over the crest of the hill, dust and smoke rose in massive, fluted columns. The valley shook and the mountains gave back the snarling rumble of explosions.' The fading echoes were then replaced by another sound – the soaring, deep-throated snarling of fighter aircraft in combat. 'Somewhere,' wrote White, 'at an altitude one could not see, there was fighting. The guns tapped plainly...A watcher called beside me, "Look, look there!" A little dark cross was drawing a line of white straight down the sky. He was one of ours.'

The Japanese had not come off unscathed, with a single Zero hit in its engine and forced to ditch in the Huon Gulf on its way home, probably taken down by either Jackson or Cox in the initial head-on contact. It was one of the many kills of Japanese aircraft during the 44 days attributed to no-one.

Ted Church claimed that Cocky Brereton witnessed the beginning of the action, right before he spun out of it. Though wounded, Brereton made it back to the airstrip but had to be lifted out of his cockpit. 'I saw a Zero right on the tail of one of ours,' he allegedly reported. 'Four or five Zeros were wheeling above. I slid in behind the Zero and fired at long range hoping to scare him off. Then I was hit and went into a spin.' The fighter he attacked may have been the one that claimed the second Australian casualty that day, Flying Officer Barry Cox. If so, it is the only clue to his fate.

Pettett had also seen an aircraft plummeting nose-first from the sky roughly seven miles west of the airstrip, but then noticed smoke beginning to rise in a column in another direction, towards the slopes of Mount Lawes. Soon after, Cox and Jackson failed to return. Taking one of the squadron's few remaining aircraft, Pettett flew off to investigate.

He found no sign of the aircraft he had seen hurtling towards the ground but its location seemed to be in the area of the large Waigani Swamp. Flying back over Mount Lawes, however, he noticed a parachute on the ground being spread out by army personnel.

Pettett reported what he had seen to the squadron doctor, Bill Deane-Butcher, who broke the news to a grim-faced Les Jackson at Moresby Hospital, where he was recovering from a bout of gastroenteritis. 'I told him two pilots hadn't returned,' Deane-Butcher said. 'John and Barry Cox.' He then announced he was heading out to the crash sight, and despite his protestations, Les insisted he accompany him. The swamp being unreachable, they decided to set off in a small truck the eight miles towards Mount Lawes.

Travelling along a rough track leading to the lower approaches, Les and Deane-Butcher encountered an army vehicle coming the other way. A macabre roadside conversation ensued – the soldiers told them they had already located and marked the crash site. 'Mercifully,' wrote Deane-Butcher, 'army personnel had attended the scene and performed the unpleasant task of recovering the remains.' Of those there was precious little. The ebony butt of a service revolver was mentioned, as was a flying boot with a foot still inside. An enquiry was made as to the size. Twelve, they were told. John's frame, like his personality, was famously large, while Barry Cox had been a small man. The realisation that John Jackson was dead struck Deane-Butcher and Les Jackson.

Jackson's burning fighter had slammed into the eastern slope of Mount Lawes so hard that its engine had buried itself six feet into the ground. The wing of his Kittyhawk was compressed from eight feet to just eight inches.

In the *44 Days* documentary, Geoffrey Robertson enquired as to Les's reaction on hearing the news of his brother's death. 'I don't think he said much,' said Deane-Butcher. 'We just drove back and he assumed temporary command and carried on.'

•

An Australian Army search party located the burning wreckage of Cox's aircraft, heavily embedded in muddy wetland soil at Waigani Swamp. Venturing there a week later, 75 Squadron pilots Piper and Tucker were unable to retrieve anything other than fragments: a panel showing the Kittyhawk's identification markings and nickname, *Sweet Adeline*; and some pieces of bone, which were later cremated. Barry Cox had begun his career in 75 Squadron in March when he and Wilbur Wackett had, in spectacular fashion, brought down the lone Sally over Moresby Harbour just hours after their arrival on the very first of the 44 days. His life ended on nearly the last.

What little was left of John Jackson was buried the following day near a village called Hanuabada. It was, according to Deane-Butcher, 'a brief but dignified ceremony'. Only four people were in attendance, Deane-Butcher, Les Jackson and ironically, no less a dignitary than Wing Commander Charles Pearce himself, who conducted the service accompanied by his colleague, Wing Commander William Gibson. 'He read appropriate passages,' wrote Deane-Butcher, 'and we buried John Jackson. That was the end of that. It was done without great ceremony.'

The effect on the squadron, however, was enormous. 'We were depressed, of course,' said John Pettett. 'Almost as though the battle was lost.' Fellow pilot John Piper similarly felt too exhausted to feel anything very much at all. 'I think by that time we were so tired that it was just one more depressing thing,' he said. 'There had been a lot of casualties.' According to Arthur Tucker, however, grief at Jackson's loss was tinged with anger. 'Lurking at the back of your mind was the way he bought it,' he told Robertson. 'He tried to do something he knew he couldn't do.'

The death of John Jackson on 28 April marks the nadir of 75 Squadron's 44-day Port Moresby campaign. 75 had fought itself to exhaustion. Despite putting up a dawn patrol the next morning with the pitiful handful of worn-out aircraft still available, a raid on the airstrip by eight Japanese bombers and their escort of Zeros went unchallenged. Gone were the days of 75 Squadron's quick hit-and-run strikes against Lae. Now, the battle had moved to right over their heads and the pilots and ground staff could only take cover and watch as the bombers came, then wait for the Zeros to swoop down and strafe, on that occasion destroying yet another Kittyhawk under repair.

With fewer and fewer fighters coming up to meet them, the Japanese sensed the waning of the Australian defences at Port Moresby and began to mount more solid attacks on the town in preparation for the planned invasion, still scheduled for May. Help was on the way, however, in the form of an increasing American presence, which the Japanese knew must soon arrive. With a growing sense of alarm, their pilots reported more and more traffic appearing in Port Moresby's once sleepy waterways. Ted Church wrote that 'The long promised help was coming. The harbour, whose placid waters had been unruffled by anything larger than a kingfish or mackerel, now resembled Woolloomooloo. Ships of all nationalities arrived to unload guns, troops, searchlights, bombs, ammunition and the many implements of war.'

Anti-aircraft defences were also strengthening, with myriad 3.7-inch ack-ack guns beginning to ring the harbour and town. 'From a place with token defence,' said Church, 'Moresby became a strong post and Australia's major centre for attack.'

75 was reinforced too, but with pilots who had no aeroplanes to fly. On 29 April, Les Jackson resumed temporary command of the squadron, as he had done throughout the fortnight of his brother's absence. He also received four fresh new pilots: Pilot Officer Cory, as well as three sergeants, H West and two coincidentally named Munro – Stewart and Don – newly arrived from 22 Squadron and Service HQ Williamtown.

Wednesday 29 April was the last action of the 44 days for Arthur Tucker, one of the few pilots who took to the air that day. Although the morning raid was unopposed, Tucker, along with John Piper, took to the air twice in response to orders to scramble. 'In late afternoon,' he recalled, 'three of us were flying between layers of cloud at about 6000 feet when we encountered six Zeros in formation. To my great surprise they sheered off!' Tucker and Piper kept looking for the raiders, but after a flight lasting nearly two and a half hours, their fuel was exhausted and they returned to the strip. Upon landing, Tucker's Kittyhawk was strafed and damaged, reducing 75's tally of serviceable aircraft still further.

The next day, 30 April, the squadron was officially relieved of its role in the air defence of Port Moresby. It was planned that Seven Mile would be handed over to the growing power of the Americans.

CHAPTER 20

Erratic leadership

In the first days of May, 75 Squadron began to get a glimpse of the next stage of the campaign, with the arrival of 26 Bell P-39 Airacobras of the 35th and 36th Pursuit Squadrons of the 8th Fighter Group, USAAF. Their ranks would have been nearly a dozen stronger if not for the series of crashes in transit from Australia due to poor training and bad weather. Some of these Americans had already trained briefly with 75 Squadron in April, but theirs would be a slow and painful integration into the realities of combat in the tropics. Like 75 at the beginning of the campaign, the American airmen were green. On their first foray over Lae, four of their number were lost.

In the meantime, 75 maintained a vigil over their airfield and Port Moresby as best they could with their three remaining serviceable aircraft. On 1 May, another Japanese raid on the strip could not be prevented, and the Zero ace Hiroyoshi Nishizawa recalled to his friend Saburo Sakai his surprise at racing low over Seven Mile Strip, guns blazing, with no opposition, the sullen faces of the weary Australians looking back at him.

The next day, 75 experienced its final battle casualty of the 44 days. The three Kittyhawks were flown by Bob Crawford, Alan Whetters and, on his first ever combat flight as Crawford's wingman, Sergeant Don Munro. Whetters became momentarily separated from his formation, but fired in the direction of three Zeros that, for once, were a couple of thousand feet below him. No results were observed, however, and the Zeros appeared to climb their way out of danger.

Crawford and Munro found themselves dead level with the main Japanese formation at about 9000 feet when they were suddenly attacked from astern and above. With split-second reactions, the seasoned Crawford 'shoved everything into a corner' and bunted away to safety at the first inkling of danger, but the newly arrived Munro had fallen to Japanese guns. His burning aircraft flew on briefly out over the sea. 'I saw him spinning and burning slightly,' stated Crawford in his combat report. 'When I finished my dive I saw an aircraft burning 340 degrees from the 'drome.' Crawford later noted a splash in the sea some miles off that may have been Munro's aircraft, indicating the young pilot possibly recovered from his dive and limped a little further out to sea.

It was a particularly bitter blow to the squadron to lose a young pilot like Don Munro on his first mission, and the circumstances of his death were just one of the contributing factors that led to ill-feeling towards 75 Squadron's new commanding officer, Les Jackson.

Arriving from Townsville a few days earlier, Don Munro, like most of the new pilots to the Port Moresby bases, was slightly dumbfounded by the apparent lack of aerial and combat tactics being discussed and imparted to new pilots. This, it seems, was just one aspect of the peculiar culture of 75 Squadron, promulgated by its equally peculiar commander, Les Jackson. Munro got onto Les's bad side early by committing the cardinal sin of speaking up. Les Jackson's notion of a perfect fighter pilot was one who simply did as he was told and did not ask questions, particularly of himself. And when Munro expressed his concerns one night in the mess tent, he was met with silent darting looks from some of the other pilots and eventually a snarl from Les. 'Shut up, Munro,' he hissed. 'You'll be pushing up the daisies by this time tomorrow.' True to his word, Munro was indeed on the battle order for the next day, and by that evening, he was dead. The whole business rankled men who had already felt Les's bitter side, such as Arthur Tucker, for years. 'I could see no advantage at all in sending up newly arrived reinforcement pilots in that stage,' Tucker said. With only a handful of aircraft available anyway, and a fiercely strong enemy who was outnumbering the Australians by ever-increasing margins, 'a new pilot wouldn't have a hope. It wouldn't have been regarded as unfair, I'm sure, by any of the pilots that those new people should not have been used in that last week or so, because there was no earthly hope they'd do any good, every chance that they'd get knocked off.'

The general feeling among the experienced pilots was that 'if you survived your first three missions, you knew your way around and you had a good chance of lasting'. In the eyes of a number of them, Don Munro's death had been a 'complete waste'.

On virtually the same day, another new arrival, Sergeant West, crashed while taking off from the difficult and much-repaired airstrip, sacrificing another serviceable aircraft and nearly taking the life of another green young pilot. Why Les himself was not electing to fly some of these final missions was a question pondered both at the time, and long after the war. This, however, was just one aspect of the atmosphere created by the odd figure of Flight Lieutenant Leslie Douglas Jackson.

•

'I liked Les Jackson very much,' insisted Bill Deane-Butcher in one of the extensive interviews he gave in later life about his experiences during the battle for Moresby. Indeed, there are many aspects of the man who led 75 Squadron throughout most of the 44 days that Deane-Butcher, who worked closely with Les, painted in glowing terms. He was 'a very tough fighter who led his men very well…a good friend in those difficult times…a fearless and courageous pilot, charismatic, swashbuckling, etc'.

Other pilots described him similarly. John Pettett didn't doubt Les's courage for a moment: 'He was just one of those sort of people. Absolutely incredible devil-may-care person was Les.'

Without question, Les Jackson was a brave and skilled airman who, like his brother, appeared completely devoid of the concept of fear. Both of them, observed Deane-Butcher, seemed as if they had been born for the adventure of combat. 'They just loved fighting. They were real extroverts, they didn't think in terms of what might happen to them.'

Les was officially credited with four kills at Moresby and several more aircraft damaged, to which he added another at Milne Bay, making him both the highest-scoring Australian pilot of the 44 days and the first Australian ace of the Pacific War. At least one of those victories, however, remained disputed by some of his fellow pilots after the war, then more recently by scholars and historians who have noted inconsistencies in the tallies of kills recorded at Moresby and then afterwards when the squadron was reconstituted back in Australia, where some claims seem to have been added retrospectively.

In March 1943, Les was awarded the DFC to which a bar was added two years later, both citations extolling his great courage under fire and his determination in pressing his attacks against the enemy as well as his leadership. After the battle for Moresby, he remained in New Guinea, eventually leading the three squadrons of 78 Fighter Wing in the long drawn out mop-up of the Japanese in western New Guinea at the end of the war. He rose to the rank of wing commander.

Like his brother, Les was an aggressive fighter who would not hesitate to attack – alone if need be – far larger formations, frequently pulling his Kittyhawk up to meet head-on assaults by diving Zeros, daring his lightly armed and armoured opponents to weather the storm of his six half-inch machine guns. It remains something of a miracle that he survived scrap after scrap, being frequently attacked from behind and above, and on one occasion surviving being shot down into the sea, all without receiving a scratch.

A full nine years younger than John, Les had run a Surat motor car garage before the war, following his brother into the RAAF reserve in 1937 before being called up for active service in November 1939. Graduating as a pilot in early 1940, he initially served with 23 Squadron on Wirraways before being posted to Singapore in July 1941 with 21 Squadron flying the wretched Brewster Buffalo. He escaped the deadly debacle of the Japanese onslaught only by being posted home shortly before Pearl Harbor.

During the 44 days, as one of 75 Squadron's flight commanders under John's leadership, Les unflinchingly took part in most of the squadron's major engagements and shared some of the squadron's operational responsibilities, but was nothing like his older brother. In many ways, Les seemed to embody 75 Squadron's particular characteristic of operating as a group of flying and fighting individuals rather than a single cohesive unit.

On the ground, Les got around in a large slouch hat and demonstrated, in Deane-Butcher's somewhat cryptic description, 'a very strong disregard for many conventions and avenues of authority'. His manner was often odd and abrupt, making it clear that he liked some people, while to others he would be sarcastic and disengaged. While such traits as these could – and frequently did – sit easily enough within the solitary nature of an individual fighter pilot, the ramifications became more serious under the blowtorch of leadership.

Sprinkled through the tributes to his bravery, Bill Deane-Butcher would reveal, as the decades went on, darker notes in his assessment of Les Jackson. In an interview for the Australian War Memorial (AWM), he said, 'I think he led his men very well but he had this rather irresponsible sort of approach to life on the ground. He got me into plenty of trouble from time to time. He'd been used to getting into trouble – and out of it – all his life, but I wasn't so used to it. Maybe he wasn't ready for leadership as he had a wild, mischievous nature which caused a few problems.'

During one of his longer recorded talks, Alan Whetters was also quick to praise Les in his slow and deliberate voice, particularly in the immediate aftermath of John's death: 'It was fortunate that his brother Les Jackson was able to temporarily command the squadron after such a terrible happening.' As the discussion progressed, however, Whetters seemed almost compelled to qualify some of his earlier remarks. 'Les Jackson had had as much experience as most of us. He was...a little unusual in his ways. It must be appreciated that the loss of his brother was a big blow, and it was obvious that he was affected. He did not have the respect of all pilots.'

Arthur Tucker typically pulled no punches whatsoever. 'Les Jackson should never have been let out of his cage,' he said bluntly in his extensive AWM interview. 'He was – well – a nasty bastard, in the kindest words I could say about him.' The quiet vehemence heard in Tucker's voice – expressed so long after the events in question – is surprisingly shocking. Tucker went on to describe Les as 'a divisive, degenerate, drunken lout, without any sense of responsibility whatsoever. He should never have been allowed to lead the squadron.' Arthur Tucker was never a man to mince words.

Few have ventured to make an assessment of the relationship between John and Les Jackson, but a number of former pilots have suggested that John was all too aware of his younger brother's personality traits, but managed to keep them in check by sheer force of his own personality. After he was gone, it was a different story. Les developed a coterie among the pilots and stuck to them, showing little interest towards the men he disliked. The criteria Les used to decide his favourites was best understood by himself, but certainly those who questioned either his methods or leadership style were ostracised, and even seniority did not seem to matter. Middle East veteran Alan Boyd fared poorly under Les, subjected to abuse and accusations of cowardice before being sent home to Australia in late April, although newcomer Don Munro, who arrived at around the same time, fared little better. A running theme of many of those who experienced his leadership was that, far from uniting his men, Les Jackson divided them, and deliberately.

Much of Les's eccentricity was seen by many through the prism of his drinking. Thanks to reasons such as the general ill-health of the squadron, many pilots eschewed their irregular – not to mention unrefrigerated – beer ration, but Les took to his, and those of others, with gusto. Always it seemed Les was scheming for new ways to acquire more booze, whether it be smuggled in under the guise of medical equipment, or purloined from the visiting American squadrons. 'One of Les Jackson's endearing features continued to be his capacity to conjure up beer,' wrote Deane-Butcher. Less endearing however, was his often demonstrated lack of responsibility.

In an interview given in the 1980s to the National Library of Australia, Deane-Butcher cited an incident after their return from Milne Bay when the squadron was camping just outside Cairns. 'We had brought down a fairly severe type of malaria from Milne Bay which did not exist in Cairns,' he said. 'We were asked not to enter certain sections of the town for several weeks. Jackson decided we should go to the pictures in an area that was in one of these sections. He just couldn't care about those things, he thought it was a great joke.' On the tape, the interviewer, Barbara Blackman, can be heard taking a breath, perhaps slightly surprised to be hearing of this kind of behaviour from an officer and respected squadron commander. 'Er, could he not be made to see reason?' she asked cautiously. Deane-Butcher – perhaps giving away a little too much – can be heard to spit out a tutt-tutting expression and a dry laugh. Later he said, 'He [Les] was a good man to have on your own side when there was a fight on and I think in the air he was probably as good a leader as they could have. But on the ground...I'm not sure that he was.'

One of the most famous – and famously bizarre – stories of Les was retold often at meetings and reunions by one of the 44-day veterans, Michael Butler. Les had disliked Butler from the start, and was particularly – even irrationally – savage at what he took to be Butler's deliberate wrecking of his aircraft by landing it in kunai grass rather than attempting to bring it back to the airstrip after sustaining damage in combat. Two days after that incident, Butler survived a long and desperate chase under fire from a number of Zeros and on his return to Seven Mile, his nerves were shattered. He requested to be taken off the next day's battle order, and despite a number of other pilots being available at the time, Les refused. The incident stirred rancour among a number of men who were sympathetic to Butler.

Later in the war both men happened to find themselves at the American-built airbase at Nadzab, constructed a short distance from the recaptured village of Lae. The story goes that Butler, having avoided Les as best he could, discovered him playing cards one night – quite the worse for wear – on the occasion of the break-up of the mess. 'I hate you, Butler,' Les hissed, scowling up at Butler as he walked in. A Thompson sub-machine gun happened to be within reach of Les, who leapt up, grabbed it and cocked it. As others in the mess began to scatter, Butler made his escape outside into the dark. Staggering after him and swearing in a drunken rage, Les then proceeded to fire the weapon at random. As unbelievable as this story sounds, it was one repeated by several of 75 Squadron's airmen, all of whom seemed to find it completely plausible.

It was also claimed that Les, similarly inebriated one evening, decided to get behind the wheel of a jeep and drive it into the occupied tent of someone he disliked. By a miracle, no-one was hurt. Again, none of 75's pilots seemed to have any trouble in believing the story. That was simply the way Les Jackson behaved. Butler never got to the bottom of Les's animosity. 'I asked him several times after the war,' he says, 'but I could never get anything out of him. Why he appeared to dislike me I've got no idea. I always did my job, to my knowledge.'

In his book *Kokoda Air Strikes*, respected aviation writer Anthony Cooper brings to light a further incident which adds little to Les Jackson's legacy. On the afternoon of 1 April, Les took part in his brother's second daring raid on the Lae airstrip, where once again the Japanese had presented their aircraft in convenient rows, ideal for ground attack. Flying with the group that day was an officer being groomed to take over 75 at some later stage, Squadron Leader Jim Wright from 22 Wirraway Squadron, then based at Richmond. Wright was the only casualty of that most successful attack, hit by what was believed to be ground fire, and receiving damage to his aircraft and injury to his shoulder, which was peppered with glass and Perspex fragments.

According to Cooper's research however, the damage had less to do with Japanese anti-aircraft fire than the inexperienced Wright – on his first combat mission – inadvertently straying across the path of the guns of the aircraft behind him. Flying tail-ender to the formation that day was Les Jackson. This was hardly Les's fault, but it was his behaviour afterwards that Cooper called into question: 'Upon landing, Jackson asked engineering officer Bill Matson to remove evidence of any .5-inch bullet hits to Wright's aircraft – which he did, confirming that the holes through the airframe were indeed .5-inch in diameter.'

As a result of his wounds, Jim Wright required a long stint in hospital, ending his prospects of commanding 75 Squadron.

Another still living 75 Squadron pilot who flew with Les at Milne Bay and later in the war, but who did not wish to be named, told me that he could not think of a single pilot who had any respect for Les Jackson. 'He wasn't a leader's thumb. Courageous, certainly, but a good leader cares about his men, both the pilots and the ground crew. Les didn't give a stuff, and he was a drunk and an idiot.'

CHAPTER 21

The last days

Spent and exhausted at every level, 75's time at Moresby was coming to an end. Now it was the turn of the Americans and they could not arrive too soon. The rampant Japanese were striking the airstrip regularly and little could be put up by way of defence. The squadron was down to a single serviceable Kittyhawk.

It was this machine that Arthur Tucker took off in on what would be the last combat mission of 75 Squadron's 44 days. Scrambled to join a detachment of Airacobras intercepting an incoming raid of twenty Japanese bombers and eight Zeros, Tucker had to wait as a detachment of American B-25s lined up in front of him – he sat with his engine running as the big Mitchells became airborne one by one. Glancing down at his control panel, Tucker noticed the yellow glow of the engine temperature warning light. It was a common enough occurrence of the big liquid-cooled Allison motor, but once airborne with the cooling gills fully open, it usually settled down. Finally airborne, however, the light stubbornly refused to go off. 'I climbed and flew around a few times at 3000 feet,' said Tucker, 'then cut my losses and came in to land.' The flight had only lasted seven minutes but taxiing back, he noticed a Bofors gun crew on the right-hand side of the runway 'jumping up and down on their sandbag enclosure, cheering me as if I'd won the Cup'. As he climbed down, he was grabbed and dragged into the gun emplacement and, in his words, 'jumped on'. Seconds later, the deep *krump* of exploding bombs was heard and the vibrations felt.

Without realising, Tucker had come in to land in the same direction as the Japanese bombers up at 18,000 feet. The anti-aircraft gunners saw catastrophe unfolding in front of them, and may well have saved him from oblivion, as one of the bombs exploded just behind his Kittyhawk, throwing it onto its nose.

Nor was this the end of the matter for Tucker, whose aircraft, despite its near-miss on the runway, was found to be relatively undamaged. Back at the dispersal bay, engineering officer Bill Matson conducted a cursory inspection and found the aircraft to be running properly, if indeed a little hot, which the P-40 tended to do on the ground anyway. As was often the case amid the culture Les Jackson engendered in the squadron, pilots who brought their aircraft back with mechanical trouble were often subject to the sly, stinging implication of cowardice – little was said, but nothing was forgotten. Tucker insisted, however, that his aircraft had been dangerously overheating and that to continue would have been irresponsible. It created a further wedge between himself and Squadron Commander Les Jackson that was never repaired.

Salt was rubbed into the wounds when the official history of the campaign was published in 1962 and the summary of that morning's events stated: 'The weariness of machine as well as man was emphasised when engine trouble forced him [Tucker] to land without making contact with the enemy.' It was seen as a back-handed slight to his courage and it was only years later that Tucker finally felt vindicated when a maintenance report surfaced from within the bowels of the RAAF records that shed a completely new light on the matter. It appears that the aircraft flown by Tucker that day was the same that Alan Whetters had landed a few days before in the kunai grass. It was only after a more comprehensive inspection in which the cowling covers were completely removed that a number of the air passages of the coolant radiators were found to have been blocked by chopped-up shards of kunai grass, causing it to quickly overheat. The maintenance regime was officially changed from then on. Tucker only belatedly received his 'pardon'.

On 5 May, Les Jackson was summoned to RAAF HQ Port Moresby to be informed that his command of 75 Squadron was now official, a somewhat ironic gesture as there was almost nothing left to command. Nor was there any time for ceremony. The Japanese, he was told as he accepted a congratulatory handshake, were on their way.

•

On 8 May, John Pettett and Pop Woods took off from Port Moresby and headed south towards Australia in two of 75 Squadron's last remaining airworthy Kittyhawks. These machines, while no longer battle-worthy, could at least be made so when the squadron regrouped and re-formed for the fights that inevitably lay ahead. Soon after taking off, however, their farewells to Port Moresby gave way to trying to make sense of what they were hearing over the radio: from somewhere way over the horizon came the sound of animated American voices engaged in fierce combat. Frantic orders and descriptions of air strikes on ships were heard through the interference, before gradually fading as the two pilots flew closer to home and safety. Although they did not realise it at the time, Woods and Pettett were listening to history unfold: the Battle of the Coral Sea.

•

Bill Deane-Butcher always remembered Les Jackson's return to the camp after his trip to Moresby to receive command of the squadron. Les came in at about six in the evening and quietly sat down on his bed in the tent they shared. Gone was the snarl, the arrogance and the swagger; this Les Jackson was quiet and subdued, as if taking a final pause before embarking on a great ordeal. 'Doc,' he said after a heavy silence, 'a massive Japanese fleet is approaching from the east. They'll be here at dawn. We have three aircraft serviceable.' In fact, officially, there were none: engineering officer Bill Matson had promised Les that he could possibly get three of the seven currently unserviceable Kittyhawks into the air by dawn. Once again, Matson's men, stripped to the waist, would have to work all night under floodlights. Deane-Butcher listened and said nothing. 'Les confided in me that we were about to be attacked at dawn next morning and we would be completely overwhelmed,' he recalled.

A ship was in Moresby Harbour, said Les, the 4000-ton troopship *Taroona.* That very night, most of the squadron's 200 or so personnel were to be transported down to the docks and taken on board. A skeleton staff would be asked to stay on to allow the squadron to make one last flight the following morning, using the last three planes. As to who would fly them on this final – and in all likelihood, suicidal – mission, the pilots who volunteered would draw straws. The third pilot, added Les, would be himself.

A short time later, Les Jackson stood on a box in the large marquee that served as mess tent at Seven Mile Strip and addressed the more than 200 assembled men of his squadron for the first time, officially, as their leader. Ironically, it was to tell them to pack up and go home. The long-anticipated Japanese fleet was, it was believed, finally on its way to Moresby and they would most likely be overwhelmed by dawn. Everyone, he said, had put up a good fight, but now the game was up. 'It was,' said Deane-Butcher, 'quite a dramatic occasion.'

Firstly, Les continued, he needed some mechanics, just one or two, also a couple of fitters and armourers. There was no shortage to choose from as almost all the men raised their hand to volunteer. The rest of them, said Les, were to go, and go now – this very minute. They were to return to their tents, grab their kit and get the hell out of here. Better still, leave your kit behind. Trucks, vehicles, and anything that would roll would ferry men the few miles to the docks, where they would board the *Taroona.* It was leaving soon, he said, and would not wait.

The men looked at each other then, without speaking, shuffled out into the evening.

Next, it was the turn of the pilots. In silence they listened as Les explained what he had been told at Moresby HQ about the situation. Masters glanced at Tucker, who glanced at Atherton. This was it, Les told them, they all knew this day would come and now the Japanese were on their way. Three pilots – himself included – would take off at dawn to meet them. No-one should harbour any great prospects of coming back. Nine pilots stood listening, and nine stepped forward. The men drew straws and Michael Butler and Peter Masters were the lucky two.

'We were told, I think it was just about tea time,' Butler later recalled, 'that we were wanted down the strip and Les said to us, "We're goin' to have possibly three planes in the morning serviceable...I'll be flying one and I want two volunteers to fly the other two." Everybody stepped forward and that was not to be unexpected in such a fine lot of fellows as they were.' Butler did not record his reaction when his name was selected, but did not sleep that night. 'I felt absolutely scared stiff knowing that all we were going to have was three aeroplanes amongst a whole heap of Japanese.'

Outside, the airstrip had taken on the appearance of a busy railway station. Lorries and other vehicles appeared from seemingly nowhere and began shuttling men down to the port where, in the fading light, the *Taroona* appeared impatient to set sail. Even Bill Deane-Butcher's ambulance was corralled into service. 'I carried about four loads in the ambulance and it was really quite difficult to know what to do because I hadn't been given any instruction,' he recalled.

On Deane-Butcher's final run down to the wharf, he watched as the last of the men he had lived every day of the past six extraordinary weeks with, disappeared into the ship's holds. Then the remaining pilots – including Arthur Tucker and Alan Whetters – went aboard. Deane-Butcher knew he had done enough. Without the briefest of shadows passing over his conscience, he could have easily walked across the wooden boards of the wharf, up the gangway and watched the big steel door of the ship close behind him. Instead, he pulled a sheet from his pocket notebook and pencilled a short note to his wife, Elizabeth, which 'said practically nothing'. Finding an old envelope in the ambulance, he tore the note into pieces to make it difficult for prying eyes to decipher, and handed it to one of the men as he approached the gangway.

The man paused, took the envelope and, looking the revered doc in the eye, swore solemnly that he would see it delivered.

Another pilot approached Deane-Butcher and made a hasty and somewhat absurd arrangement to rendezvous in a year to the day at a certain spot along the coast, where he would try to get in a flying boat to spirit him away to safety – providing of course that he was still alive. With a wish of good luck, the pilot boarded the ship.

Deane-Butcher propped himself up against his clapped-out ambulance and watched as the ship pulled away from the dock. 'The ship floated off into the night, and that was that.'

Meeting up with Les Jackson a short time later, Deane-Butcher reflected that they were now the only two officers left in the squadron. Given the option of returning to the base, Les, true to form, instead suggested they break down the door of the nearby mess and help themselves to the beer.

Soon afterwards, arms laden with beer, the men made their way down to the beach and planted the bottles in the wet sand to keep cool. A couple of plush armchairs were purloined from somewhere, which they arranged facing out to sea, ready for the first sign of the invasion fleet expected in just a few hours. At that point, they would return to Seven Mile, where Jackson would take to the air and Deane-Butcher would lead the rearguard and ground party to Rouna Falls in the hills. In the unlikely event that any of the pilots returned, they were to destroy their aircraft and join them. However, neither men considered that to be a likely option.

The two men sat, and according to Deane-Butcher, 'an embarrassed quiet' settled between them. Behind them, Moresby appeared silent and deserted. Just faintly, they could trace the darkened outline of the *Taroona* as she slid quietly into the night. 'I cursed myself for having made such a rash decision and recalled my father's last words of advice, "Do your duty, but never volunteer."'

The soldier who had Deane-Butcher's letter to his wife kept his word, and Elizabeth kept the torn-up pieces of notepaper for the rest of her life.

•

What Pettett and Woods had been hearing in their headphones as they flew south were the hammer blows exchanged between the American, Australian and Japanese navies in the first great sea battle of the Pacific War. Operation Mo, the Japanese carrier force sent to clear a path to Port Moresby for an amphibious invasion like the one that had crushed Rabaul three months earlier, sailed into a trap. American naval intelligence broke the Japanese code and rushed a carrier group to intercept them in the great expanse of ocean defined by the eastern tip of Papua, the Solomon Islands and the Queensland coast. For four days, the aircraft of the carrier fleets pounded each other. The Americans lost their carrier *Lexington*, the Japanese *Shoho*. All in all, however, the Japanese fared worse, and were forced to withdraw their battered fleet north to Rabaul, Truk and even Japan. Throughout the historic four-day engagement, fought entirely with air power, the opposing ships never came within sight of each other.

Had the Japanese struck earlier, rolling their juggernaut straight to Port Moresby, they would have proved irresistible. Their delay for consolidation – giving time for the power of the United States to be brought to bear – robbed them of a chance they would not be handed again. For 75 Squadron, reduced now to a rump of three pilots and 27 ground crew out at Seven Mile Strip, it would mean relief.

•

Seated on their armchairs on the beach at Moresby, having spent the night talking quietly and sipping stolen beer in resigned anticipation of imminent destruction, Les Jackson and Bill Deane-Butcher caught the first glimpses of a clear and peaceful dawn. A short time later, the two men were officially informed that contrary to predictions, no Japanese invasion fleet would, for now, be headed for Moresby. It was a not unwelcome anticlimax. 75's three remaining aircraft it was planned would join several American Dauntless dive bombers stationed at nearby Three Mile Strip and escort them south to Horn Island, where they would refuel before continuing on to Townsville.

On their final evening at Seven Mile, Deane-Butcher and Jackson hosted what Deane-Butcher loosely described as a 'banquet' for the Americans of the arriving Airacobra squadrons. After several faltering toasts to kings and presidents, the defence of Moresby was passed to the men of the USAAF. 75 Squadron would never operate from Port Moresby again. The official history records that over the next month, as the air war over Moresby intensified, the Americans would lose 30 aircraft and endure 21 bombing raids on the strip.

The next morning, 9 May, the three Australian Kittyhawks and four US Dauntless dive bombers lined up along Three Mile Strip in preparation to take off and head south. Deane-Butcher was there too, and remembered the day as clear, calm and exquisite. His turn to leave would come, he knew, when arrangements had been made to evacuate the remaining ground crew. That, hopefully, would be at the first available opportunity.

As the aircraft were being prepared, Les Jackson suddenly bolted over to Deane-Butcher. 'Doc! You've got ten minutes to learn to be a rear gunner. You're riding home in the back seat of one of the dive bombers...Now get going fast!'

Deane-Butcher was staggered. After a frantic change into flying gear, he climbed into the Dauntless's cramped rear cockpit as an American armourer leaned over the side of the fuselage and gave him a three-month gunnery course in approximately 30 seconds. Clutching the enormous twin-mounted 50-calibre machine guns in front of him, he took in information about aiming, reloading and trajectory. 'I was hypnotised,' recalled Deane-Butcher. 'It was like trying to learn golf from photographs in a manual.'

'Good luck, doc,' said the American. 'By the way don't forget the safety catch and for Christ's sake keep it on till you get away from here!' His pilot however, was more encouraging, informing him that they 'weren't likely' to be jumped by Japanese fighters. He spoke too soon, as just at that moment, 'the next shattering surprise was on its way', and aircraft with red circles on their wings suddenly appeared, totally unannounced, above the far end of the runway.

Joining a scramble of bolting bodies, Deane-Butcher managed to throw himself into a deep gutter just as the blast of machine-gun fire and the zoom of aircraft engines flashed overhead. 'Men were diving into holes everywhere.' When they emerged, all thankfully unharmed, two of the Kittyhawks and one Dauntless had been hit. Michael Butler, due to take off in one of them, likewise remembered this final attack on 75. 'We just had time to climb into a slit trench before the strafing by Zeros commenced. My aircraft was hit in three places and in particular a large junction box of 20 to 30 different circuits was hit.' For the moment, Butler was going nowhere.

'The bastards!' cried Les, who appeared relatively unruffled. 'They won't be back...let's go!' And he proceeded to climb into the single undamaged Kittyhawk. The formation, suddenly reduced from seven aircraft to four, started up and taxied out along the runway, waved off by the small party remaining on the strip.

Les led the formation, with the three Dauntless following behind, one of them carrying a very nervous air gunner who clutched the big half-inch guns and scanned the skies frantically for signs of Japanese aircraft that thankfully did not appear. Later, Deane-Butcher remembered flying over a glassy sea on a perfect day as the mainland of New Guinea slipped away into a bluish haze behind him.

After landing at Horn Island, Deane-Butcher's stint in the back seat came to an end when his Dauntless received minor undercarriage damage in a rough landing. Lacking the patience to wait the several days for parts to be flown in from the mainland, he hitched a ride on a US Fortress that was headed to Townsville. Lying asleep in the aircraft's belly, Deane-Butcher was awoken and asked to come up to the cockpit to lend some assistance. Landing at night, the American pilot, who had not been to Australia, was confused and asked Deane-Butcher if the lights below looked like Townsville to him. Deane-Butcher, of course, had absolutely no idea, but the pilot, unimpressed by the doctor's ignorance of his own country, elected to land on the much-too-short runway anyway. It was a nervous touchdown, but at least Deane-Butcher was home. He was not, however, in Townsville – the American pilot had mistakenly landed at Cairns.

The next morning, Bill Deane-Butcher caught a ride into town and strolled into the famous Hides Hotel where, perhaps not unexpectedly, he encountered an equally astonished Les Jackson. It was a happy reunion neither of them would ever forget.

•

On the *Taroona*, the men of 75 Squadron awoke the morning after their hurried departure from Moresby to the same idyllic conditions that greeted Bill Deane-Butcher and Les Jackson, but most were too done-in to enjoy them. Arthur Tucker, his weight now down to under ten stone, recalled that 'all of us were dead from "here up"'. Apart from the 160 or so men and pilots of 75 Squadron, the ship carried another passenger on that trip, 24-year-old Petty Officer 3rd Class Yoshimitsu Maeda, the sole Japanese prisoner to be captured during the 44 days. Having taken off in his Zero on 28 April to conduct a combat patrol, Maeda failed to return to his base at Lae and was reported missing. In fact, he had become separated from his fellow Tainan pilots and, about to turn back to his base, had spotted a small vessel just off the beach about 160 miles east of Moresby. This was the tiny runabout *Laurabada*, a familiar sight in New Guinea waters pre-war, but recently commandeered by the navy, who bestowed on her a somewhat grandiose HMAS, despite her armament consisting of a solitary machine gun of doubtful vintage.

With little else to account for his day's action, Maeda swooped down to strafe the vessel, but perhaps received his deserts after pulling up slightly too late over the coconut trees dotting the shore line and ploughing straight into the fronds. This, oddly enough, did not so much damage the Zero, but catch it as though in a fly trap, its motor still running in the tree tops. Eventually, the tree relinquished the aircraft and Maeda's Zero fell gently to the ground, level and virtually intact, its pilot unharmed.

A local army detachment that had witnessed the bizarre incident was soon on the scene and captured the mortified Japanese pilot, who immediately requested the soldiers execute him to save his honour. They would have none of it, and he was handed over.

Maeda's Zero, one of the first intact examples ever to fall into the hands of the Allies anywhere, was extracted from the jungle and transported to the wharf at Moresby, where it was soon stripped of virtually every useful part by souvenir hunters, rendering it useless to intelligence officers once it was shipped to Brisbane for inspection. In future, it was decreed, captured enemy aircraft would be rigorously secured.

Sitting on the deck of the *Taroona* and under guard lest he run for the side rail and hurl himself overboard, Maeda, on his way to Cowra prisoner-of-war camp, cut a somewhat pitiful sight. Arthur Tucker recalled that he refused to look anybody in the eye. 'We felt a bit sorry for the poor bugger. No-one intruded on him or made him uncomfortable. He was obviously unhappy. I think we would have liked to have communicated with him.' The only other aspect of the voyage Tucker could recall was the occasional decent meal.

Alan Whetters, for his part, couldn't remember a thing. His robust constitution, having held up all through the 44 days, finally gave out once the pressure was off, and he collapsed unconscious into sickness. He would wake up a few days later in a Cairns hospital, minus the precious bag of combat reports with which he had been entrusted.

As for the other pilots, they were too exhausted to think about anything much at all – about Moresby, about John Jackson and the young faces of the other pilots who would not be coming back, about the fact they had survived or, particularly, about what lay ahead. All there was to contemplate was the flat calm of the sunlit sea, and the reassuring throb of the ship's motors taking them home.

Epilogue

The 44-day battle for Port Moresby was not a victory, nor even the beginning of the end of the Japanese presence in the South Pacific and their threat to Australia. Far greater battles lay ahead. In his thorough account, *The Decisive Factor*, author David Wilson described the battle as 'one of those intangible points which occur in a campaign when courage and fortitude create a rock against which the tide of enemy aspirations pounds relentlessly, but to no avail'.

Green pilots, flying in a green squadron, frustrated constantly by inferior aircraft, appalling conditions and at times questionable leadership, had thrown themselves against a powerful enemy at their zenith, shocking them into the realisation they were not, after all, invulnerable. From the moment in March when the Kittyhawks arrived at Seven Mile Strip, the Japanese knew they would always be met, and always be attacked. Sometimes it was by a half-dozen Australian pilots, sometimes just two, occasionally even one solitary Kittyhawk. But they would always be met.

These young pilots of 75 Squadron left a lasting impression on war correspondent Osmar White:

> The men who lived an hour or a night or a week removed from death were in tent camps near the field. They conformed to no physical type, only to a standard of courage. Some were big fellows with stubble beards on their cheeks; others were small, delicately made boys with pimples and hardly any beard at all.

According to the records of Intelligence Officer Stu Collie, 75 Squadron's claims against the enemy between 21 March and 3 May were eighteen aircraft destroyed in the air and seventeen on the ground, with a further 50 or so damaged or claimed as 'probables'. On the Australian side, fifteen aircraft were lost in air combat and two to ground attack, with another five Kittyhawks written off in accidents. During the period, 37 Australian pilots served with the squadron, of whom eleven were killed, as well as Squadron Leader Barney Cresswell, lost on attachment from 76 Squadron.

Many of the pilots, after heading south to regroup, would return to New Guinea in August to fight in another battle of significance at Milne Bay, where, once again, a Japanese amphibious force was defeated primarily by air power. Then, for many, it would be on to unknown dots on the map such as

Goodenough Island, Nadzab, Cape Gloucester and Morotai to continue the long, slow – and arguably pointless – grind against an effectively neutralised enemy till the end of the war in 1945.

Only in later years did the men of the 44 days seem to come together – occasionally – to recall the six weeks at Port Moresby. Like many veterans of the Second World War, some chose – as best they could – to simply forget. For many, that was not easy; they still fought the battles and railed against the culture of unfairness they perceived to be the particular toxin of the squadron, particularly under Les Jackson. In those days, accusations – even inferences – of cowardice stuck hard and compounded the awful scar of what today would be identified as post-traumatic stress.

The neglect shown to the men of 75 Squadron from the higher echelons of the air force during the campaign seemed to have continued well into the war and after. It is worth noting that barely a single decoration was handed out to any of the pilots of the 44 days either at the time or afterwards. This, it was said, was part of the culture of the squadron under Les Jackson, who, as commander, refused to recommend any of his men for a medal, his opinion being that they were just doing the job they were paid for. It was an attitude that did not change even during the desperate Battle of Milne Bay the following August, where not a single pilot was recognised.

Even the official history talked of 'the parsimony with which decorations were awarded to members of the RAAF in the South-West Pacific'. One or two Distinguished Flying Crosses were given to the officers, including John Jackson, but these, as the history again noted, 'were won overseas in 1940–41 by men whose service against great odds in the SWPA received no further recognition'. For the sergeant pilots, or the ground crew, there was nothing.

It would be left to an American general, Henry 'Hap' Arnold, credited with being one of the founders of the doctrine of modern air power, to praise the men of 75 Squadron. Speaking well after the war, he said, 'Victory in the entire air war against Japan can be traced back to the actions which took place from that dusty strip at Port Moresby in early 1942.'

In a letter to Bill Deane-Butcher written in the 1990s, John Pettett summed up his own experiences.

> I would never wish, ever, to go back to Port Moresby to live that six weeks again. That was horrendous. It was bad conditions, bad living, a bad situation – until the end of it, towards the end of it – but most it was just drudgery; terrible drudgery. I know I wasn't, I suppose, as healthy as I could have been...We didn't even get good beds to lie in, to be comfortable in, to get a good night's sleep in. In fact, towards the end of it, I couldn't even push the rudder pedals; I was weak...I was very happy to say goodbye to Port Moresby.

In the months after the 44 days, the Japanese, frustrated at their defeats in the Coral Sea – not to mention their bloodying in the skies over Port Moresby – attempted a doomed overland invasion across the abyss of the Owen Stanley Ranges. Unlike the men of the 44 days, however, the men of the Kokoda battles did not go unrecognised. It may have taken many decades, but those brave men of the army who fought the Japanese to a standstill in the steaming jungles of New Guinea finally received the accolades due to them. By and large, such accolades have yet to be bestowed on the now long-departed men of 75 Squadron who fought the 44 days. One or two scholarly books, and a single hour-long documentary is all that has been created to commemorate the six weeks when Australia and a handful – really, a handful – of boys stood alone. Their story, worse perhaps than being forgotten, has never really been known. We Australians are peculiar in how we choose our heroes.

Notes

Prelude

The final scenes of 75 Squadron's 44 days in Port Moresby are vividly conveyed in both Peter Ewer's *Storm over Kokoda* and Mark Johnston's *Whispering Death*. The atmosphere of that last day was confirmed by the descriptions given in the Keith Murdoch Australian War Memorial (AWM) interviews of pilots Arthur Tucker, Alan Whetters and John Piper.

Chapter 1

Johnston and Ewer give an excellent account of the RAAF's pre- and inter-war deficiencies, as does Douglas Gillison in Volume 3 of his official history of the RAAF's war in the Pacific. Osmar White's classic, *Green Armour*, and AE Church's *They Flew Alone* provide a picture of Moresby and its airstrips on the eve of war.

Chapter 2

Graham Sivyer's *Seek and Strike* describes much of the coming together of the squadron; the online *Australian Dictionary of Biography* (adb.anu.edu.au/biography/jackson-john-10599) and Peter Jeffrey's AWM interview give some details regarding John Jackson's earlier career. Bill Deane-Butcher's autobiographical *Fighter Squadron Doctor* describes his early medical career and his unconventional path into the RAAF; further information was gathered from his son, Richard Deane-Butcher. Details of sale of John Jackson's Klemm monoplane were obtained in interview with Charles Hill, son of Viv Hill. Arthur Tucker and Michael Butler's AWM interviews were also excellent sources for this chapter. John Piper likewise describes the chaos of 75's first disastrous flight north in his AWM interview. Ray Cooper's *Crash of the Kittyhawk* is the best description of the details and aftermath of the deaths of Norton and Holliday.

Chapter 3

Butler in his AWM interview and Deane-Butcher in *Fighter Squadron Doctor* both give vivid descriptions of Townsville as 75 Squadron arrived. John Pettett's AWM interview is also first used here. Butler likewise describes, in his AWM interview, the problems with the Kittyhawks' aerials and other technical problems. Arthur Tucker's AWM interview describes some of the early tensions among the newer pilots of the squadron and the Middle East veterans.

Chapter 4

Many descriptions of the Kittyhawks' arrival at Seven Mile Strip exist; it is described well in Johnston's *Whispering Death* and also in David Wilson's *The Decisive Factor*. Osmar White in *Green Armour* describes the destruction of the Japanese bomber over Moresby harbour, as well as the sense of euphoria it created for the men on the ground. Johnston's *Whispering Death* was a valuable source in this chapter, and John Pettett's AWM interview is also used. AE Church in *They Flew Alone* also describes the atmosphere of relief as 75 Squadron was finally able to offer some resistance to the Japanese air attacks. Wilson's *The Decisive Factor* gives a full description of the first attack by 75 under John Jackson against the Japanese airfield at Lae. John Piper's AWM interview provides a potent description of the scene as he flew on his first sortie.

Chapter 5

Much of Wackett's description of his month-long ordeal across the jungle after being shot down comes from Wilson's *The Decisive Factor*.

Chapter 6

Deane-Butcher's *Fighter Squadron Doctor* and Church's *They Flew Alone* were excellent sources in this chapter: they provide the best descriptions of the Japanese counter-strike on Seven Mile Strip.

Chapter 7

Arthur Tucker's AWM interview, as well as his speech, *Blind in an Unsighted World*, provide a detailed description of his background and attitudes to 75's early days at Port Moresby. John Pettett's AWM interview likewise describes the squadron's living conditions at Seven Mile Strip.

Chapter 8

The history of the Mitsubishi Zero fighter and P-40 Kittyhawk is well described by both Ewer and Johnston, and technical data is drawn from a variety of online sources, including Wikipedia (https://en.wikipedia.org/wiki/Mitsubishi_A6M_Zero) and HistoryNet (www.historynet.com/myth-of-the-zero-fighter.htm). Wilson's *Decisive Factor* was a valuable source for descriptions of the air fighting in this chapter.

Chapter 9

An excellent description of the difficult birth of radar at Port Moresby is given in one of the *Radar Returns* historical newsletter series compiled by former RAAF radar operators, and the privately published work, *Echoes over the Pacific* by Ed Simmonds and Norm Smith. A description of the operations of No. 4 Fighter Sector is also given here. There are several accounts of the work of observer Leigh Vial, but I have drawn in part on the biography provided by the *Australian Dictionary of Biography* website (adb.anu.edu.au/biography/vial-leigh-grant-11923).

Chapter 10

The description of the arrival of American air power at Seven Mile Strip in David Wilson's *The Decisive Factor* was very useful.

Chapter 11

John Pettett's AWM interview is drawn on to describe his air fighting experiences. Ewer, Johnston and Wilson provide much of the detail of the daily combat, and Anthony Cooper's *Kokoda Air Strikes* is first drawn on, giving detail of Les Jackson's accidental firing on fellow pilot Jim Wright's aircraft. One of John Jackson's letters is also quoted, provided by Wilson.

Chapter 12

A solid description of the work of the 75's ground crew and their leader, Bill Matson, is drawn from Deane-Butcher's *Fighter Squadron Doctor* and Church's *They Flew Alone*, the former also describing the difficult medical conditions encountered.

Chapter 13

David Wilson describes the departure of John Jackson on his fateful flight on 10 April, plus the aftermath following his disappearance. Alan Whetters's AWM interview also is drawn upon here, as is the letter Jackson penned detailing his experience of trekking through the jungle, supplied by Wilson.

Chapter 14

In *Kokoda Air Strikes*, Anthony Cooper gives a detailed description of the Japanese dispositions throughout the period of the 44 days. Japanese pilot Saburo Sakai's autobiographical *Samurai!* is also extensively drawn upon to describe life for the Japanese. The National Archives of Australia's website provides a great deal of the documents pertaining to the disappearance and subsequent investigation into the fate of Sergeant David Brown (recordsearch.naa.gov.au/SearchNRetrieve/Interface/ViewImage.aspx?B=106490).

Chapter 15

Peter Masters' words are taken from his comments in Geoffrey Robertson's 1992 *44 Days* documentary for ABC television. Bob Crawford is likewise quoted here.

Chapter 16

The torrid but confusing action of 17 April is drawn from a variety of sources, including Wilson, Cooper, Ewer, J. Vader's *Pacific Hawk* and the personal recollections of Arthur Tucker, as related to his son Peter. From the Japanese side, Sakai's *Samurai!* is also drawn upon. Personal recollections of flying and the visit of dignitaries to Seven Mile Strip are taken from pilot Alan Boyd's recently discovered diary of the period.

Chapter 17

Cooper describes the growing ascendancy of the Japanese in *Kokoda Air Strikes*, as do the recollections of Tucker and Boyd. Michael Butler's AWM interview outlines in vivid detail his crash-landing in kunai grass. Alan Whetters describes his similar experience of a few days later in his AWM interview. The death of Barney Cresswell is effectively described by Wilson, Ewer and Johnston.

Chapter 18

Produced by David Salter and presented by Geoffrey Robertson, the sole television documentary of the period, *44 Days*, is an excellent source, as is Osmar White in his *Green Armour* on Jackson's return to the squadron. The details of Jackson's grilling of his pilots as to what had taken place in his absence comes in part from Alan Whetters' AWM interview and recollections from Arthur Tucker's son, Peter. The *Australian Dictionary of Biography* provides descriptions of the early flying careers of New Guinea RAAF commanders Pearce (adb.anu.edu.au/biography/pearce-charles-william-11356) and Gibson (adb.anu.edu.au/biography/gibson-william-norman-bill-12536). Johnston discusses their attitudes to some of the early RAAF pilots of the Pacific campaign. Cooper also provides most valuable insights here. Details of the final briefing of Jackson to his men were provided by the recollections of pilot Peter Masters from several sources including his *44 Days* documentary appearance.

Chapter 19

Deane-Butcher in *Fighter Squadron Doctor* gives an account of John Jackson's death and the discovery of his crash site on Mt Lawes. The action itself is described by Peter Masters in the *44 Days* documentary, and the action is given close attention by David Wilson, and was also observed by White in *Green Armour*. AE Church tells of the growing reinforcements of Port Moresby Harbour in *They Flew Alone*, and Arthur Tucker and Piper recall some of the squadron's last flights in their AWM interviews.

Chapter 20

The character of Les Jackson is examined by many sources including Tucker, Pettett, Deane-Butcher, Piper and Whetters in their respective AWM interviews. Deane-Butcher offers more insights into the man in his work *Fighter Squadron Doctor* and another recorded interview conducted for the National Library of Australia in the 1980s. A personal opinion of Jackson was given to the author by a former 75 Squadron pilot who served with Jackson slightly later in the war but who did not wish to be named. A formal description of Les Jackson's career and achievements can be found on the *Australian Dictionary of Biography* website (adb.anu.edu.au/biography/jackson-leslie-douglas-10709) as well as that of the Australian War Memorial (www.awm.gov.au/people/P10679908/). Anthony Cooper offers additional scholarly insights into Jackson, which further fills out the picture of the man's character.

Chapter 21

Wilson, Ewer, Church and Johnston all describe 75's final days at Port Moresby in great detail. Deane-Butcher recalls the night of the departure of the squadron's personnel vividly in *Fighter Squadron Doctor*, as does Michael Butler in his AWM interview. Arthur Tucker likewise recalled his impressions of the forlorn figure of the captured Japanese Zero pilot onboard the ship heading back to Australia.

Chapter 22

Osmar White's *Green Armour* and David Wilson's *The Decisive Factor* are quoted in the summing up of importance of the 44 days. Gillison's official RAAF history is also drawn upon here, as is a letter written by John Pettett to Bill Deane-Butcher in the 1990s.

Sources

Primary Sources

Boyd, A., 'Port Moresby Diary of Alan Boyd', Australian War Memorial, Canberra.

Butler, M., Keith Murdoch Sound Archive, AWM S00738, transcript of interview.

Deane-Butcher, W., *Fighter Squadron Doctor*, published by the author, 1990.

Dean-Butcher, W., Keith Murdoch Sound Archive, AWM S00559, transcript of interview.

Dean-Butcher, W., and Blackman, B., National Library of Australia, BIB ID 2653591, interview recorded in 1984.

Jeffrey, P., Keith Murdoch Sound Archive, AWM S00951, transcript of interview.

Pettett, J., Keith Murdoch Sound Archive, AWM S00515, transcript of interview.

Pettett, J., letter to William Deane-Butcher in 1990s, private collection.

Piper, J., Keith Murdoch Sound Archive, AWM S00577, transcript of interview.

Sakai, S., *Samurai!*, Doubleday, New York, 1957.

Tucker, A., 'Blind in an Unsighted World', transcript of speech delivered to the Sydney Regional Aircrew Reunion, 9 February 2000.

Tucker, A., Keith Murdoch Sound Archive, AWM S00701, transcript of interview.

Whetters, A., Keith Murdoch Sound Archive, AWM S00592, transcript of interview.

White, O., *Green Armour*, George Allen & Unwin, London, 1945.

Secondary Sources

Buggy, H., *Pacific Victory: A Short History of Australia's Part in the War against Japan*, Department of Information, 1946.

Deane-Butcher, R., interview with the author, 16 August 2014.

Church, A. E., *They Flew Alone*, Frank Johnson, Sydney, 1947.

Cooper, A., *Kokoda Air Strikes,* NewSouth Books, Sydney, 2014.

Cooper, R., *Crash of the Kittyhawk,* Wauchope District Historical Society, Wauchope, 2002.

Day, G., *Eight Hundred Million Candlepower: Journals of the 67 AASL 1942–45*, Prominent Press, Shepparton, 1999.

Ewer, P., *Storm over Kokoda.* Murdoch Books, Sydney, 2011.

Gillison, D., *RAAF: 1939–42,* Australian War Memorial, Canberra, 1962.

Hoy, A., 'From Zeros to Heroes', *The Bulletin*, 30 April 2002, p. 30.

Johnston, M., *Whispering Death,* Allen & Unwin, Sydney, 2011.

RAAF Directorate of Public Relations, *RAAF Log*, Australian War Memorial, Canberra, 1943.

RAAF Directorate of Public Relations, *RAAF Saga,* Australian War Memorial, Canberra, 1944.

Radar Returns, 11, No. 2, November 2006.

Robinson, H., 'Scramble – The Story of Australia's Few', *Weekend Australian Magazine*, 25–26 April 1992.

Salter, D., *44 Days*, ABC Television Science and Talks, 1992.

Simmonds, E., and Smith, N., *Echoes over the Pacific*, Radar Returns, Hampton, 1995.

Sivyer, G., *Seek and Strike: The Magpie Fights Back,* published by the author, Toowomba, 1992.

Thomas, A., & Holmes, T., *Tomahawk and Kittyhawk Aces of the RAF and Commonwealth*, Osprey, Oxford, 2002.

Tucker, P., interview with the author, 1 September 2015.

Vader, J., *Pacific Hawk,* Macdonald and Co, London, 1970.

Wilson, D., *The Decisive Factor,* Banner Books, Melbourne, 1991.

Index

INDEX

INDEX

INDEX